LEGAL RIGHT AND SOCIAL DEMOCRACY

LEGAL RIGHT AND SOCIAL DEMOCRACY

ESSAYS IN LEGAL AND POLITICAL PHILOSOPHY

NEIL MACCORMICK

CLARENDON PRESS · OXFORD
1982

Oxford University Press, Walton Street Oxford OX2 6DP

London   Glasgow   New York   Toronto
Delhi   Bombay   Calcutta   Madras   Karachi
Kuala Lumpur   Singapore   Hong Kong   Tokyo
Nairobi   Dar es Salaam   Cape Town
Melbourne   Auckland
and associates in
Beirut   Berlin   Ibadan   Mexico City   Nicosia

Published in the United States by
Oxford University Press, New York

British Library Cataloguing in Publication Data

MacCormick, Neil
Legal right and social democracy.
1. Law—Philosophy
I. Title
340'.1   K230

ISBN 0-19-825385-0

Library of Congress Cataloging in Publication Data

MacCormick, Neil.
Legal right and social democracy.

Includes index.
1. Law and politics—Addresses, essays, lectures.
2. Sociological jurisprudence—
Addresses, essays, lectures.
I. Title.
K487.P65M33   1982   340'.11   82-8020
ISBN 0-19-825385-0 (Oxford University Press) AACR2

Typeset by Oxprint Ltd., Oxford
Printed in Great Britain
at the University Press, Oxford
by Eric Buckley
Printer to the University

PREFACE

THERE is a standing tension between liberty for individuals and equal well-being of individuals. Individual freedom in a market economy can and does result in great inequalities of material well-being. Programmes for equalization of well-being erode or abolish the liberties exercised by citizens in market societies. These liberties are guaranteed under an order of universal 'legal right'—'the rule of law' as we sometimes say. If 'social justice' demands equalization of well-being, is it then an ideal incompatible with respect for legal right?

Some say it is, and urge us therefore to abandon any pursuit of this mirage of social justice; others say it is, and urge us therefore to abandon our bourgeois attachment to legal right and the rule of law. What I understand as the 'social democratic' view is that there must be a middle way. Despite the admitted tensions between liberty and (material) equality, the good society is one which aims to hold them in balance.

This book sets out from an attempt to back that 'middle way' with rigorous arguments rather than mere assertions. The principles upon which these arguments depend are also relevant to, and further explored in, the subsequent essays upon other issues of legal and political philosophy. The underlying concern of the whole is with *justification*—the attempt to justify claims of right and assertions of duty both at the grand level of civil liberty and political obligation and at more detailed levels such as those of privacy, promises, and reparation. What are the proper spheres of individual and of collective or even national right? Although what I here present is a collection of separately written essays each tackling a specific theme in a spirit of controversy, I hope that the whole work does express a coherent view grounded in mutually compatible principles. The work was commissioned and the title decided before the formation of the new Social Democratic Party in Britain. I am not a member of that party, and would contest its sole proprietorship in the concept 'social democracy'. So I decided not to change my title (or my views), despite the risk that I might be deemed rather a propagandist for a party than for a set of principles.

Whether the theses I state are well or ill made, convincing or unconvincing, I have no doubt that their subject-matter is of more than academic concern. In my professional life as a jurist and a teacher of jurisprudence it is my job to aim at and encourage in others a respect for analytical clarity and rigorousness of argument rather than to urge upon my students one view or another in matters of political controversy. Yet in the end such scholarly virtues would be pointless in such a field as that of legal or political philosophy if one did not also proceed further, as a citizen over and above an academic, to putting forward one's own view upon such matters of controversy.

D.N.M.

ACKNOWLEDGEMENTS

THE first chapter of this book, 'Legal Right and Social Demo-cracy' was originally delivered as the Corry Lecture at Queen's University, Kingston, Ontario, in March 1981, and will also be published in due course in the *Queen's Quarterly*. I record my gratitude to Queen's University for the honour it did me in inviting me to act as Corry lecturer, and for its hospitality; also to the Universities of Sydney, Auckland, and Brisbane, and to the New Zealand Society for Legal Philosophy, where I gave similar addresses on the same theme during the summer of 1981. The second chapter was originally prepared as a paper for the ICUS Conference in Florida in November 1980, and will be published with the proceedings of that conference, which I was, however, unable to attend. I also received valuable criticisms of it at seminars conducted in the universities of Glasgow and Wollongong in 1980 and 1981.

The remaining chapters, some of them substantially revised, were originally published as follows, and I gratefully acknow-ledge the permission granted me by the editors and publishers to republish the papers in the present volume:

Chapter 3 is the amended text of a special lecture given in Heriot-Watt University, Edinburgh, in 1977, and published in that year by the university. Chapter 4 was the Austin Lecture delivered to the UK Association for Legal and Social Philosophy in 1978, and was published in LXV *Archiv für Rechts-und Sozialphilosophie* (1979) 387–410. Chapter 5 was a lecture to the University of the Saarland in 1975, published subsequently in 3 *Dalhousie Law Journal* (1976) 367–84. Chapter 6 was published in 15 *Valparaiso University Law Review* (1981) 243–63 under the title 'Adam Smith on Law'. Chapter 7 was published in 87 *Philosophical Review* (1978) 585–607, under the title 'Dworkin as Pre-Benthamite'. Chapter 8 was published under its present title in LXII *Archiv für Recht-und Sozialphilosophie* (1976) 305–16. Chapter 9 was published under its present title in

Censorship and Obscenity (ed. R. Dhavan and C. Davies, Martin Robertson and Co., Oxford, 1978), pp. 76–97; Chapter 10 was published in rather different form under the title 'Voluntary Obligations and Normative Powers' in *Aristotelian Society Supplementary Volume* 46 (1972) 59–78. Chapter 11 was published under the same title in *Proceedings of the Aristotelian Society* (1977–8) pp. 175–83; Chapter 12 is to be published under the same title in the forthcoming Proceedings of the 1979 World Congress in Philosophy of Law and Social Philosophy, ed. P. Trappe; and Chapter 13 was published under the same title . in *The Crown and the Thistle* (ed. C. MacLean, Scottish Academic Press, Edinburgh, 1979), pp. 99–111, that work being commissioned by the St. Andrews Jubilee Trust.

Besides these debts, I must acknowledge generous help and criticism offered by many colleagues on various parts of the work. I can do no more than name them and thank them as follows: Alessandro Baratta, Zenon Bankowski, Eric Clive, Eric Colvin, Nicola Franklin, Knud Haakonssen, Vinit Haksar, Donald Harris, Anthony Kenny, Richard Kinsey, Alistair MacLeod, Michael Machan, David Nelken, David Raphael, Wojciech Sadurski, Alice Tay, and Alan White. I can impute to none of them responsibility for the faults remaining in the whole of the work, though each saved me from error in one or more of its parts.

Neil MacCormick
Sydney
August 1981

CONTENTS

I.
LEGAL RIGHT AND SOCIAL DEMOCRACY

THE term 'Social Democracy' has an odd history. Now the name for politics of the moderate left, it originally denoted a Marxist approach to socialism (by contrast, for example, with Fabianism). Social democratic parties in Continental Europe, such as the Austrian one led by figures like Karl Renner, were explicitly and avowedly Marxist in approach. Only since the Second World War have European Social Democrats made the final break with Marxism, a crucial turning-point (or mark of a change already achieved in substance) being the Bad Godesberg congress of the West German SPD in 1959. By now, at any rate, it is clear enough that 'social democracy' has come to be regarded by most English-speaking people as a philosophy of the moderate left, or even the centre, of the political spectrum. We may take it as an alternative to, rather than a form of 'socialism'.

My understanding of such a philosophy encompasses four main points:

i. That social justice cannot be realized through free market institutions premised on the classical rights of liberal individualism as protected by the classical liberals' minimal state.

ii. That it is therefore necessary for state (and other collective) agencies to take an active role in economic affairs with a view to securing fair shares and fair opportunities for all citizens.

iii. That the civil rights and liberties proclaimed by classical liberalism are, however, of fundamental importance to human beings, as moral persons, and ought to be qualified only so far as necessary to the securing of fair shares and fair opportunities.

iv. Because of the importance of classical rights and liberties, and because these require recognition of private property, no proposal for a completely collectivized or state socialist reorganization of, or revolution in, post-liberal societies is either acceptable or desirable.

That is no doubt contestable as an adequate description of 'social democracy',[1] and vague upon the key issue of what constitutes 'social justice' or 'fairness' of shares, etc. But my purposes are argumentative rather than descriptive, so I can ignore the charge of misdescription. Within the general field of what is called 'social democracy', I shall argue that the above is a *good* version of a social democratic philosophy and I shall try to make it at least a little clearer what versions of 'social justice' and 'fairness' I am commending. In particular, I shall argue that such a version of social democracy is, contrary to the view of F. A. Hayek,[2] fully compatible with respect for legal right and the rule of law. I shall also contend, contrary to the views of some Marxist socialists, that respect for legal right and the rule of law is a vital condition of social justice.

Let me start by showing why it is a serious question whether the ideas of 'legal right' and 'social democracy' are mutually compatible or mutually exclusive. Can there be a social democratic conception of legal right, or must any social democratic programme lead always to some form of antinomian corporate state? Must such a programme lead always to a governmental system of managerial direction by men rather than to a principled governance of laws?

Those who nowadays press such questions often base their case on arguments first advanced by David Hume in Part II of Section III of his *Enquiry Concerning the Principles of Morals*.[3] In any event, Hume's arguments have a challenging forcefulness and clarity. I shall take them as a starting-point.

Hume treats of justice as the virtue we exhibit when we strictly respect other people's legal rights, especially their rights over property. His explanatory reason for the existence of property rights at law lies in his view of the nature and circumstances of human beings. They are beings of limited altruism and yet of a social disposition who inhabit a planet of limited resources requiring effortful cultivation for survival of indivi-

---

[1] See Shirley Williams, *Politics is for People* (London, 1981), for an alternative description of 'Social democracy' from within the new Social Democratic Party. While my view was not based on hers, the two seem reasonably compatible.

[2] See F. A. Hayek, *Law, Legislation and Liberty* (3 vols., London, 1973, 1976, 1979), especially vol. 2, *The Mirage of Social Justice*.

[3] David Hume, *Enquiries concerning Human Understanding and concerning the Principles of Morals* (ed. L. A. Selby-Bigge and P. H. Nidditch, 3rd edn., Oxford, 1975), §§ 154–63.

dual and species. Such beings naturally develop common social rules for allowing possession of particular useful or desirable things to individuals and to family groups or other groups of individuals. The justifying reason for observing these rules is their usefulness in maintaining the possibility of human life and in creating the circumstances whereby men can make their life more commodious by their own reasonable efforts and by commercial collaboration with each other.

Further reflection on this justifying reason reveals to Hume the necessity of treating the property rules, and positive laws in general, as being rigid and universal in their application, even in individual cases where their rigid application yields adverse consequences.

As against this thesis, Hume considers various alternatives. Perhaps assets should be distributed always in direct proportion to the moral meritoriousness of individuals?—Impossible, for '. . . were mankind to execute such a law, so great is the uncertainty of merit, both from its natural obscurity, and from the self-conceit of each individual, that no determinate rule of conduct would ever result from it; and the total dissolution of society must be the immediate consequence'.[4] The Duke of Wellington's chief praise of the Knighthood of the Garter in England was that 'there is no damned merit in it'. Hume's view of property is much to the same effect; it is justified by its general social usefulness, not by its appropriateness as a reward of the moral deserts of those who hold it. Yet on that very view there seem to be compelling objections to the actual system of property distribution which prevails. Under it, different individuals and families may have very different fortunes and therefore very different fortune each from another. The rigorous upholding of property rights is a rigorous upholding of gross inequalities in resources. And yet this, by Hume, is said to be justice; nor does he fail to observe the difficulty of his position:

It must, indeed, be confessed that nature is so liberal to mankind, that, were all her presents equally divided among the species, and improved by art and industry, every individual would enjoy all the necessaries, and even most of the comforts of life; nor would ever be liable to any ills, but such as might accidentally arise from the sickly

4 Ibid., § 154.

frame and constitution of his body. It must also be confessed, that, wherever we depart from this equality, we rob the poor of more satisfaction than we add to the rich, and that the slight gratification of a frivolous vanity, in one individual, frequently costs more than bread to many families and even provinces. It may appear withal, that the rule of equality, as it would be highly useful, is not altogether *impracticable*; but has taken place, at least in an imperfect degree, in some republics, particularly that of Sparta; where it was attended, it is said, with the most beneficial consequences.[5]

Having posed for his own thesis this most formidable difficulty, Hume proceeds to demolish it. He has three arguments which concur to defeat the egalitarian case. These we may label the arguments from impracticability, from inefficiency, and from perniciousness.

The argument from *impracticability* is that one may establish at any given time a perfect equality of material possessions, but that such a distribution cannot last, for 'men's different degrees of art, care and industry will immediately break that equality'.[6] The argument from *inefficiency* is that if one prevents people using their art, care, and industry to improve as they choose the productivity of their initial share, one might succeed in preserving equality, but only the equality of universal destitution: 'instead of preventing want and beggary in a few, [you] render it unavoidable to the whole community'.[7] The argument from *perniciousness* rests on the suggestion that any attempt to prevent unequal outcomes supervening upon the original scheme of equal distribution must involve the erection of a tyrannical form of government to maintain a perpetual inquisition into every possible case of supervening inequality, and a perpetual re-distribution of the fruits thereof: 'But besides, that so much authority must soon degenerate into tyranny, and be exercised with great partialities; who can possibly be possessed of it, in such a situation as is here supposed? Perfect equality of possessions, destroying all subordination, weakens extremely the authority of magistracy, and must reduce all power nearly to a level, as well as property.'[8] Thus does Hume in a way anticipate

[5] Ibid., § 155.
[6] Ibid.
[7] Ibid.
[8] Ibid.

Orwell's *Animal Farm*, in supposing that a paradoxical but necessary outcome of the equality of all animals is that some end up more equal than others. Nor need one accept his somewhat time-bound and culture-bound supposition that magisterial powers must for efficacy be vested in those who are already of socially superior rank in virtue of wealth; it is sufficient to the argument that the task of continued equalization of property shares, even if possible, entails a considerable inequality of power and privilege (if only in a technical Hohfeldian sense) as between the equalizers and the rest of the community. Even if the strongly empowered equalizers do not take unto themselves extra material perks, the scheme ·for equality of possession necessarily yields inequality of power; and any prima-facie moral claim in favour of interpersonal equality seems as good a claim in respect of legal power and privilege as in respect of material possessions.

Hence Hume's argument comes to this: If we want a system of free government under law rather than tyrannical and in-quisitorial rule, we cannot accept any principle of absolute equality of all persons in material wealth. This is bolstered by an argument for efficiency in favour of the established property system:

Who sees not, for instance, that whatever is produced or improved by a man's art or industry ought, for ever, to be secured to him, in order to give encouragement to such *useful* habits and accomplishments? That the property ought also to descend to children and relations, for the same useful purpose? That it may be alienated by consent, in order to beget that commerce and intercourse which is so *beneficial* to human society? And that all contracts and promises ought carefully to be fulfilled, in order to secure mutual trust and confidence, by which the general *interest* of mankind is so much promoted?[9]

Not merely is acceptance of inequality of possessions necessary to ward off tyranny, but it is also a key part of an arrangement which encourages people to act in a way which promotes the general interest through the pursuit of their own interest in the well-being of themselves and their families and close associates.

Hume's arguments and conclusions to this effect have been powerfully and extensively restated in recent times by F. A.

[9] Ibid., § 156.

Hayek, who has perceptively shown the close similarity to it of the moral and political arguments of Kant, for all the supposed absolute mutual opposition of Humean and Kantian philosophies.[10] Hayek carries forward the argument into a denunciation of any attempt to use government institutions to implement schemes of social justice, even schemes falling far short of perfect equality in material benefits available to all citizens. Every such attempt Hayek characterizes as implicitly if not avowedly antinomian in seeking to bring humans under a rule of governmental and legislative directives rather than leaving them free under law, that is, free to pursue the good as they see it within a universally applicable set of 'rules of just conduct' prohibiting each from intentionally impinging on any other's sphere of unimpeded free action.

It is interesting that some at least of the acutest Marxist thinkers about law substantially agree with Hayek's descriptive as distinct from his prescriptive thesis. E. B. Pashukanis and his contemporary supporters agree that relationships of legal right between individuals are intrinsically and essentially part of the capitalist economic order.[11] The ideal type of bourgeois law is

[10] For Hayek's reconciliation, see his *Law, Legislation and Liberty*, vol. 1, *Rules and Order*, p. 113, and vol. 2, *The Mirage of Social Justice*, pp. 27–9, 43, 166–7. On the latter passages, Hayek rightly observes that Kant's theory about universalizability, as applied in his *Rechtslehre*, requires us to test out the universalizability of our maxims of conduct in the context of the legal order of 'civil society'; see Kant, *Metaphysical Elements of Justice* (tr. John Ladd, Indianapolis, 1965), pp. 76–7. With respect, it seems to me a sound view that Hume's insistence on the universal application of legal rules, regardless of particular outcomes in particular cases, comes in effect very close to Kant's notion of universalizability as gathered from the *Rechtslehre* as well as *The Groundwork of the Metaphysic of Morals* (tr. H. J. Paton as *The Moral Law*, London, 1966).

[11] See E. B. Pashukanis, *Law and Marxism: A General Theory* (ed. C. Arthur, tr. B. Einhorn, London, 1978). See, e.g., pp. 121–2: 'Only when bourgeois relations are fully developed does law become abstract in character. Every person becomes man in the abstract, all labour becomes socially useful labour in the abstract, every subject becomes an abstract legal subject. At the same time, the norm takes on the logically perfected form of abstract universal law.' With this, Hayek seems to agree almost entirely: see his *Rules and Order*, ch. 5, on 'Nomos: the Law of Liberty'. See again Pashukanis, op. cit., p. 160: 'The proletariat may well have to utilise these forms [morality, law and the state], but that in no way implies that they could be developed further or permeated by a socialist content. These forms are incapable of absorbing this content and must wither away in an inverse ratio with the extent to which this content becomes reality.' Hayek again agrees, almost word for word. See, e.g., *The Mirage of Social Justice*, p. 142: 'The current endeavour to rely on a spontaneous order corrected according to principles of justice amounts to an attempt to have the best of two worlds which are mutually incompatible.' What Pashukanis and Hayek disagree about is the relative desirability of these incompatible things.

indeed that of a normative order which perfectly confers on all individuals the abstract equality of legal personhood and which impartially and universally regulates the actions and relationships of legal persons through such categories as 'obligation', 'duty', 'right', 'contract', and 'property'. These categories are enshrined in general abstract rules rigidly applicable according to their terms, not subject to exceptions for the needs and abilities of the particular concrete individuals to whom in given cases they apply. So far from commending this, however, Pashukanis contends that the abstract legal equality enjoyed by every legal person in the capitalist order is no more than a primitive foreshadowing of material socialist equality. The real live human beings behind the persona, the bourgeois legal mask, are not merely contingently unequal in material well-being; they are necessarily so given the bourgeois economic and legal system. The workers, who suffer under this regime of inequality, are necessarily exploited through their contracts of employment. Such contracts may be formally fair bargains between legal equals, but their effect is to legitimize an expropriation of the surplus value or 'profit' created by the labour of the working class over and above the payments made to workers as wages.[12]

The abstractly equal legal liberty ascribed to every person beyond the confines of the law's universal prohibitions and prescriptions is likewise for concrete men a travesty—being for the masses the liberty to work or want, to be exploited at work or to be excluded from the common stock of society. The system does not even, as Hume supposes, secure to every man 'whatever is produced or improved by [his] art or industry', given the intrinsically exploitative character of the employment relationship. Hence (a) a socialist order of real material equality and real equal freedom ought to supplant the capitalist order; and (b) the hallmark of the socialist order will be its abandonment of the apparatus and categories of legal right, in particular in respect of private property (except 'personal' property). From such theses flow the standard socialist and Marxist proposals for the replacement of 'abstract' legal equality with 'material' economic equality and the supplantation of 'formal' legal

---

[12] Pashukanis, *Law and Marxism*, p. 157.

liberty with 'substantive' freedom from want and exploitation.[13]

Tyranny must, however, be the immediate consequence of any such proposals, according to Hume and to Hayek. The latter explicitly argues that the order of legal right, what he calls 'nomos', is the only guarantee of the only thing which it is intelligible for humans to call by the grand name of 'liberty', a condition attainable only under abstract and universal laws.[14] In powerful alliance with Hayek, we find Robert Nozick asserting that the freedom of individuals and respect for their persons requires recognition of their possession of Lockean natural rights which are logically and morally prior to any arrangements by way of positive law.[15] Justice is and is only respect for the momentary outcomes of a system of fair trading, exchange, and voluntary giving among individuals. It cannot be defined in terms of any desired pattern or end-state.[16] Nor, therefore, can any end-state in the form of a planned and principled distribution of social goods justify any invasion of rightfully acquired possessions. Justice is not teleological but purely and simply procedural. Whatever distribution of goods results from free and fair exchanges among persons whose original acquisitions were just is itself just.[17] Compulsory redistribution of fairly acquired goods, e.g. through a system of income tax, is the moral analogue of slavery.[18] He who is taxed is forced to work for others' good. So are slaves.

These oppositions of view between Whig and Marxist are for me thesis and antithesis. My aim is to achieve an acceptable synthesis. At a time when, at least in parts of Western Europe, there has arisen a new polarization in politics, between an increasingly Hayekian right, and and increasingly Marxist left, it becomes an urgent question whether there is any middle way. Is there no morally and intellectually defensible ground between individualist Whiggery and Marxist collectivism?

I am bound to say that I hope there is. For all of the optimism and moral seriousness of an Adam Smith, the social evils which

---

[13] Ibid., pp. 60–1.
[14] Hayek, *Rules and Order*, ch. 5.
[15] R. Nozick, *Anarchy, State, and Utopia* (Oxford, 1974).
[16] Ibid., pp. 153–5.
[17] Ibid., pp. 150–79.
[18] Ibid., p. 169.

high capitalism in the mid to late nineteenth century brought in its wake are scarcely deniable. For all the optimism and moral passion of a Karl Marx, the social evils which have in this century been attendant upon the full dress socialism of the peoples' republics of Eastern Europe are equally plain to the eye of candid enquiry. Nor does it seem reasonable that apologists of either position be permitted the refuge of an argument which each group has deployed for its own favoured case. I mean, the argument, or assertion, that the system was never given a fair try in ideal circumstances. Just as some argue, Dicey-like, that liberal capitalism had only just got under way when weak-kneed politicians started to corrupt it with all manner of collectivist adulterations,[19] so others argue, Lenin-like, that economic underdevelopment within and capitalist encirclement without denied the socialist republics a fair testing-ground for the flowering of humane praxis under the guidance of benign theory.[20]

Political philosophies are practical philosophies for the real human world we inhabit. To let political philosophers play Procrustes and lament that the actual human frame has needed some trimming to bed nicely into their theories is a luxury we cannot in all reason afford them.

In fact, there is some truth in both the Whig thesis and the Marxist antithesis. Each identifies weaknesses in the other's view. Of what I call, in deference to Hayek, the 'Whig' position, it is true as Marxists say that it gives undue priority to securing liberty in a certain sense of the term, 'negative liberty' as it is sometimes called.[21] This is the liberty to do whatever one is not legally required not to do. The requirements of law draw a moral boundary round each individual in his person and assets and forbid a person to cross any other person's boundary. If such legal requirements are kept to the minimum necessary for preventing anyone from directly obstructing others' free choices, then each person is as free as possible to pursue whatever he sees as his, or the, good.

[19] See A. V. Dicey, *Law and Public Opinion in England* (2nd edn., London, 1914), Introduction and chs. 8, 9.
[20] See V. I. Lenin, *Selected Works* (London, 1960–70), IX. 254 f.
[21] See I. Berlin, *Four Essays on Liberty* (Oxford, 1969), ch. 3, 'Two Concepts of Liberty'; J. N. Gray, 'On Negative and Positive Liberty', 28 *Political Studies* (1980) 507–26.

A policy of maximizing such liberty is indeed commended by its defenders as defining the only form of community in which every person accords to every other the respect due to an autonomous moral agent.[22] But advocacy of this stern regime of liberty under minimal law and equality before minimal law commonly ignores the morally unacceptable consequences of grave economic disparities. Of the equal freedom of rich and poor alike to sleep or not sleep under the bridges, Anatole France said in effect all that needs be said.[23] Freedom from the law's coercion is an instrumental not an ultimate good, and it is not the only instrument humans need in pursuing their good. Enormous disparities in the other instruments, 'economic goods' let me call them for short, exclude impoverished masses or even impoverished minorities from any reasonable opportunity to pursue their idea of the good life on anything like equal terms with the wealthy. And the tyranny of pressing needs and necessities exposes them to exploitation and undue influence by their better-off sharers in what Burns called 'nature's social union'.

The socialist critique of the Whig position seems entirely convincing in its assertion of the moral unacceptability of these consequences of maximizing liberty. But in admitting the socialist diagnosis of Whiggish ailments, I do not go so far as to accept Dr Marx's prescribed remedy. Indeed, the diagnosis itself starts to go wrong from this point onwards.

Having noted that equal liberty before formally universal laws is no fair guarantee of a universal opportunity for access to the good life, some socialists proceed to the fallacy that formal legal liberty is not a valuable form of freedom at all. Freedom from want and freedom from exploitation by the economically dominant are presented as the fundamental freedoms, which ought in turn to be coupled with freedom to commit oneself to collective and democratic decision-making as an autonomous member of a self-determining community. Here, we are told, lies the true and positive liberation of the human spirit, here

---

[22] Hayek, *Mirage of Social Justice*, p. 27.
[23] See Anatole France, *Le Lys Rouge* (Paris, 1894), p. 114; denouncing 'the majestic equality of the law that forbids the rich as well as the poor to sleep under the bridges, to beg in the streets, and to steal bread'.

material freedom and material equality, over against the merely abstract liberty and formal equality of bourgeois legal order.[24]

The error of diagnosis is this: freedom cannot but be both negative and relative. Freedom is the state of not being subject to some presumptively undesirable state of things.[25] And equality is always abstract, since, as Elizabeth Wolgast points out, things and people can only be equal or unequal in terms of some measurable quality considered in abstraction from the other qualities which make up the whole person.[26] It seems contingently impossible as well as practically undesirable actually to procure that every human being be or be made equal in every conceivable quality or attribute, starting only with age, sex, height . . .

From these trivial truths it follows that negative civil liberty can be a real and valuable condition even though not itself a complete guarantee of the good for any or all citizens of a state. It further follows that equality in civil liberty is no guarantee that the liberties equally ascribed to all will be of equal value or worth to all. An analogy: a benign government might provide identical and excellent electric cookers to all its citizens. But this equally distributed boon may not lead to equal beatitude if one-tenth of the recipients are too young to cook, three-tenths have no access to electric supplies, and a further three-tenths no food to cook. We may observe, however, that even these extravagant suppositions could justify neither the conclusion that the items distributed were not real electric cookers nor the conclusion that electric cookers are not after all good things to have.

This analogy has some point if it can be shown that on some reasonable supposition civil liberty is at least instrumentally good. On one supposition it is, namely this: human beings have a capacity to be responsible self-regulating persons whose chief satisfactions lie in the arduous pursuit of goals and conditions

---

[24] See, e.g., Z. Bankowski and G. Mungham, *Images of Law* (London, 1976), pp. xi–xxiii.

[25] Even in the case of so-called 'positive freedom' (see references cited above, n. 21) this seems to be true; for what is in issue there is a person's (or a group's) freeing himself (itself) from domination by some subjective 'internal' failing or inhibition, or from some 'external' deficiency such as poverty or lack of education.

[26] E. H. Wolgast, *Equality and the Rights of Women* (Ithaca and London, 1980), pp. 18–55.

they think good within the context of a communal life along with other like beings. For such beings, the capacity to make and follow out individual and joint plans of life without arbitrary impediment set by other persons is a rewarding exercise of their practical reasonableness. The absence of arbitrary impediment is then of instrumental value to that which on my supposition is a basic, or at least a more basic, good. The only known way of discouraging and discountenancing such arbitrary impediment is, however, governance under pre-announced laws mainly negative or prohibitive in tenor. Civil liberty is, precisely, the sphere of freedom to make and pursue one's individual and joint plans in the area of indifference of such laws.

To the extent that the same laws of like tenor apply to the whole body of citizens, or adult citizens, this liberty is possessed equally by all. What is more, special restrictions upon some or special exemptions for others are prima facie indicative of some differentiation in status superimposed upon the presumptively equal status of all sane adults as autonomous moral agents. Such inequality of treatment is prima facie inconsistent with according the *same* respect to *all* persons.

The socialist prescription for scrapping the 'formal' liberty and 'abstract' equality of bourgeois law therefore seems a quack remedy based on an incoherent diagnosis. Yet a real evil was diagnosed at the first stage of the present discussion. Once we have identified civil liberty as a genuine but instrumental good, and seen the strong presumption in favour of distributing it in abstractly equal terms, we shall stand as resolute as so many David Humes against schemes for dismantling it.

But, as with our electric cookers, we shall at least wonder if we cannot do something to remedy the contingencies which make the instrument practically valueless[27] to some of its possessors. Allowing that youthfulness is the one disability which necessarily makes its own cure by effluxion of time, we have to attend to those deficiencies of external economic good which as much impede the exercise of liberties as of electric cookers.

---

[27] See H. L. A. Hart, 'Are there Any Natural Rights?', in *Political Philosophy* (ed. A. Quinton, Oxford, 1967), pp. 53–66, at p. 53 on the distinction between the existence of liberty and its value to an individual. Cf. J. Rawls, *A Theory of Justice* (Cambridge, Mass., and Oxford, 1971 and 1972), pp. 204–6 on liberty and the worth of liberty.

Can we do anything about these deficiencies without infringing the admitted good of governance under universally applicable laws? Of course we can. There is nothing non-universal about a law which ascribes to every adult citizen a right to enjoy an annual minimum income of £3,000, and to obtain this or the balance from the appropriate authorities of the state in the event that he/she can prove that reasonable personal efforts have failed to procure an income so large. The mere fact that not every adult citizen *could* prove this in any given year is irrelevant to the question of whether the rule is formally universal. The fact that not everyone can prove that someone has wrongfully injured him is in the same way irrelevant to the universality of the rule that whoever has been wrongfully injured is entitled to compensation from his wrongful injurer; to accept that the tort rule is universal is to accept that my imaginary rule of 'welfare law' is in the same sense universal.

But how can the state raise the money? Answer: by taxation whether on the basis of property owned or on the basis of income earned or on the basis of money spent, or some amalgam. Again, there is nothing formally non-universal about laws which prescribe that all citizens holding property over the value of £x must pay half of the excess in tax; or that all citizens earning more than £x shall pay income tax at flat rates or, for that matter, progressive rates; or that of every £1 spent, 20 pence (or whatever) shall be paid in tax.

Such are, of course, abstractly simple models for schemes of redistribution aimed at diminishing disparities of economic goods as between citizens. Citizens of modern states need no reminder of the vastly greater complexity attending most existing systems of redistribution. Most existing schemes are, I might mention, ludicrously over-complex, and offensively paternalistic or (as I prefer to say) parentalistic towards the recipients of state welfare or equalization payments in cash or (perhaps more largely) in kind; not that a certain degree of complexity is avoidable in any reasonable attempt to make diverse provision for diverse forms of need.

Merely to show that redistribution is a practical possibility and a possibility which need not entail any infringement of formal universality in laws is of course neither to show that it is just nor to show that it is desirable in itself. I shall now sketch the reasons why it is both just and desirable.

As to justice, John Finnis has recently restated most eloquently the old natural lawyers' insight that the stock of material goods available for human use and exploitation is in principle a common stock of mankind.[28] It is not the less so even if the enterprise of particular individuals and groups and the sweated labour of individuals and groups is a precondition of anyone's using the common stock. For such enterprise and labour go forward only in communities and yield no fruits save under the protection of laws communally evolved, sustained, and enforced. It lies ill in the mouths of those whose appropriations from common stock require communal protection, to hold themselves entitled to exclude other more needy people from any share in the goods they have appropriated; *a fortiori*, if they found this asserted entitlement upon the sanctity of the respect equally due to all moral beings. The claim of those whose economic means are too small to endow legal liberty with any substantial practical worth against those whose means are larger is a claim of justice.

But is such a claim one which we can ever afford to meet? What about Hume's arguments for the impracticability, the inefficiency, and the perniciousness of schemes for wealth- or income-equalization?

It is indeed, as Hume said, impracticable to insist upon any absolute equalization of holdings. For at any moment different degrees of art, care, and industry will break the equalized balance of goods. What is more, it would be grossly inefficient to discourage the exercise of these virtues of art, care, and industry. They are our best hope for expanding and improving the common stock of societies.

Nothing has been said here in favour of any exact and permanent equalization of every person's possessions with everyone else's. The argument has been an argument for diminishing inequalities of fortune, not for abolishing them. But where does one stop such a process? Why take (as my earlier example took) a sum such as £3,000 per annum? Is this not arbitrariness in new guise, a number plucked from the air?

An answer to that question may lie in the consideration of efficiency and inefficiency. If we choose to rely upon the art,

---

[28] J. Finnis, *Natural Law and Natural Rights* (Oxford, 1980), pp. 165–77.

care, and industry of individuals and freely collaborating groups as our method for procuring movement of common stocks, then at any given time there is some threshold beyond which our schemes for redistribution become self-defeating. We kill the goose whose golden egg we meant to scramble for the poor. I am not sure how much is really known about disincentive effects of high taxation, but it seems intuitively obvious that excessively high rates and *a fortiori* 100 per cent taxation of property or income have twofold ill effects: on the one hand they discourage enterprise and on the other they encourage the wasted ingenuity and the injustice of schemes of tax-avoidance and evasion.

Here we remind ourselves again of Hume's argument from perniciousness several times over. Taxation beyond limits perceived as reasonable by most taxpayers leads to tax-evasion which can be countered only by vesting state tax officials with increasingly arbitrary discretions and powers. That way lies tyranny. On the other hand wholesale abandonment of reliance on free individual and group enterprise seems by the experience of our times to lead both to inefficiency and to an aggrandisement of state power wherein again lies tyranny. And it is, to say the least, the grossest of ironies that schemes which commence from moral indignation over inequalities of material assets end up not merely countenancing but entrenching vast disparities of power.

As you see, my dissent from both Whiggism and socialism leads me to a somewhat Rawls-like conclusion, albeit by a route wholly other than Rawls's hypothetically contractarian one.[29] My contention is that legal right and civil liberty indeed matter, and matter for the Kantian reasons our new Whigs give, for they are indeed essential conditions of respect for persons. But I deny that the protection of civil liberty adequately justifies the inequalities of fortune which a *merely* libertarian legal order facilitates. I assert a debt of justice owed by the haves to the have-nots, a debt payable by redistribution of assets to the latter to secure to them adequate worth for their legal liberties. But there are practical limits on such distribution, bounded by the moral imperative against schemes productive of tyranny.

---

[29] Rawls, *Theory of Justice*, pp. 11–22. See also ch. 5 below.

And these are well captured by Rawls's 'difference principle',[30] in a simplified, not to say crude, form. Establish as the minimum income of the worst off the highest sum achievable without such disincentive effects through the taxation system as to reduce the real value of the income of the poorest in a self-defeating way.

Such a policy is not aimed at a 'patterned' or an 'end-state' view of justice, as Nozick contends.[31] It is not a matter of social statics but of social homeostatics, a matter of the continual self-adjustment of the body politic to changes in external and internal circumstances. I use the term 'adjustment' deliberately here because of its etymological root in the idea of securing a just balance among members of a larger whole.

I have rested a good deal on the Humean argument about tyranny. I shall perhaps run the risk of condemnation from my more absolutely democratic-spirited friends and critics.[32] Fully communal humans, I hear, would not have to rely on individual enterprise and initiative, or on the competitive social environment these presuppose. There is no freedom, I hear, to parallel the freedom achieved by those who in the true community of a whole nation (or whatever) exercise the most perfect autonomy in the collective politics of democratic action. So some say, but I reply that all such assertions are not merely reminiscent of, but ultimately derived from, Rousseau's romancing about the General Will.

May I therefore conclude my statement in favour of what I am pleased to present as a social democratic conception of justice and legal right by quoting from William Godwin his conclusive demolition of the romance of the general will:

[I]f government be founded in the consent of the people, it can have no power over any individual by whom that consent is refused. If a tacit consent be not sufficient, still less can I be deemed to have consented to a measure upon which I put an express negative. This immediately follows from the observation of Rousseau. If the people, or the individuals of whom the people is constituted, cannot delegate

---

[30] Rawls, *Theory of Justice*, pp. 75–83.
[31] Nozick, *Anarchy, State, and Utopia*, pp. 173–5; cf. Hayek, *Mirage of Social Justice*, pp. 65–72, 114–15.
[32] For an example tending towards the position I refer to, see Bankowski and Mungham, *Images of Law*, pp. 29–30.

their authority to a representative, neither can any individual delegate his authority to a majority, in an assembly of which he is himself a member. That must surely be a singular species of consent the external indications of which are often to be found in an unremitting opposition in the first instance, and compulsory subjection in the second.[33]

A singular species of consent indeed; and a funny sort of freedom. I do not say this with a view to decrying democratic processes. On the contrary, the right of adult citizens to equal participation in the elective processes of representative democracy is essential to the ideal of social justice and equal citizenship which I here advocate. It must also be remembered that majority votes do not themselves guarantee justice. In the next chapter I attend to the question of the limits that ought to be acknowledged to the proper exercise of governmental and legislative power, even where governments and legislatures genuinely represent majority opinion or choice.

---

[33] See W. Godwin, *Enquiry Concerning Political Justice* (ed. I. Kramnick, Harmondsworth, 1976), p. 216 (1798 edn; bk. III, ch. 2, last para.).

2.

AGAINST MORAL
DISESTABLISHMENT

I. INTRODUCTION

THIS chapter is about the question of whether laws should be
used for the enforcement of moral values. Chapter 1 plainly
commits me to the view that there are some moral values which
ought to be enforced in law—for I meant not only to imply that
a social democrat's conception of social justice is compatible
with the rule of law; I also meant to imply that a good legal
order would be used to implement that form of social justice. So
if it is always a mistake to use laws for upholding or enforcing
moral values, my thesis is grounded in a mistake, and cannot
stand. And some might say that it is a mistake.[1] The legitimacy
of using laws to moral ends has been a much disputed point in
modern times. I must therefore defend my position by arguing
out a view on this question: how far, if at all, the law ought to be
used for the enforcement of moral values.

The starting-point for discussion of the question is to recognize
that it is itself a question of morality, rather more specifically a
question of political morality. For it is a question about the right
exercise of the public powers vested in agencies of state—legislatures, governments, judges, police, and prosecutors. Whoever
attempts to give a general answer to the question about the
right exercise of such powers is necessarily committed to stating
practical principles for the guidance of those who exercise them.
And practical principles of right conduct are moral principles.

At this point it may falsely seem that our discussion is at an
end. For if there must be some principles governing the right
exercise of state powers, and if these principles are moral
principles, then the proper use of law is that which respects
these principles. The issue is not then *whether* state power should

---

[1] See, e.g., works cited at nn. 3, 4, 7 and 16 of this chapter, and accompanying text.

be used in accordance with moral principles, but *what* moral principles should be observed in the exercise of state power. Is that not, in effect, the question what morality the law ought to enforce?

It is important, as has often been stressed, that we avoid treating these two points as being identical. To show why, let me draw an analogy. Suppose we were discussing the proper practice of psychiatry.[2] One view might be that in treating patients a psychiatrist ought to avoid making any moral judgment of or moral prescriptions for his patient, and ought only to treat patients with the aim of restoring them to health. Another view might be that in treating patients with a view to restoring them to health the psychiatrist must apply a moral conception of what health is. Both these views would be moral views ('ethical' views) about what it is morally incumbent on the psychiatrist to do. The former holds that the psychiatrist is morally bound not to refer to moral values in treating patients. The latter holds that the psychiatrist is morally bound to refer to moral values in treating patients. On either view, a good psychiatrist is one who observes a certain moral principle when acting as therapist; but only on the second view ought therapy to be conducted by reference to what are deemed moral values *for the patient.*

A similar distinction could be made between two possible views about the proper exercise of state powers. One view might be that the responsible persons are morally bound to exercise their powers of legislation, etc., without reference to the question of how it is morally right or wrong for citizens to behave. An opposed view would be that the responsible persons are morally bound to exercise their powers of legislation, etc., by reference to what are deemed moral values for the citizens of the polity in question. Both views are moral views. Both concern what is morally required in the exercise of state power. But the former view is that the morally proper exercise of state power should be based on no further moral presuppositions as to the values citizens ought to observe; whereas the latter view requires such power to be exercised in accordance with further

---

[2] These questions are canvassed in many works. See for example T. Szasz, *The Ethics of Psychoanalysis* (London, 1974).

moral presuppositions as to the values citizens ought to observe. The former view is perhaps akin to the view that there ought to be no legal establishment of an official state religion; the latter, to the view that it is a proper exercise of state power to require conformity to the creed and forms of worship of an established state religion. For that reason, let me call the former view 'the principle of moral disestablishment'.

Although the principle of moral disestablishment is itself a moral principle concerning the right use of state power, what it prescribes is that such power never be used to enforce moral values. Those who hold it, hold, of course, that it is of moral value that the holders of public powers abstain from enforcing moral values. The question today is whether state power should be exercised in accordance with the principle of moral disestablishment, or in accordance with some rival principle which in some form requires or permits state power to be exercised with respect to moral norms and values extraneous to the rival principle in view.

We should be clear from the outset that this question has important practical bearing on many currently controversial issues. Let it be supposed, for example, that the majority of the members of a legislature or of the electors in a democratic state holds that each of the following types of conduct are morally wrongful:

1. Deliberately killing people—murder
2. Deliberately doing violence to people—assault
3. Deliberately taking another's property—theft
4. Procuring abortions—abortion
5. Publishing obscene articles—obscenity
6. Participating in homosexual intercourse—sodomy
7. Extra-marital heterosexual intercourse—fornication and adultery
8. Treating animals cruelly—cruelty

Let it be further supposed that the criminal law of the state under consideration contains provisions under which murder, assault, theft, abortion, obscenity, sodomy, fornication and adultery, and cruelty to animals are all criminal offences subject, upon trial and conviction, to punishments of varying severity. Would it then be a sufficient justification for upholding (or, in the first place, enacting) all these provisions, that all these forms of conduct are sincerely considered by the relevant majority to be morally wrong—even gravely morally wrong?

According to the principle of moral disestablishment, the answer must be 'No'. For under that principle no consideration of the moral wrongfulness or rightfulness of any way of acting is of itself a consideration which holders of state power may treat as relevant to the exercise of their powers. To this the existence of democratic or non-democratic institutions is irrelevant. For state power—power to legislate, power to administer, power to adjudicate—is no less state power when it is controlled by majority choices among the citizens than when it is controlled by minority choices. The principle of moral disestablishment is as binding on the democratic legislative process as on a undemocratic one, if it is valid at all.

Its validity has been a hotly contested issue in debates over law reform in many countries in recent decades. Laws against sodomy, against abortion, against obscene publications, and against fornication and adultery have been criticized as merely enforcing moral values—whether or nor majority values. Under the weight of criticism and debate, they have in many states been repealed partly or entirely, and some have in the United States been struck down as unconstitutional because infringing basic constitutional rights. Then the counter-arguments are raised. Why let these forms of wickedness be practised with impunity when similarly, or less, wicked doings like murder, assault, theft, and cruelty to animals remain punishable? Should excessive legal liberalization not be reversed? In the recent history of Iran, for example, we have seen the Islamic revolutionaries denouncing the former regime's tendency to moral (and religious) disestablishment and exacting the most extreme penalties from sodomites, fornicators, and adulterers, in a triumphal re-establishment of the proclaimed values of Islam.

Whether we should embrace or reject the principle of moral disestablishment is thus an urgent question. It bears acutely upon live issues in contemporary societies. If we reject it, we face a no less urgent question, that of what to accept in its stead.

In the rest of this chapter, I shall do three things: first, I shall expound the best case I can for the principle of moral disestablishment; secondly, I shall show why it seems to me untenable; finally, I shall suggest an alternative principle of limited moral establishment, which I believe admits all that is sound in the case for moral disestablishment while carefully guarding against any allowance of moral totalitarianism.

II. THE CASE FOR THE PRINCIPLE OF MORAL DISESTABLISHMENT

Those who argue against a legal establishment of a compulsory state religion do not necessarily attack the importance of religion or religious belief and practice. On the contrary, they commonly argue that religion is too important to come under the control of any state. Its importance is as a conscientious expression of the faith of each individual. True religion is the expression of true conviction; healthy churches are those sustained by nothing other than the free and dedicated commitment of the believers. State-coerced professions of faith, compulsory exactions of tithes, and enforced attendances at acts of worship are hence inimical to true religion and healthy churches.

The fundamental basis of the case for what I am calling 'moral disestablishment' is materially the same as that for religious disestablishment, or non-establishment. Its proponents do not devalue, but stress, the importance of morality for human beings; too important for the state, they say. The demands of morality are demands incumbent on each human being as an autonomous (or self-regulating) human being. True moral values are those realized in the free and uncoerced choices of persons, acting conscientiously in accordance with the principles to which they willingly subject themselves. True moral virtue is not constituted by outward conformity to externally imposed standards backed by the deterrence of lawful penalties. It is constituted by free self-commitment to inwardly accepted standards and values, and by choices motivated by that self-commitment. Moral discipline is self-discipline, not the discipline of police, courts, and prisons.

Hence, precisely because the cultivation of true moral values and of true virtue depends on self-discipline rather than external discipline, it requires liberty of choice. This view, despite its obvious roots in Kantian moral philosophy, is also central to the utilitarian John Stuart Mill's argument in his classical statement of legal liberalism, his *Essay on Liberty*;[3] and it has been forcefully restated in our own time in H. L. A. Hart's *Law, Liberty and Morality*, and related works.[4] As Ronald Dworkin points out, Mill's ideal of liberty is thus grounded in a belief in the necessity of independence of action for moral personality.[5] The independence of a moral agent is at least qualified, if not even wholly abrogated, if state powers are exercised with a view to laying down through criminal law the moral norms to be observed by every citizen under threat of coercive punishments in case of disobedience.

That would be so even where there were perfect conformity between a person's own moral standards and the norms of the criminal law. But such perfect conformity is by no means guaranteed. If moral principles are those which are autonomously embraced by individuals as independent moral persons, it is possible that state power exercised in the name of moral standards may prescribe norms in conflict with one or other of the principles to which a person is conscientiously committed as his or her moral principles. Then not merely does the deterrent effect of coercive punishment qualify the freedom of the individual's choice; it operates as a direct deterrent against his/her doing what he/she thinks right, or at least as a coercing motive against his/her doing something which it seems in principle morally acceptable to do, and perhaps preferable in a given context.

This argument from a possible diversity or conflict of moral views, as between those of particular citizens and those of the holders of legislative power, is not one which presupposes moral subjectivism or relativism in a radical sense. Mill, in particular,

---

[3] J. S. Mill, *On Liberty and Considerations on Representative Government* (ed. R. B. McCallum, Oxford, 1946); cf. Godwin's *Enquiry Concerning Political Justice* (ed. I. Kramnick, Harmondsworth, 1976), anticipating many of Mill's arguments, and applying them also to religious disestablishment.

[4] H. L. A. Hart, *Law, Liberty and Morality* (London, 1963); *The Morality of the Criminal Law* (London, 1965); 'Social Solidarity and the Enforcement of Morality', 35 *Univ. of Chicago Law Rev.* (1967–8) 1–13. See also MacCormick, *H. L. A. Hart* (London, 1981), ch. 12.

[5] R. Dworkin, *Taking Rights Seriously* (London, 1977), ch. 11 on 'Liberty and Liberalism'. I agree with Dworkin's ascription to Mill of the idea of 'liberty as independence'; cf. ch. 7 below.

certainly believed that there was an objective truth in questions of morality.[6] Indeed, because he believed that, he believed that there was a special urgency in the independent search for truth by every man and woman. The difficulty for him was not *whether* there is a truth, but *what* is true, *who* can claim to know the truth, and *how* best to secure that truth can be discovered. His answer was, in moral and other matters, that there ought to be the greatest possible freedom of argument, enquiry, and experimentation as the most reliable process whereby over time humans may approximate more closely to the truth. To repress particular ways of thinking and living on the grounds that they conflict with what state authorities or temporary democratic majorities conceive to be morally true is thus inimical both to the pursuit of moral truth, establishable (if at all) only by free discussion and experimentation, and to the moral independence of truth-seeking individuals.[7]

Cumulatively, the arguments sketched above make out a powerful moral case for the principle of moral disestablishment as a guiding principle for the exercise of state powers, at least in respect of the criminal law. Considerations such as that of self-discipline as essential to moral behaviour, autonomous self-commitment or moral independence as being potentially endangered by state-enforced moral norms, and freedom of discussion and experimentation as conditions for getting at the truth, all seem to tell heavily in favour of requiring the state to abstain from establishing a single moral code for the whole polity in the coercive forms of criminal law.

Of itself, however, the principle of moral disestablishment is negative only. It tells us how state power ought not to be exercised. If we accept it, there remains the question of what are the permissible grounds for the exercise of such public power.

The classical answer of moral disestablishmentarians has been recourse to what Joel Feinberg helpfully dubs the 'harm principle'.[8] This is the principle that the legislative and law-enforcement powers of the state may rightfully be used to

---

[6] See for example Mill's argument in *Utilitarianism* (London, 1863); cf. again Godwin's *Enquiry*.

[7] A major part of Mill's case for freedom of discussion in *On Liberty* is the argument that in conditions of free discussion the truth will prevail on its own merits.

[8] J. Feinberg, *Social Philosophy* (Englewood Cliffs, NJ, 1973), pp. 25 f.

prevent persons from doing harm to other persons. John Stuart Mill indeed held that the *only* purpose for which in a civilized society coercive power could rightfully be used over any person was the prevention of harm to others.[9] Feinberg helpfully elucidates the concept of harm thus: 'A humanly inflicted harm is conceived as the violation of one of a person's interests, an injury to something in which he has a genuine stake.'[10] Further, as he points out, Mill must be understood as including within the harm principle not only violations of individual interests but also violations of public interests, in the sense of attacks upon those public institutions which are essential to the ordering of a liberal state.[11]

Some, such as H. L. A. Hart (though not Feinberg) extend the concept of 'harm' to include the perpetration of offences upon people's feelings or sensibilities by public displays and manifestations.[12] Let us suppose this to be an acceptable extension. Let us also follow Hart's proposal (again rejected by Feinberg) to allow that the harm principle may have some admissible paternalistic applications.[13] If some conduct by an individual may be gravely harmful to him/herself, then at least in the case of children and the mentally incapacitated it is justifiable to prohibit such conduct; and in case of the severest permanent harms, even adults may justifiably be restrained by law from self-injurious conduct. Where this requires another's collaboration, the consent of the harm-victim is, in these cases of justifiable paternalism, properly excluded as a defence available to the collaborator if prosecuted for the harmful act perpetrated.

The reason offered for accepting the harm principle in any form is thoroughly compatible with the arguments against moral establishmentarianism. These arguments, we saw, rest

---

[9] J. S. Mill, *On Liberty*, ch. 1.
[10] Feinberg, *Social Philosophy*, p. 26.
[11] Ibid., pp. 25–6.
[12] Hart, *Law, Liberty and Morality*, pp. 43–8; cf. Feinberg, *Social Philosophy*, pp. 28–9.
[13] Hart, op. cit., pp. 30–4; cf. Feinberg, op. cit., pp. 45–52. For the purposes of the present argument, nothing turns on interpreting the 'harm principle' broadly rather than with the greater exactitude on which Feinberg insists. In particular, my criticism of the 'harm principle' as supposedly compatible with 'moral disestablishment' holds good in either case. For other purposes, Feinberg's distinctions are extremely illuminating.

on respect for persons as autonomous moral agents. But just as a person's capability for free moral choice can be inhibited or rendered nugatory by legal prohibitions backed with threatened punishments, so can it be inhibited by actual or threatened harms inflicted by other individuals. Hence to prohibit and to deter as far as possible such actually or threateningly harmful acts is justified on the same grounds as justify the principle of moral disestablishment. The point is perhaps at its weakest in the case of simply offensive behaviour, but at least the grosser forms of offensive public display can be said to inhibit the freedom of ordinarily sensitive people to go about their affairs in public places. In the case of the paternalistic extension of the harm principle, people are indeed inhibited by law from exercise of momentary freedoms, but only with a view to preserving their longer-run freedom and independence.

A further point can here be made, which goes back at least as far as to Adam Smith's *Theory of Moral Sentiments*.[14] Punishment involves harm wilfully inflicted on individuals, through seizing of property and/or deprivation of liberty and/or imposition of physical suffering up to and possibly including death. Criminal laws in providing for liability to punishment put people in fear of undergoing such suffering. This seems to be morally objectionable in itself. But at least if criminal laws were restricted in ambit to those justified by the harm principle, it would follow that such wilfully imposed suffering and wilful arousal of the fear of it were used by the state only so as to diminish or restrict the infliction on innocent individuals of commensurably similar forms of suffering.[15] This would not be so if the whole range of moral values were admitted to enforcement by criminal law.

Hence a further moral argument for the principle of moral disestablishment when coupled with the harm principle is the argument that their conjoint implementation would tend to secure the minimization of human suffering deliberately inflicted by other humans. In implementing the principle of

---

[14] Ed. D. D. Raphael and A. L. Macfie (Oxford, 1976). See pt. VI, § 2, intro.: 'Proper resentment for injustice attempted, or actually committed, is the only motive which, in the eyes of the impartial spectator, can justify our hurting or disturbing in any respect the happiness of our neighbour. To do so from any other motive is itself a violation of the laws of justice, which force ought to be employed to restrain or punish.'

[15] See Mill, *On Liberty*, ch. II.

moral disestablishment we restrict exercises of the state's power to harm people by punishing them; in implementing the harm principle, we allow the state to threaten and to impose harms by way of punishment, but only in order to prevent private perpetration of greater harms essentially similar in kind. The case seems all in all a strong one.

If we ask as to the practical implications of the principles for the matters taken as instances earlier, we find that murder, assault, and theft—as harms to individuals—are clearly within the admitted sphere of criminal law; that the legitimacy of prohibiting abortions depends on whether the human foetus is deemed a person; that cruelty to animals is covered only if we extend the harm principle to preventing harm to sentient beings generally; that obscene publications legislation is justified only in case of public displays having a grossly offensive character; that sodomy and fornication in private between consenting adults must fall beyond the reach of the criminal law; and that adultery is problematic depending on the weight placed on harm to the cuckolded spouse in cases where he or she experiences the other's adultery as an injury.

The trend of criminal-law reform in many democratic states has been exactly that which would be justified by conjoint acceptance of the principle of moral disestablishment and the harm principle. These principles have had powerful advocates, and their advocacy, it seems, has had persuasive effects on legislators' minds. We must therefore consider the counter-arguments which might be raised against accepting these principles.

III. ARGUMENTS AGAINST MORAL DISESTABLISHMENT

Of all the moral evils there are in the world, human suffering wilfully inflicted by other human beings seems among the worst. Whatever else is a requirement of morally acceptable conduct, it seems an evident moral requirement that one abstain from wilfully hurting or harming others, save under some exceptional justification or excuse.

If the above position is accepted, there is reason to doubt the claim that the harm principle is a satisfactory corollary or complement to the principle of moral disestablishment. If it is permissible in principle for the criminal law to prohibit harmful ways of acting, and if the criminal law does—I know of no criminal code which does not—prohibit most sorts of harmful violations of person and property, then at least it is the case that the prohibitions of the criminal law coincide with all but universally accepted moral requirements. With or without the Hartian addenda about offensiveness and paternalism, the harm principle itself seems to legitimize the legal enforcement of a central moral value, that of securing individuals from harms wilfully inflicted by others. The criminal law, in prohibiting wilfully harmful behaviour and subjecting harm-doers to punishment seems directly to enforce requirements which are also moral requirements. This is justified by the harm principle.

But the principle of moral disestablishment is here defined (and, no one else having used the phrase, my say as to its definition is the last word on the subject) as the principle that state power must never be used to enforce moral values. If the harm principle authorizes the use of state power to enforce certain moral values, then it is not a corollary to, but a partial contradiction of or exception to, the principle of moral disestablishment.

A possible reply is that laws authorized by the harm principle only coincide or overlap with moral requirements, but do not actually enforce moral values as such. What the state authorities are properly concerned with is the harmfulness of harmful behaviour, not its immoral character—even though the moral values offended by harmful actions are, as H. L. A. Hart observes, 'universal values' upheld in some form by all human societies.[16] This seems a plausible interpretation of the harm principle, but it is subject to at least two radical objections, the first rooted in the concept of harm and the relationship of the criminal law to other branches of the law; the second rooted in the nature of punishment as an institution.

As to the concept of harm, this presupposes our identification of certain interests of persons as individuals ('private interests') and as citizens of a body politic having some common good ('the public interest'), which interests are capable of being adversely affected by human actions. Hence, to specify the application of

[16] Hart, *Law, Liberty and Morality*, p. 70.

the concept 'harm' in order to put the harm principle into operation, it is necessary to specify the interests which are to be protected. This necessarily involves the making of choices which are morally loaded however we make them. After all, we saw that the justification of the principle of moral disestablishment coupled with the harm principle depended on an appeal to the (moral) value of respecting persons as autonomous moral agents, and thus to the derivative value of protecting persons from invasions of their autonomy. Hence, to frame a conception of the interests of humans as moral persons which require protection is (whether or not the matter be controversial) to elaborate the content of a fundamental moral value.

Moreover, when we turn to consideration of the public interest or the common good, while some of us may wish to protest against definitions of the public interest (such as Lord Devlin's[17]) which take it to include a public interest in the maintenance and vindication of shared standards of moral decency even in private behaviour, we thereby again demonstrate that the question of what are the interests to be protected against harmful violations is a controversial *moral* one.

These two grounds for supposing that 'harm' is itself a morally loaded (and essentially contested[18]) concept can be further reinforced by adversion to the necessary interrelationships which hold between criminal law and other branches of law. Exponents of the harm principle treat theft and related offences as clearly covered by their principle. But theft presupposes property. Here is an obvious example of one of the points of intersection between private law and criminal law, necessarily relevant to applying the harm principle. The interest protected from invasion ('harm') by the criminal laws concerning theft and related offences is the interest of an owner in his/her property.

Nothing, however, could be more obviously a moral question than the question whether individual interests in private property are always, sometimes, or never legitimate. The issue of the justice of systems of private property is a central one in the great clash of ideologies in the contemporary world. As an issue

---

[17] See P. Devlin, *The Enforcement of Morals* (London, 1965), pp. 115 f.
[18] See W. B. Gallie, 'Essentially Contested Concepts', 56 *Proceedings of the Aristotelian Society* (1955–6) 169.

of justice, it is obviously an issue of moral as well as political and economic import.

No less moral issues, nor less controversial ones, are those concerning such matters of public law as taxation on the one hand and welfare rights on the other: how much ought people to contribute in tax to the common revenues of the state; how much ought they to receive in cash or kind for the relief of what needs? However legislatures answer such questions, they universally find it necessary to hedge in the taxation and welfare systems they set up; to hedge them in behind the protection of the criminal law, by legislation prohibiting under penalty various statutory offences whose commission would be inimical to the system established.

As these examples suggest, resort to the criminal law is always parasitic on or ancillary to an established legal order of rights and duties in the spheres of private law and public law. Such an order of rights and duties (et cetera) has to be founded on some (however muddled and patchwork) conception of a just ordering of society. The interests protected from invasion by criminal laws are interests legitimated by a given conception of a just social order. And the harm principle would be vacuous without some such conception of legitimate interests. Hence, naturally, the laws which are justified by the harm principle on a given interpretation of 'harm' do indeed coincide with widely held precepts against 'harmful' behaviour. But they do not *merely* coincide; the criminal law in so far as it is concerned with fending off harmful behaviour is *necessarily* geared to protection of what are legitimate interests *according to a certain dominant political morality*—the 'ideology' which, as Gramsci and his followers put it, enjoys 'hegemony' within a given polity.[19]

These propositions are supported by the second set of considerations I wish to adduce in denying that the concept of 'harm' as it figures in the harm principle can plausibly be interpreted as a morally neutral concept. These further considerations concern the nature of punishment.

The act of 'punishing' as such is always and necessarily an expressive and symbolic act, expressive of an attitude of serious

---

[19] I am indebted to my colleagues David Nelken and Richard Kinsey for this point. See Antonio Gramsci, *Prison Notebooks* (London, 1971), esp. p. 260.

disapprobation of the thing done by the person who is punished, punished on the very ground that he is held guilty of that thing. This point has been so well made by many before me, including for example Emile Durkheim, Sir Walter Moberley, and Joel Feinberg,[20] that I need not linger long in restating it here. When parents punish naughty children, they do something more than merely invest the child's need (undesired by the parents) with consequences of an undesirable kind (undesired, they hope, by the child). In doing that they also evince their own more or less severe *disapproval* of the child's act. Whether this is a good way of imparting moral attitudes or not, it is certainly a way of doing so, and one commonly in use.

State-imposed punishments require a more complicated account, because the state is an artificial rather than a natural person. Legislatures legislate against offences, prosecutors prosecute particular alleged offenders, judges preside over the trials, juries convict or acquit, judges pass sentence on convicted persons, and other officials implement the punishment according to the judicial sentence. Many human minds and wills must collaborate together in the criminal process of the state, and the individual persons concerned have doubtless diverse and varying personal opinions and attitudes upon moral and political questions. As *organized* activity, however, the acts of all the disparate individuals involved in the process must cohere together under common or interrelated norms of official conduct directed by some supposed common purpose and expressive of what would be a single attitude were it possible for one individual to accomplish all (as could the paterfamilias of old within his own family).

As Hans Kelsen and John Chipman Gray both showed, the very facts which enable us to personify 'the state' and conceive of it as a single acting subject are the facts of coherently organized systems of action involving many individual human beings exercising various sorts of authority under law.[21] The inter-

. [20] See E. Durkheim, *The Division of Labour in Society* (tr. G. Simpson, New York and London, 1964), pp. 108–10; Sir Walter Moberley, *The Ethics of Punishment* (London, 1968), chs. 8, 9; J. Feinberg, *Doing and Deserving* (Princeton and London, 1970), ch. 5, 'The Expressive Theory of Punishment'.

[21] See H. Kelsen, *General Theory of Law and State* (tr. A. Wedberg, Cambridge, Mass., 1945), pp. 181–206; J. C. Gray, *Nature and Sources of the Law* (2nd edn., ed. R. Gray, New York, 1929), ch. 3. Cf. MacCormick, 'A Political Frontier of Jurisprudence: John Chipman Gray on the State', 65 *Cornell Law Quarterly* (1980–1), forthcoming.

related acts of many individuals and groups acting in their
'official' capacity are imputed to 'the state' as its acts. The
purposes and attitudes of the state are those postulated official
purposes and attitudes which make rational the interrelated
acts of officials—rational, because they can be understood as
subserving some reasonably coherent scheme of values.[22]

Hence, while we can give a simple account of the way in
which an individual person (a parent, for example) punishing
another individual (a child, for example) thereby expresses an
individual moral attitude, a more complicated account is required of the way in which the punishments of the criminal law
express an attitude. But the complicated account follows the
lines I have sketched above. When legislators prohibit some
type of action under a provision of criminal law, they represent
such a way of acting as being in some way and on some ground
reprehensible or worthy of disapprobation. When, after
prosecution, trial, and conviction, a judge sentences an offender
to some legally allowed or prescribed punishment for that
offence, he thereby publicly as an officer of state sets the seal of
public disapprobation upon the wrongful act of which the
offender has been found guilty. He expresses the state's condemnation of the deed done.

Judges themselves have frequently given voice to this view of
their own activity.[23] They often speak of themselves as expressing in appropriately forceful terms 'society's' denunciation
of wrongful or even wicked acts. They visit misdeeds with
'condign' punishments. The judges' claim to be acting on behalf of 'society' is as much (or as little) tendentious as any claim
by any other officer of state to be acting 'for the whole of society',
'for the community', and so forth. The citizen body of any
modern state—the polity as a whole—is a large and diverse
group of persons, a group of groups and classes and cultural
communities and political parties and sectional associations of
many kinds. Multinational states like the United Kingdom
contain diverse national traditions within them. And so on. To
claim that for every state there is one 'society', and that officers

<hr>

[22] See MacCormick, *Legal Reasoning and Legal Theory* (Oxford, 1978), ch. 7, on the
notion of coherence in the values expressed within a legal system.
[23] See the quotations from the English judiciary given by Hart in *Law, Liberty and
Morality*, pp. 60–9, and in *The Morality of the Criminal Law*, ch. 1.

of state speak in the name of 'society', is to make doubtful claims about the unity of consensus within an entire polity. Often if not always it is a rhetorical and self-legitimating pretension rather than a testable assertion of fact.

While it is on such grounds doubtful how far or in what sense judges express 'society's' condemnation of the offences to which they apportion sentences, it is certain that they thereby express the state's condemnation of the acts which state legislation stigmatizes as offences. And an attitude of condemnation or disapprobation is *per se* a moral attitude.

Hence, since what the harm principle authorizes is the exercise of public powers, in particular powers of criminal legislation and *punishment*, with a view to repressing or restraining harmful conduct, it follows that the harm principle does directly contemplate the (supposedly) immoral quality of harmful acts. Indeed, any principle whatever which allows that the state may resort to *punishment* necessarily allows state enforcement of *some* moral values. Hence any such principle is incompatible with the principle of moral disestablishment.

Some thinkers, most notably Barbara Wootton,[24] have indeed argued that precisely because of the moralistic implications of such concepts as 'crime', 'offence' 'guilt', and 'punishment', it should be at least a long-run aim to expunge them from legal use and practice. Her rival principle is one of 'social hygiene', aimed at identifying and curing propensities to socially harmful behaviour whenever and however these manifest themselves in individuals' behaviour.

To this, my first objection is that the morally loaded concept of 'harm' remains intrinsic even to such a radical proposal. Since that is so, it is preferable to retain the moral and morally contestable concepts of criminal law as we have them, including the requirement that persons be not, at least not normally, liable to state interference unless by some wilful or reckless act they infringe some provision of the published criminal law. Secondly, I would argue (with H. L. A. Hart[25]) that only such a regime secures the sort of freedom which enables people to plan their lives and live according to their own plan. Thirdly, I

---

[24] B. Wootton, *Crime and the Criminal Law* (London, 1963), esp. ch. 3 and *Social Science and Social Pathology* (London, 1959), ch. 8.

[25] Hart, *Punishment and Responsibility* (Oxford, 1968), ch. 7.

would argue that only where we deal in the coinage of 'crime' and 'punishment', with all the associated moral stigma, do we have a system which is apt to have any useful deterrent effect upon the commission of socially harmful deeds (according to some moral/ideological conception of 'harm').[26]

Fourthly and finally, I would object along lines laid down by Durkheim and partially retraced by Lord Devlin that the cohesiveness and solidarity of any large and complex polity does require some common morality.[27] It is tendentious in the extreme to claim that the criminal law captures or enforces the norms of some pre-existing or independently existing moral code upheld by the consensus of the whole citizen body. But there is a powerful and plausible case for supposing that, precisely because of its symbolic force as the public morality of the state, the criminal law with its public drama and symbolism of trials and punishment can be to some extent *constitutive* of a common morality for the body of citizens as such. The criminal law does not always and necessarily *reflect* a moral consensus; but it tends to generate one.[28] Since some degree of moral consensus is a prerequisite of social solidarity, it is a *useful* aspect of the system of criminal law and of the institution of criminal punishment that they are morally 'loaded'.

I conclude not merely that the harm principle is a principle which entails the enforcement of some moral requirements, being thus incompatible with the principle of moral disestablishment, but also that there is an independent and compelling reason to reject the principle of moral disestablishment. According to the argument from social solidarity, the criminal law is, and in some degree ought to be, concerned with enforcing moral values. The powers of the state are, and in some degree ought to be, used for the enforcement of moral values. Since I find the argument from social solidarity convincing, my remaining question is: in what degree?

---

[26] Ibid., p. 209, and cf. my *H. L. A. Hart* (London, 1981), ch. 11, section *b*.

[27] Durkheim, *Division of Labour*; Devlin, *Enforcement of Morals*; and see Hart's discussion of Devlin's and Durkheim's views on this point in 'Social Solidarity'.

[28] Cf. K. Olivecrona, *Law as Fact* (1st edn., Copenhagen, 1939), pp. 54–5; M. D. A. Freeman, *The Legal Structure* (London, 1979), ch. 3.

IV. A RIVAL PRINCIPLE: LIMITED
MORAL ESTABLISHMENT

The regulation and ordering of any polity must comprehend or cover what our eighteenth-century predecessors called 'duties of justice'.[29] These they took to be a subset of the whole set of moral duties, demarcated by the following criterion: performance of such duties can properly be *exacted* coercively, whereas higher duties such as those of benevolence (charity) and the demands of superior virtue beyond the call of duty cannot properly be subjected to coercive exaction. Duties of justice between persons are moral duties, but they constitute a part only of morality. The law, in systematically regulating the exaction and vindication of such duties, has a decidedly moral function. But the proper function of law relates only to this restricted moral sphere, not to the whole of morality.

The upshot of the two preceding sections seems to be to favour a revival of that way of dealing with the subject-matter, though to revive the terminology might be misleading. What we need is a principle of limited moral establishment—unequivocally moral, for the reasons accumulated in section III above; severely limited, for the reasons accumulated in section II.

Section II suggested that respecting the autonomy of persons as moral beings is not merely a moral value but a prerequisite of morality itself. If there is any fundamental moral value, that of respect for persons as autonomous agents seems the best candidate for that position.

If it is morally incumbent on us to respect moral personality in all its manifestations, then for each of us that has two implications: we are required to respect moral personality in ourselves and we are required to respect it in others. The requirements of morality are requirements as to self-respect and as to other-respect.[30] These are related: if it were not obligatory that I act in a self-respecting way, why should it be obligatory on others to treat me as a being worthy of respect?

The idea that moral requirements ('duties', 'obligations') are

---

[29] See, e.g., Adam Smith, *Theory of Moral Sentiments*; also Hume, *An Enquiry Concerning the Principles of Morals*, § V.

[30] See R. S. Downie and E. Telfer, *Respect for Persons* (London, 1969).

in this way bifurcated is helpful towards getting at the reasons for only allowing a limited state establishment of morality via criminal law—or otherwise.

If I were to treat another person as a being incapable of acting as self-respect requires save under pressure of external coercion or external allurements and rewards administered by me, I would prima facie deny that other the opportunity of self-respect as an autonomous moral being. Unlike me, who choose the coercions and allurements for him, he is not capable of morally proper choice—so I necessarily imply in treating him as I treat him. Hence, what I do for the sake of his self-respect paradoxically denies him the possibility of self-respect; except in one case. The one case is that of parentalism, where an adult, a parent or one *in loco parentis*, assists another to actualize the potential in himself/herself for full moral personality.

Hence there is a particular inappropriateness in enforcing upon others performance of any duties which we conceive as duties of self-respect. For example, if obscene publications tend to deprave or corrupt a person, and if it is a duty of self-respect to avoid temptations to self-depraving experiences, there is nevertheless a good reason not to use coercions or coercive punishments against one who breaches that duty.

There is a contrast in relation to duties of other-respect. So far as the acting individual is concerned, the value of his autonomy and self-respect is indeed depreciated to the extent that someone else forces him to act as he ought rather than leaving it to him to choose freely the right act. But since we are contemplating an *other*-regarding duty, there is another moral interest at stake. That other person's opportunities for self-respect as an autonomous moral agent come under threat from the former's possible breach of duty. The very considerations which prohibit us from enforcing on anyone the requirements of *his* self-respect require us to intervene when the conditions of a person's self-respect are endangered by another person's disrespectful acting towards the former.

Hence, of the requirements of morality, the only ones which outside of parental and quasi-parental relationships it is permissible to *enforce*, are other-regarding requirements of respect for persons. Unfortunately, as I remarked in section II, there is a possible diversity of moral views, including a diversity of views as to the requirements of other-regarding respect for persons. So we cannot say for certain in abstract terms what these are. But that does not debar us from requiring that those who exercise legislative power exercise it only with a view to enforcing those duties of respect for persons which they honestly and for good reasons hold to be other-regarding duties.

Even in this sphere we may further require them to exercise it with regard to the inevitable risk that some people will be coerced to act against conscience and that others will be liable to punishment for actions they conscientiously performed in accordance with what they honestly considered to be requirements of respect for others (some cases of euthanasia might arise here; also abortions). Hence I prescribe a twofold limitation on the proper use of state power, in the context of a principle of limited moral establishment: state powers may be and ought to be exercised so as to enforce moral requirements, but only those which are other-regarding duties of respect for persons, and only to the smallest extent necessary for securing to all the conditions of self-respect as autonomous beings.

Such a principle has much in common with what the harm principle covers; indeed the harm principle is thoroughly compatible with this, and the arguments for it can be applied to my above-stated principle. The advantage of the present statement is that it faces clearly the morally laden quality of the concept 'harm', and recognizes that legislators' and others' conceptions of what respect for persons requires may be varied. Also, my present formulation fits in with the thesis propounded in chapters 4 and 7 that securing the conditions of self-respect requires positive intervention by the state through general welfare and educational provision, as well as negative intervention to prevent private harms. Subject to all that, I should like to repeat the point that social cohesiveness or solidarity does depend on *some* common moral precepts which can constitute a moral consensus. The consensus I should wish to see would be upon the disapprovability of acts invasive of others' self-respect and bodily security or damaging to public institutions required for securing people's conditions of self-respect. Beyond that, moral issues should be left to the autonomous persons whose autonomy and self-respect would then be hedged in by adequate legal protections. That would be a good basis for social solidarity.

It remains to add here only the admission that the notion of 'duties of justice' used in the concluding section of the present chapter has been left somewhat vague and lacking in content. So also the notion of those rights of persons which we ought to observe in justice to them remains undefined and vague. The following chapters constitute an attempt to render these notions more exact, sometimes through discussion of the works of other thinkers, sometimes through discussion of particular problem cases of legal and moral rights and duties.

3.
CIVIL LIBERTIES AND THE LAW

PERHAPS no words could serve better as an introduction of this chapter's theme than the best-known lines from Barbour's *Bruce*, that great medieval epic of the Scottish War of Independence:

> Ah Fredome is a noble thing
> Fredome maiss man to have liking
> Fredome all solace to man givis
> He livis at ease that freely livis.

In a modern idiom we might put the same thought by arguing that freedom is a condition of human self-respect and of that contentment which resides in the ability to pursue one's own conception of a full and rewarding life. That is the case. Solzhenitsyn's and many other contemporary writings confirm the point that Barbour goes on to make. Those who have never lost freedom are scarcely aware how precious it is. Those who have tasted, and then escaped from, 'foul thralldom', 'think fredome mair to prize/Than all the gold in warld that is'. I agree, and shall here try to show why I agree.

What I have to say will fall into three sections: first, what liberty is and why people have a right to it; secondly, the idea of civil liberty, which is necessarily liberty under law, against the anarchist idea of natural liberty; thirdly, whether civil liberty is a necessary condition of true law. Throughout, I shall use the terms 'liberty' and 'freedom' as identical in meaning and entirely interchangeable.

I. LIBERTY AND THE RIGHT TO LIBERTY

By 'liberty' and 'freedom' I understand the absence of constraint on one's actions. There are two relevant kinds of constraint: factual and normative.[1]

Factual constraints are external forces which prevent or impede us from doing something we might otherwise have done, especially forces of constraint constituted by human actions aimed at such prevention or impediment. A nightwatchman gagged and bound, a prisoner locked in a cell—both are factually constrained from going where they wish as they wish. A speaker shouted down at a meeting is factually constrained from giving his speech.

As for normative constraint: a person is normatively constrained against doing something whenever it is his or her duty not to do it. Such duties, and thus such normative constraints, can be legal, moral, or social. Indeed whatever norms of conduct may be applicable to human action, so many are the dimensions of normative constraint. Legally, I have a duty not to publish a libel concerning any one of my readers. That is a normative constraint, entailing that I am not in law free to libel you. I have a moral duty to keep my promises, under which moral constraint, as it follows, I am not morally at liberty to break my word.

There being two relevant kinds of constraint, liberty as the absence of constraint has two aspects, factual and normative. They do not necessarily coincide. If I publish a libel or break a promise and get away with it, I have exercised factual freedom in defiance of normative constraint. A speaker who is shouted down is being denied the factual freedom to express the views which he is normatively at liberty to express, in all too many cases.

Happily, it is sometimes and indeed quite often the case that both aspects coincide. There is, as we say, 'nothing to stop us' doing something, and 'nothing against doing it'—neither factual nor normative constraints apply. We need a phrase to

---

[1] Some theorists of so-called 'positive freedom' seem to imply that absence of constraint is not a necessary condition of freedom; others, however, seem simply to wish to extend the list of undesirable constraints beyond the constraints of state coercion envisaged by 'negative libertarians'. The former opinion is to me unintelligible; the latter is consistent with my view. It seems to me odd that most political writing on liberty seems simply to ignore the notion of *normative* constraint and its absence, despite the fact that this is *definitive* of 'legal liberty' in one sense. Cf. sources cited ch. 1, nn. 21 and 25 above, and associated text.

cover this: let us adopt the usage that somebody is 'fully free', 'fully at liberty' to do something whenever there is neither factual nor normative constraint upon his/her doing it. An example: nothing and nobody is stopping me from writing this book, and I am in breach of no legal, moral, social, or other duty in doing so. I am fully free to write it.

Observe that it does not follow that I am capable of doing it or *a fortiori* of doing it well. My freedom to do it is already established; my capability awaits the test of your judgment. And that is a general truth: freedom to do something neither entails nor is entailed by capability to do it. Freedom is the absence of constraint in either or both senses, and that, in my judgment, is all there is to it.

When then is freedom a noble thing, the right to which may exercise us so deeply? In what aspects is the denial of freedom objectionable?

At the beginning of this chapter I spoke of freedom as 'a condition of human self-respect and of that contentment which resides in the ability to pursue one's own conception of a full and rewarding life'. To be able to decide what to do and how to do it, to carry out one's own decisions and accept their consequences, seems to me essential to one's self-respect as a human being, and essential to the possibility of that contentment. Such self-respect and contentment are in my judgment fundamental goods for human beings, the worth of life itself being on condition of having or striving for them. If a person were deliberately denied the opportunity of self-respect and that contentment, he would suffer deprivation of his essential humanity.

Rights, I have argued elsewhere,[2] concern those goods which it is wrong to deny to or to withhold from individuals. The more basic the good, the more basic the right. Life and factual liberty of action being among the conditions of what I shall abbreviate as self-respect and the pursuit of contentment, there are necessarily rights to life and to liberty of action and inaction.

But these are not rights to total and unfettered liberty of action, for a very simple reason. One person's freedom can be another person's unfreedom. A slave-master has a factual

---

[2] Ch. 8 below; see also 'Rights in Legislation', *Law, Morality and Society* (ed. P. M. S. Hacker and J. Raz, Oxford, 1977).

freedom to deal with other human beings in ways open to no one in a society such as ours. He has that freedom precisely because his slaves are utterly subjected to his power of factual constraint. Yet if the conditions of self-respect and the pursuit of contentment are a good for any human being they are a good for everyone. If on that account there is for anyone a right to freedom, the same right must hold for everyone. Therefore I agree with Kant and Rawls.[3] A person's right to liberty is, as a moral right, a right to so much liberty as is consistent with every other person having as much.[4]

What we are speaking of here is a right to liberty in its aspect as an absence of factual constraints imposed by other human beings. In concluding that there is a moral right to non-constraint only up to the point at which each can equally enjoy the same extent of non-constraint, we are concluding also as to the proper extent of moral liberty as a normative liberty. Each has a duty to respect the liberty of every other up to that point at which everbody can factually be equally free of constraint. Any freedom which one person enjoys at the cost of another's disproportionate unfreedom is not an exercise of the former's right, but a denial of the latter's.

Is the right to liberty in this sense absolute and unqualified? I think not. I have argued that it is a right because liberty is a condition of self-respect and the pursuit of contentment. But there are other conditions of self-respect and the pursuit of contentment, among them what may be crudely identified as a full stomach, a roof over one's head, and the opportunity to maintain these by a decent way of work. An economic order which denies such goods as these to some persons, or which systematically distributes them in grossly unequal measure, is as inimical to the equal claim of every person to self-respect,

---

[3] I. Kant, *Metaphysical Elements of Justice* (tr. J. Ladd, Indianapolis, 1965); J. Rawls, *A Theory of Justice* (Oxford, 1972), discussed in ch. 5 below.

[4] I agree with Rawls (more or less) that this should be made subject to one particular qualification. An institutional structure well adjusted to securing the right to equal liberty can justifiably grant special or exceptional liberties to holders of institutional positions and offices, but only in so far as these are necessary to securing the regime of equal basic liberties; a possible example is the granting of special privileges in speech to MPs or judges, so far as is essential to their doing their tasks 'without fear or favour'. See Rawls, *Theory of Justice*, p. 302.

etc., as is a political order which represses liberty unduly or distributes it in systematically unequal shares.

My fifth chapter deals with fairness in access to economic goods. What is obvious here is that although economic fairness can and does compete in some spheres with the claim of liberty, there are many vital spheres of liberty in which economic fairness cannot even in principle compete. Liberty in speech, in religion, in opinion, in political activity and organization, liberty from arbitrary arrest and seizure, liberty from abusive exercises of public power—such aspects of liberty are neutral in their bearing on the distribution of economic goods. Whether justified or not, proprietary and market liberties are different, since they do bear upon the distribution of economic goods.

The great heresy of the political right wing is to pretend that there are no liberties which compete with economic fairness, and the more that heresy is pressed (as by some of today's Conservatives, if I may say so) the more it generates a counter-heresy of the left: that a concern for liberty in any aspect is merely a manifestation of bourgeois ideology fit to be swept away with all else therein. An alternative fallacy is the assertion that giving someone a full stomach, a decent house, adequate health care, and a decent job is making him free in a way exclusively preferable to other freedoms. It is not. That these are unquestionable goods, to which people have right, does not make them liberties.[5] Liberties concern what you can do, not what you have.

In that sense of liberty, we each have a right to as much liberty as everyone can equally enjoy; where, but only where, liberty competes with fairness in access to economic goods, the right is qualified to the extent necessary to satisfy our conception of economic fairness.

II. CIVIL AND NATURAL LIBERTY: LAW AND ANARCHY

Civil liberty is liberty as conditioned by civil society, that is, society organized under the governance of an authoritative and announced system of law. The origin of the expression 'civil

[5] Of course, hunger or disease can be envisaged as constraints on human action, from which it is obviously desirable to set people free. But this depends on settling a system of fair access to economic goods, so the question of fairness here has priority.

liberty' is in contrast to 'natural liberty', the form of liberty which would prevail in a state of nature—the condition of mankind postulated by philosophers on the supposition of an absence of institutionalized laws and governments.

To understand the idea of civil liberty it is therefore necessary to consider the interaction of the concepts of law and of liberty. The primary characteristics of 'positive law' are that law is normative and that it is coercive.[6] A legal order is normative in that it comprises rules and principles in various ways guiding human social conduct and establishing criteria of judgment as to its rightness or wrongness. It is coercive in that for breaches of some of the duties laid down by legal rules and principles penalities are provided and are subject to coercive enforcement, while for other of the law's duties direct means of coercive enforcement of obligations are provided. Persons determined by law are legally empowered to cause such acts of coercion to be carried out, and likewise other ancillary acts of coercion such as commital to prison pending trial. In advanced societies, the organization of the state secures that these legal powers are supported by great, usually overwhelming, factual powers of coercion.

It follows as a necessary truth that law limits freedom, in both possible ways. Normatively, law imposes duties, and legal duty is the negation of legal liberty. Factually, the coercive machinery of the law is an engine of constraint, and factual liberty exists only where such constraint does not apply.

From that, however, it does not follow that law is necessarily inimical to the right to liberty as I have described it. That right is a right of each person to so much liberty as everyone can enjoy, subject to satisfaction of other conditions of self-respect and the pursuit of contentment, a proviso which covers at least the right to economic fairness according to some conception of economic fairness (which would have to be argued out within a general theory of distributive justice).

That right is then by its very definition a right to liberty delineated by a set of normative constraints. Every human being owes to every other a duty not to act so as to invade any other's factual liberty in any matter in relation to which equal

---

[6] Though not coercive by definition. See ch. 12 below.

freedom for everyone is possible. Even without positive law human beings 'in a state of nature' would rightfully enjoy only 'liberty, not licence' as John Locke put it.[7] That follows from the moral argument previously enunciated in this chapter.

It is possible therefore that the normative constraints prescribed by a legal system could be perfectly in accordance with the normative constraints which our particular conception of the right to liberty prescribes, allowance made for the competing claims of other basic rights. Of course it is essentially contestable among us what particular conception of the right should prevail. But it is not necessarily the case that a legal system will fail to conform to some reasonable conception of rightful liberty.

Since that is no more than a possibility, it is of course also possible that some of the law's constraints may be conceived as infringing the right to liberty. In my judgment the decision in the recent *Gay News* trial[8] in London enunciated an unjust rule. It was laid down that blasphemy is still a crime by the law of England, and the editor of *Gay News* was convicted and fined heavily for publishing a poem found by the jury to cast scandalous aspersions on the person of Christ. I have since seen the poem, and while I found it both mawkish and lacking in taste, I am astonished that a work written with such evident honesty of purpose could be judged a criminal blasphemy. Quite apart from any aesthetic judgment, it is simply unacceptable that the law's penal prohibitions should give special protection to the tenets of one religious faith, even the faith of the majority in the country. That is incompatible with equality of liberty for all citizens. The state of Scots law in this matter, as Sheriff G. H. Gordon, QC, describes it in his authoritative work on *Criminal Law*[9] is preferable: 'it may be said that blasphemy is no longer a crime. Blasphemous publications which are indecent in their terms may be dealt with as indecent publications, and blasphemous statements made in circumstances likely to cause a breach of the peace may be dealt with as breaches of the peace.' Unsatisfactorily broad and vague as are the criteria of

---

[7] John Locke, *Second Treatise of Civil Government* (many edns.), ch. 2, § 6.
[8] *R. v. Lemon* [1979] QB 10.
[9] 2nd edn., Edinburgh, 1978, p. 998.

indecency and breach of the peace in our law, these crimes are at least not in principle unequal in their restriction of liberty, though their vagueness creates a risk that they could be so in their practical enforcement.

When we consider practicalities of enforcement, we direct ourselves to the question whether the factual constraints of law are necessarily intrusive upon rightful liberty. Again, it is evident that they are not necessarily so.

Let us first consider the possibilities in total disregard for the content of laws in a particular legal system, that is, disregarding the extent to which the normative constraints of law fit our conception of rightful liberty, or do not fit it. What is necessary is that law imposes some normative constraints. What is possible is that the factual constraints wielded by legal officials are operated always and only to restrain or punish clear breaches of those normative constraints. It is further possible for a legal system to embrace the principle that no one, citizen or official, shall use coercive force upon any other person save as provided by law on the ground of some breach of legal duty, or for some necessary ancillary purpose such as imprisonment pending trial in serious cases. And it is possible that that principle be observed in most cases, or effectively vindicated as against those few who act against it.

Of course that is an ideal possibility which is and has been nowhere perfectly realized. Always there are some individuals and groups willing to exercise physical, economic, or social power to the detriment of the freedoms left to citizens by the law, and they are not all fully (or, in some cases, at all) brought to book. But as a matter of practical, real-world, possibility, legal orders can be administered faithfully, conscientiously, and effectively by honest people in such a way that the ideal possibility tends to be realized. In that case the law is imbued with a promise of full freedom for citizens within the ambit of legal liberty.

In a purely formal sense, the ideal of the Rule of Law is none other than what I have just described: the ideal of laws clearly delimiting citizens' duties and officials' powers, under which every abusive exercise of public or private power against the legal liberty of any person is suppressed or penalized, and with no one going in peril of coercion for anything other than breach of a pre-announced law.[10] Civil liberty as a formal idea is identifiable as the form of full freedom which prevails whenever, or to the extent that, the ideal of the rule of law is realized.

Substantive civil liberty requires more than that. It requires that the laws faithfully administered be themselves actually compatible, in the normative constraints they impose, with the favoured conception of rightful liberty.

That a legal system successfully secure formal or *a fortiori* substantive civil liberty is a possibility, not a certainty. It is therefore a possibility also that the order secured will be at the expense alike of justice and of liberty. The explicit normative constraints of the law may be unequal in their application to different groups of persons. As under the new Soviet Constitution, the members of one political party may be favoured at the expense of all others. Or members of one church may be unduly favoured, or freedom of opinion, of association, of political activity, may be unjustly limited. And over and above all that, the power of factual constraint exercised by state officials may be abused so that people are subjected to coercion even beyond the limits set by bad laws. Laws can indeed be bad, but their pretended execution worse.

To have legal systems at all is then to incur a grave risk of just such forms of tyranny. Is the risk too high to be worth taking? In my opinion it is not; and for this reason: it is altogether too easy to suppose that state power is the only kind of power which can be abused, whereas in truth abusive exercises of power are by no means confined to officials. Determined and ruthless people can nowadays, perhaps more easily than ever before, acquire means of coercion on a massive scale. Acts of terrorism by the Red Army Faction and their like are an abuse of power of human over human infinitely more horrifying than anything likely to be done by the forms of government against which their rhetoric is directed. It is doubtless naive to suppose that ideals of the *Rechstsstaat* or the Rule of Law do fully restrain governments and public officials, but there is plain evidence that a popular conviction of their importance can and does in many countries procure a real and effective limitation of the abusive

[10] For a fuller and more satisfactory statement of *all* the elements of the Rule of Law, see J. M. Finnis, *Natural Law and Natural Rights* (Oxford, 1980), ch. 10; and J. Raz, *The Authority of Law* (Oxford, 1978), ch. 6.

exercise of public power, even if nowhere in a fully ideal way. I am far more afraid of the power which acknowledges no legal limit and which does not have to justify itself in the public arena of courts and parliaments, than of the power which is necessarily vested in a liberal state.

There is debate in Britain now over what to do about such bodies as the National Front. Mr Tyndall, one of the leaders of that group, some time ago in a *Times* interview disclosed that his organization is (to paraphrase him with appropriately crude brevity) even more against liberals than against blacks.[11] His organization's prime target is subversion of the set of values which I am propounding here. Nevertheless, I condemn most roundly the tactics deliberately avowed by the Socialist Workers' Party, of forcibly breaking up lawful meetings and processions held by the National Front. A secondary objective of such tactics is of course to secure that such processions are attended by sufficient likelihood of disorder to procure their banning under the Public Order Act.

The use of mob rule as a method directly and indirectly to prevent the expression of opinion which it is otherwise lawful to express is as much and as objectionable a threat to civil liberty as is the abuse of public power. In its longer run tendencies it is highly dangerous to the cause of rightful liberty, since if it really comes to mob rule there is no sure way of predicting which mob will win and a high likelihood that neither of the mobs in question would be restrained in power by any respect for either formal or substantive civil liberty.

Current rhetoric about banning the National Front on the grounds of its racist convictions is also objectionable though of course less dangerous. The law does, and it ought to, restrain most vigorously acts of incitement to racial hatred and *a fortiori* any kind of physical harrassment of a racial (or indeed any other) kind. It seems clear that that law is not being enforced as strictly or rigorously as it might be. But the remedy for that is to procure the due and rigorous enforcement of the law, not to deprive members of the National Front of the right to an equal liberty with the rest of the citizen body, a right which necessarily includes the right of every person to advocate changes in the

---

[11] *The Times*, 30 August 1977.

law, even changes repugnant to other opinions. I respect Mr Denis Canavan's right to argue that the National Front be denied access to public halls and meeting places.[12] I respect the National Front's right to argue that my kind of liberalism be abrogated by law. I think it would be a great tragedy if either such argument should prevail in legislation, for they are arguments for an unequal liberty which to my judgment is unrightful liberty.

In both this and the blasphemy case I have deliberately chosen highly controversial examples, and ones in which my views will no doubt cause offence in roughly the opposite ends of the spectrum of opinion. What comes within the right to liberty is an essentially contestable question and even those who believe in liberty may disagree over its proper limits. But it is also the case that our sincerity in holding to any conception of rightful liberty is tested not by our reaction to exercises of liberty by those of whom we approve or with whom we only marginally disagree. He who believes only in the liberty of others to support and act in accordance with his own tenets does not believe in liberty at all but in his own tenets. The real challenge in my opinion is to take seriously and use unapologetically one's own moral tenets in approving or condemning acts of human beings without desiring that everyone share these tenets, save in relation to the delimitation of equal liberty for all. For me to have and to pursue my own tenets is a condition of my self-respect; so I conceive it to be for others. Therein is the ground of the right to equal liberty for all, within those constraints in which liberty can be equal, subject to securing economic fairness.

To all this there is a possible objection made in the name of philosophical anarchy. For example, my colleagues Bankowski and Mungham have argued that capitalist law necessarily prevents the free self-expression and self-development of the working class.[13] So long as there is positive law there are officials and experts who pursue legal definitions of problem situations, mystifying and ensnaring their clients, the more so the more poor and inarticulate. 'Good law' becomes in such a thesis an

[12] *Scotsman*, Monday 17 October 1977.
[13] Z. Bankowski and G. Mungham, *Images of Law* (London, 1976). See also R. H. S. Tur, 'Anarchy versus Authority', and Z. K. Bankowski, 'Anarchy Rule: O.K.?', 63 *Archiv. für Rechts- und Sozialphilosophie* (1977) 305–25 and 326–37 respectively.

evident contradiction. The risks which I concede to be inherent in legal order they conceive so inevitable of realization as to outweigh any pretended benefits it can bring about.

Arguments of this stamp in effect invert the old 'social contract' arguments of such as Locke and Rousseau. Locke and Rousseau and others postulated a prior or primitive condition of natural liberty from which by agreement human beings emerged into civil society, which under impartial governors could guarantee to each an equal measure of civil right better secured than mere natural liberty could be. Our contemporaries present a mirror-image.

They make no ahistorical assumptions about pre-social states of humanity. Instead, they envisage a future transition from what they deem the delusion of civil liberty to a true and genuine natural liberty, the trammels of positive law thrown off, each person free to make his or her own life within a framework of democratic mass action.

I do agree with such thinkers as to the risks of abuse of legal order, and I welcome their harping on the real distance which lies between the actuality and the ideal of civil liberty. But I reject that as an argument for dinging down the whole edifice. The vision of a future golden age seems to me no less fantastical, in the strict sense, than fictions about a past golden age. Hobbes's vision of the state of nature, of the war of all against all, more nearly replicates what actually supervenes when legal order is discarded in favour of mass action than does Locke's or Rousseau's more optimistic picture. From such convulsions what actually in experience emerges is Hobbesian tyranny, not Lockean civil liberty: order with little liberty and much arbitrariness of command. Napoleon, Lenin, Stalin, and Pinochet, were none of them historical accidents.

Such are indeed the reverse of the ideals which philosophical anarchists embrace. Like Locke, but without his exaggerated deference to property rights, they favour a natural order of 'liberty not licence'. But in my judgment that is not what would come about if their advocacy were heeded.

A normative order of 'liberty not licence' is necessarily one in which each recognizes his freedom as limited by respect for every other's equal right. Only the most fatuously fashionable Marxian pretence that 'right' is a purely 'bourgeois' concept could obscure that truth. Any belief in 'liberty not licence', even as a purely autonomous natural order, necessarily employs the concept 'right', though of course a different word could be adopted to represent it. Since that is so, those who believe in the withering away of law and the state need to address themselves better than anyone has yet done to a problem posed at least as long ago as the late seventeenth century, by both Stair[14] and Locke.[15]

The problem is this: nobody is normally, nor is normally conceived by others to be, a fair and objective judge of his own rights in a case of conflict with others. To have organized adjudication by people not party to the particular disputes they adjudicate is therefore an all but essential condition of social peace. Moreover, there is little utility in systems of adjudication if judgments are backed by insufficient power of enforcement. The history of Scotland abounds with illustrations of this truth, none more pointed than the following one culled from Mr John Prebble's *Glencoe*:

> The first raid which Glencoe and Keppoch made upon Breadalbane was a terrible failure . . . Mad Colin Campbell, the Laird of Glenylyon, captured thirty six of them . . . and hanged them in rows outside his castle of Meggernie. He was as independent a spirit as any Maclain, and as reluctant to acknowledge any authority but his own. When he was asked by the Privy Council if he would put his hand to a deed swearing that he had executed the MacDonalds in defiance of proper justice, he said that he would not only put his hand on the paper but his foot as well.[16]

Without the factual constraints essential to securing it as full freedom, a merely normative order of liberty is apt to prove chimerical. The strong can, though they ought not to, oppress the weak. And the absence of a capitalist system is, to say the least of it, no secure guarantee that some will not build up strength against others. Moreover, since it is an essentially contestable question what are the rightful limits of liberty, it is also necessary, as Stair and Locke pointed out, to have some

---

[14] See James, 1st Viscount Stair, *Institutions of the Law of Scotland* (ed. D. M. Walker, Edinburgh, 1981), I. i. 15.
[15] Locke, *Second Treatise of Civil Government*, ch. 9; cf. ch. 4 below.
[16] J. Prebble, *Glencoe* (London, 1966), p. 51.

method of settling by public decision what the exact limits of liberty are to be.

No doubt both of these points partly account for the stress which anarchist and Marxist writers put upon the urgency for a united will among 'the masses'. But there is no such thing as a literally united will of a mass, though there may fleetingly be a common purpose in a crowd. To any group or mass of people over time we can only ascribe a common will by the utilization of some such procedure as voting. But such procedures imply already recognition of some, albeit skeletal, public law. And we are right back to our old problem: how to secure limits on the exercise of legal power so as to protect the equal right of every person to as much freedom as each can enjoy equally with every other. Even granted satisfaction of that, we still face the need to secure that acts against the public resolutions are restrained, but only such acts. In short we are back to law and the problem of civil liberty.

My conclusion is to be deeply unimpressed by the anarchist and Marxist critique of civil liberty and the rule of law.

III. IS SUBSTANTIVE CIVIL LIBERTY A NECESSARY CONDITION OF LAW?

Having concluded that law is both a necessary condition of civil liberty and a better guarantor of rightful freedom than anything the opponents of legal order can offer, I turn to my third question. Is the fair and equal protection of liberty an essential feature of true law? The idea that it is so belongs to one branch of the tradition in Western legal and political thought known as 'natural law' theory. I do not agree with that view, so I am going to take an extreme test-case against the more positivistic approach which I espouse.

In 1941 the National Socialist Government in Germany issued a decree which deprived of German citizenship every German Jew whose place of abode then was or would in future be outwith Germany, and which declared confiscated to the state all property in Germany of such former citizens, the confiscated property 'to be used to further aims connected with the solution of Jewish Problem'. We all know, with an appropriate horror or revulsion, just how effectively that decree and its ancillary aims were put into practice. The government which promulgated it was indubitably in effective control of the German state, and the act of promulgation was formally valid under a law of 1935, itself formally valid under the Constitution.

In more recent times the courts of the Federal Republic of Germany, established under the Basic Law of 1949, have on several occasions had to consider the effect of that decree in the context of litigation arising in post-war Germany. The clearest expression of their view is this, taken from a decision of the Federal Constitutional Court in 1968: 'The decree of 1941 violated fundamental principles. It is to so intolerable a degree irreconcilable with justice that it must be considered to have been null and void *ex tunc.*'[17] There could scarcely be a clearer practical affirmation of the Lockean doctrine of natural law.[18] Nor is it at all surprising that inspiration should have been found in natural law doctrine by those who with such energy, determination, and indeed success have since 1945 gone about restoring a decent and civilized legal and political order in Western Germany, expunging the miasma of the Third Reich.

To treat every question arising in the present on the footing that no authority whatever is to be accorded to the decree of 1941 is the nearest that can now be done to achieving practical restitution to those who suffered under its baneful constraints. It is right to do that, and its being actually done is of course of infinitely greater human importance than any fine theoretical questions as to the validity of the particular principles appealed to in doing it.

But it is therefore also possible for me to agree profoundly with what the German courts have done—as indeed I do—without sharing their particular philosophical premises. Whereas their thesis is that the decree never was a law, mine would be that it was indeed all too really a law, one whose injustice was so awful and palpable that the decision retroactively to strip it of legal effect (so far as that is now possible) is not merely justified but clamantly demanded.

---

[17] Quoted from F. A. Mann, 'The Present Validity of Nazi Nationality Laws', 89 LQR (1973) 194, q.v.

[18] This Lockean doctrine is not (as many suppose) a defining or omnipresent feature of natural law theory. See Finis, *Natural Law*, chs. 1 and 12. The doctrine itself is more fully discussed in ch. 4 below.

I reject the natural law view because in my opinion it makes unsustainable ontological assumptions about the existence of objective and rationally discoverable principles of right. Such principles exist in, not beyond, the reasoned convictions and will of human beings. Law exists, not necessarily in accordance with such principles, but as a complex kind of social fact—what I have elsewhere called 'institutional fact'.[19] That is a 'legal positivist' opinion, which entails for me a further crucial proposition: that the existence of law never necessarily implies a moral obligation of conformity with it.

The view which I would espouse is thus rather close to views expressed by a majority in the House of Lords in the recent case of *Oppenheimer* v. *Cattermole*,[20] in which (in the course of a complicated tax appeal whose complexities I can for present purposes happily ignore) the question arose what status the 1941 decree had for the purposes of law courts in the United Kingdom. The question arose because Mr Oppenheimer's liability to British tax on a compensatory pension awarded to him by the Federal Republic in 1953 in compensation for his persecution by the Third Reich, depended on whether or not he had in 1941 or on any later date lost the German nationality he had had by birth.

In the course of his speech in the case, Lord Salmon had this to say: 'Whilst there are many examples in the books of penal or confiscatory legislation which according to our views is unjust, the barbarity of much of the Nazi legislation is happily unique. I do not consider that any of the principles laid down in any of the existing authorities require our courts to recognise such a decree and I have no doubt that on grounds of public policy they should refuse to do so.'[21] What that says, rightly in my submission, is that there may be laws which trench so fundamentally upon the right to equal liberty (and other requirements of justice), that British courts should deem them inoperative for any purpose of litigation. That does not involve denying that they actually are laws, nor therefore does it delude us into supposing that that which is a legal order is necessarily by the supposition in some reasonable measure a just order.

[19] MacCormick, 'Law as Institutional Fact', 90 LQR (1974) 102–29.
[20] [1976] AC 249.
[21] Ibid., p. 282.

Lord Cross of Chelsea, who was of the majority on this question, took more than a step further towards endorsing or adopting the natural law view. The 1941 decree, he pointed out, did not deprive all *émigré* Germans of citizenship:

It only deprived *Jewish* émigrés of their citizenship. Further . . . this discriminatory withdrawal of the rights of citizenship was used as a peg on which to hang a discriminatory confiscation of their property . . . What we are concerned with here is legislation which takes away without compensation from a section of the citizen body singled out on racial grounds all their property on which the state passing the legislation can lay its hands and, in addition, deprives them of their citizenship. To my mind a law of this sort constitutes so grave an infringement of human rights that the courts of this country ought to refuse to recognize it as a law at all.[22]

The whole of my argument to date indicates plain agreement with Lord Cross that one of the plainest modes of fundamental injustice is what he called 'discriminatory withdrawal of the rights of citizenship'. But what of his view that in case of 'so grave an infringement of human rights' the enactments infringing rights should not be recognized 'as law at all'?

The acid test, I think, would be if we could find an example not by way of enactments by a foreign state but in legislation of the UK Parliament. The sad fact is that we can find such an example. It is provided by the law on immigration. The Immigration Act 1971 in its first section defines the 'right of abode' in terms that all who have it 'shall be free to live in, and to come and go into and from, the United Kingdom without let or hindrance'. The second section proceeds to exclude from that right various categories of citizens of the United Kingdom and Colonies, including persons in that category who hold what are with wholly unintentional jocularity known as 'United Kingdom passports'. This policy had already been adopted in the Commonwealth Immigrants Act of 1968, the plain purpose of which was to restrict the inflow into Britain of UK and Colonies citizens of Asian extraction, resident in Kenya, whom in many cases then and since the Kenyan Government was illegitimately obstructing from effectively exercising their constitutional right to take up Kenyan citizenship. But whatever the wrongs to

---

[22] Ibid., pp. 277–8.

which our Act was a response, it involved depriving UK and Colonies citizens, who were resident in a country whose citizenship they did not have, of their right freely to enter the only other state of which they did have citizenship. It is a pretty plain example of 'discriminatory withdrawal of the rights of citizenship'.

In other ways also the 1971 Act affected fundamental rights. In one case the House of Lords by a majority held that by its express provisions it enabled the executive to deport from the UK people who had previously had the right as British subjects to live here, on the ground of illegality in their original entry, but despite the fact that at that time deportation was not stipulated as a penalty for or consequence of such offences.[23] As Lord Salmon, a distinguished judge, not a provocative professor, said, the Act so interpreted 'imposed on [the people affected] the liability to be imprisoned and deported by the executive in place of the right which they have previously enjoyed to live here and to go free'.[24] Until Mr Roy Jenkins as Home Secretary declared an amnesty, it was as though new penalities had been invented for old offences in place of the lesser penalities authorized by the law at the time when the offences were committed.

It is of course as foolish to exaggerate analogies between different cases as to ignore them. By contrast with the Nazi decree, the British legislation is not confiscatory, nor is it attached to any sort of a 'final solution' of racial problems. It was introduced into Parliament and passed through by decent and humane men and women faced with genuine problems as to the capacity of British cities to absorb coloured immigrants in large numbers. Its effects in the case of UK citizens in East Africa have been mitigated by the adoption of the 'special voucher' system. And so on. But there is no blinking the fact that it is an instance, implicating us all, of legislation effecting a discriminatory withdrawal of rights of citizenship drawn on essentially racial lines.

Supposing that it were a more grave infringement of human rights than it actually is (and no such infringement can be taken

---

[23] *Azam* v. *Home Secretary* [1974] AC 18.
[24] Ibid., p. 74.

lightly); supposing the judges thought it bad enough to fall within the ambit of Lord Cross's doctrine in the *Oppenheimer* case; on these suppositions could the courts, and should they, refuse to recognize such Acts as law at all? Could they, and should they, adopt with respect to present legislation of the UK Parliament, the natural law doctrine espoused by the German courts, that enactments which breach fundamental principles are legally null and void *ab initio*?

They certainly could. But I do not think they should. In addition to thinking that natural law doctrine is philosophically unsound, I think that its practical adoption in this context in this country would be inexpedient in the highest degree, for two reasons.

First, it would be all too easy for a government of any political colour to raise a populist hue and cry against non-elected judges having the temerity to defy an elected Parliament. Of late years Labour and Conservative governments alike have shown themselves ready to resort to retroactive legislation to undo court decisions displeasing to them, as the War Damage Act 1965 and the Education (Scotland) Act 1973 amply testify. Left-wing populist outcry has greeted judgments such as that in the Tameside Affair, where the judges pushed their existing powers to the limit. An upholding of civil liberty in the face of immigration legislation would doubtless release a different genie from the same lamp.

Secondly, as a matter of principle, all the dangers of vagueness associated with judge-made law would be attendant on a decision by the judges to set out in pursuit of their own conceptions of natural law and human right. An arbitrary and unreviewable judicial power, which in its nature such a jusnaturalist resolution would entail, is scarcely if at all preferable to the arbitrary and unreviewable power now asserted for a Parliament effectively dominated by the executive branch of state.

There is a real problem, but the assertion of the Lockean natural law doctrine is not the way to solve it. Bad laws are not merely thinkable as law; they are all too often present in human societies. Law and order can suppress rightful liberty. It was so in Germany under the Third Reich. It is so today in the Soviet Union and its satellite states; it is so in South Africa; it is so in many other states.

Even with us in the United Kingdom where jealousy in the defence of substantive civil liberty has a long and honourable place in our traditions, there are grave blemishes on the record. Sometimes these have resulted from a panic reaction to a problem situation, as in the Commonwealth Immigrants Act of 1968. Sometimes, as with the Immigration Act of 1971, established injustices are consolidated, and in addition a complex interaction of barely comprehensible sections and schedules can pass through Parliament barely noticed yet giving the executive power to divest individuals of previously vested rights. Sometimes, as in recent industrial legislation, differential protection is given to religious and non-religious consciences, as in the provision that the right not to join a trade union is to be guaranteed only to those who have a conscientious objection grounded in the tenets of some religious faith.[25] (It is all the more incomprehensible that this discrimination should have been embraced by people who rightly and honourably objected to discrimination of that kind being applied by British Conscientious Objectors' Tribunals and by American Draft Boards.)

If bad laws are a possibility, and they are, the only remedy is better laws and better legal institutions. That, in a nutshell, is the case for adopting an entrenched and justiciable law guaranteeing fundamental rights and civil liberties. Such laws do not involve giving judges that measure of potentially arbitrary power with which a pure doctrine of natural law necessarily clothes them. For such laws can specify a fairly clear and determinate conception of fundamental rights and civil liberties, and they are not necessarily unamendable. What is required is only that they be difficult to amend. Then amendment occurs only when there is a strong and well-considered will in parliament and people to change the definition of, or even to forego, some right.

We have available for consideration and adaptation the European Convention on Human Rights, to observation of whose provisions the country is already committed. If it be said that to entrench such provisions would breach the traditional sovereignty of Parliament, the answer is: none the worse for

---

[25] This was the effect of section 1(e) of the Trade Union and Labour Relations (Amendment) Act 1976.

that. When the Parliament of Great Britain was created in 1707 by agreement of, and by interlocking legislation enacted by, the English and the Scottish parliaments, the new Parliament was expressly limited in its powers.[26] The assertion of absolute parliamentary sovereignty is and always has been assertion of a usurped power. None the worse, then, if it be now by express decision limited again.

I said that the only remedy for bad laws is better laws. That is not quite true. Better laws are the necessary but not a sufficient condition of secure civil liberty. We would do well to remind ourselves of the arguments of Adam Ferguson, not the least enlightened member of our Enlightenment, from whose *Essay on the History of Civil Society* spring many of the ideas essential to a discussion of civil liberties and the law. There is some exaggeration in his thesis that liberty in society is gained and held not by the adoption of laws and institutions, however well designed, not by the evolution of this or that social, economic, or political structure—republic or monarchy, tribal, feudal, or commercial society—but solely by the will and vigilance of a people determined to sustain their liberty. Yet it is true that laws alone do not guarantee either liberty or social justice. There must also be an attitude among citizens of vigilance for their own and others' liberty. And this must surely be coupled with a recognition that the values subserved by civil liberty require also fair opportunities for all persons to have access to the economic means for a decent way of life.

[26] See MacCormick, 'Does the United Kingdom have a Constitution?' 29 *Northern Ireland Legal Quarterly* (1978) 1.

4.
LAW, OBLIGATION, AND CONSENT: REFLECTIONS ON STAIR AND LOCKE

I. BIOGRAPHICAL OBSERVATIONS

THE theme of this chapter is to be Law, Obligation, and Consent; my subtitle obliges me to proceed to that theme by way of reflection upon the work of two great men of the seventeenth century: John Locke, whom we may perhaps call the greatest of English political philosophers, and James Dalrymple, 1st Viscount Stair, whom we may certainly recognize as the greatest of Scottish legal writers. A graduate of the University of Glasgow, Stair served there for some years as Regent Master in philosophy, before proceeding to practise as an advocate before the Scottish Courts in Edinburgh from 1648 onwards, in due course achieving the eminence of Lord President of the Court of Session. His great masterpiece, the *Institutions of the Law of Scotland*,[1] indubitably owes much in structure and content to the Aristotelian philosophy which he both learned and later taught in the old College of Glasgow.

Stair and Locke were almost exact contemporaries—1619–95 and 1632–1704 are their respective dates. They were both deeply involved in the troubled politics of their respective countries in the seventeenth century, Stair contriving to serve as a judge both under the Protectorate and after the Restoration, Locke being a member of the household of Anthony Ashley Cooper, 1st Earl of Shaftesbury. Both were in exile in the Netherlands in the 1680s, Stair retiring there in 1681 just before the publication of the first edition of the *Institutions*, Locke in 1683 following the involvement of Shaftesbury (Dryden's Achitophel) and others in the plot to put the Duke of

[1] Ed. D. M. Walker, Edinburgh, 1981 (text based on Stair's second edition of 1693). See generally on Stair, *Stair Tercentenary Studies* (Stair Society vol. 33, ed. D. M. Walker, Edinburgh, 1981).

Monmouth on the throne. Stair returned with King William in 1688, Locke with Queen Mary in 1689; Stair resumed the Presidency of the Court of Session in Scotland; Locke was appointed a Commissioner of Appeals in England. Stair brought out an improved second edition of the *Institutions* in 1693; Locke's *Two Treatises of Civil Government*[2] appeared in 1690. Their fundamental doctrines of 'Law, Obligation, and Consent' are strikingly similar, though Stair's is expressed in smaller compass. It is nice to speculate on the question whether during their common period of exile they ever met and discussed these matters. One of my greatly respected teachers, W. D. Lamont, first drew my attention to this possibility in a course of lectures on political philosophy in Glasgow University twenty or so years ago, and I am glad to have this opportunity of recording the debt.

But there is no evidence known to me that they met, and no sure evidence that either read the other's work. On the main lines of the common doctrine Stair's first edition must have been available to Locke, but it is not recorded among the books he owned. In the second edition Stair added a short passage to the opening section of Book II, dealing with property, which brusquely and by implication dismisses the view of Filmer that God's original gift of the earth and its creatures was to Adam and his heirs in tail male rather than to mankind in common. That addition strongly suggests a borrowing from Locke's *First Treatise*. But, as I say, the main body of Stair's doctrine was laid down by 1681 and remained unaltered.

So it is only possible that they met each other or read each other's work. What is certain is that they shared common assumptions: (1) that there is a law of nature disclosed to men by reason; (2) that men need also positive (human) laws and instituted legislators and judges to amend the insecurity of a state of nature; (3) that these instituted legislators and judges are instituted by the agreement of men; (4) that the obligation to conform with laws and judgments derives from that agreement, and extends only so far as that free consent extends. These assumptions are of course not wholly original in either

[2] The texts cited are from the Everyman Edition, by W. S. Carpenter (London, 1924), and are identified by an italic '*L*' followed by Treatise number (I or II), chapter number (i, ii, etc.), and paragraph number (1, 2, etc.) as in the Everyman Edition.

case. They belong in one form or another to the traditional natural law thought of Western Europe, and in particular to the seventeenth-century rationalist version of that tradition associated particularly with the names of Grotius and Pufendorf.

That is well known. Less well recognized I believe is the influence of George Buchanan's *De Jure Regni Apud Scotos* (most recently translated in 1964 by D. H. MacNeill under the title *The Art and Science of Government among the Scots*[3]). First published in 1579, Buchanan's work expounded a general theory of kingship and *inter alia* justified the actions of the Scottish people in deposing Mary Queen of Scots from her throne for misgovernment and complicity in her husband's murder. Partly on that ground it enjoyed a considerable success (*succès de scandale?*) in contemporary Europe, and it was adopted by English Parliamentarians including Milton as a text for the times of the Civil War. Not surprisingly it was banned by the Privy Council in 1660, and again in 1688. In 1683, while Locke was still a student of Christ Church, the University of Oxford caused it to be burned publicly by the common hangman.

Beyond having had the chance of being present at its incineration, it is certain that Locke knew Buchanan's work, and sympathized with it. In the concluding chapter of the Second Treatise, where he expounds his doctrine of justified revolution, he takes pains to confute William Barclay's essay *Contra Monarchomachos*—an essay which was itself written to confute Buchanan (see *L.* II. xix. 232–9). Stair's familiarity with Buchanan's work is too obvious to require argument.[4]

To indicate the significance for our authors of a work now little regarded by scholars, let me quote a passage (in MacNeill's translation, pp. 95–6) from sections LXXXV and LXXXVI of *De Jure Regni*, the passage being in dialogue form:

BUCHANAN. There is scarcely any other cause of war that is propounded among peoples and kings than injuries which cannot be dealt with by ordinary law, but require the arbitrament of the sword.

MAITLAND. These are the usual reasons for making war against foreigners. But it is different when one takes up arms against one's

---

[3] Ed. W. Maclellan, Glasgow, 1964.
[4] Cf. especially *Inst.* I. i. 16, as quoted on p. 67, with §§ XI and XII of Buchanan.

own king, to whom obedience is due in respect of a most sacred oath of loyalty.

B. We are indeed under that obligation; but, on the other hand, our kings likewise have taken an oath in the presence of our leading men that they will administer the law with fairness and with justice.

M. That is so.

B. There is then a mutual contract between king and people.

M. So it would appear.

B. Whoever repudiates any contract or violates its terms has thereby cancelled the matter agreed on or contracted, has he not?

M. Certainly he has cancelled the bargain.

B. The bond which binds the king and the people being therefore broken, he has therefore forfeited any particle of legal right which might pertain to him from the contract he has upset.

M. He has indeed forfeited it.

B. And the other party to the contract is in law as free as he was before the contract was made.

M. Clearly he has the same right and the same freedom.

B. Now if the king does something to upset the social order, the preservation of which was the reason for appointing him king, what name does he receive?

M, Tyrant, I should say.

B. Now a tyrant does not hold lawful power over the people but is even their enemy.

M. He is indeed their enemy.

B. War against an enemy is justifiable if it arises out of great and intolerable injuries . . .

Not for the first time, the dialogue form strikes me as a pleasing way of lining up an argumentative fall-guy whose ready assent to the propositions put makes light of the task of persuasion. More seriously, I suggest to you that Buchanan's argument very obviously sets up a theory of legitimate political power of which Locke's, in particular, seems but a more fully developed version[5]—and one which universalizes a thesis which Buchanan had located more particularly in Scottish legal and constitutional history.

[5] Locke's conception of the social contract is, of course, concerned primarily with the foundation of civil society by agreement of individuals, the (collective) act of conferring power on governing authorities being described in terms of 'trust' rather than contract. Sections XI and XII of Buchanan's work should be read before it is assumed that they are pursuing quite different ideas; also, in the light of the passage quoted from Buchanan, *L*. II. xviii.

Be that as it may, I hope that these introductory remarks have sufficiently indicated that this chapter has a subject as well as a title. My claim is that Stair and Locke hold strikingly similar opinions on certain key issues, and that they do so at least because they drew upon common sources belonging to a common tradition. In what follows I propose to do two things: first, to expound in more detail the arguments of Stair and Locke, giving slightly more emphasis to Stair than to Locke, because his work is the less familiar of the two; secondly to advance some ideas of my own on law, obligation, and consent arising from a discussion of elements of similarity and difference in the Stair/Locke position.

II. THE DOCTRINES OF LAW, OBLIGATION, AND CONSENT

In this second section, then, my task is to set out the theory of law and political power which we find in Stair and Locke. I mentioned a moment ago four basic assumptions which they derive from their common tradition; those concerned with rationality of law, the need for positive law to secure a rational order in human society, the derivation of positive law from a fundamental social contract, and the existence of a resultant obligation to conform with law. To start with the first of these:

For both of them a central tenet is the rationality of law; rather, the *identity* of law and reason. For Locke, the state of nature has a law of nature to govern it, and 'reason . . . is that law' (*L*. II. ii. 6); for Stair, 'law is the dictate of reason determining every rational being to that which is congruous and convenient for the nature and condition thereof' (*Inst*. I. i. 1). Rightness in conduct is conformity to reason, and albeit imperfectly and with necessary aids from revelation men can by reason know the right. But reason alone does not sufficiently explain the obligatoriness of law. Both Stair and Locke (I think) hold a view which was common to the tradition. Although reason sets the standard of rightness, the obligatoriness or *vis obligandi* of law—natural law or positive law—is another matter. Obligations bind the will, and only an act of will can bind the will. Our obligation to act in accordance with reason can then depend only on the will of God or on the will of man. Thus

Locke justifies his claim that the law of nature 'obliges every one' by reference to the will of our 'omnipotent and infinitely wise maker' (*L.* II. ii. 6). Stair, arguing from what he takes to be the three basic principles of natural law (the principles of 'obedience, freedom, and engagement' he calls them, *Inst.* I. i. 18), divides all our obligations into two classes: obediential and conventional (*Inst.* I. i. 19, 21, 23). Obediential include obligations to refrain from harmful conduct to one another and to make reparation for harm done, familial obligations, and obligations of recompense and restitution: they are defined as 'obligations upon man, which are not by his own consent or engagement, nor by the will of man, but by the will of God' (*Inst.* I. i. 19). The contrast with conventional obligations is, precisely, that these latter are by 'the will of man'. Reason indeed has primacy for both Stair and Locke in this sense: reason discloses that *if* God wills men's acting in certain ways, men are then obliged to conform their wills and actions to his. So our fundamental obligations, reason tells us, are dependent on what God actually does will for us, indeed on whether he wills anything for us. Since he does will our obedience on certain fundamental matters, the class of obediential obligations is not an empty class.

If it is a matter of reason that man the inferior obey God his superior, can there be like reason why human inferiors should obey human superiors? The answer plainly depends on men's natures: is there *natural* superiority of one to another? Stair and Locke answer 'No'. Men are created free and equal, although, being subject in nature to 'obediential obligations' as Stair calls them, their natural condition is one of 'liberty not licence' (*L.* II. ii. 6) as Locke puts it.

Against proponents of divine right and social hierarchy such as Filmer, whom Locke elaborately confutes in the First Treatise, the counter-thesis is established that the earth and all is fruits and creatures were given to the whole progeny of Adam in common as free and equal beings. But this asserted equality presents us with two evident problems: how can individual property be justified on this premiss, especially if possessions are unequally distributed? and how can there be any political authority among men?

Locke's solutions are well known; that Stair's are strikingly similar is less well realized. Let us start with his theory of property. Recognition of the fundamental obediential obligations entails recognition that men have rights to life and liberty. The right to life, for Stair, necessarily entails the right in each to appropriate from the common store of nature objects to use 'for his necessity, utility and delight' (*Inst.* II. i. 1). The right to permanency of possession is over those 'things which [have] received specification from his art and industry' (ibid.), where that represents a permanent improvement, as in the taming of wild animals, or the erection of permanent buildings, or the digging of wells for irrigation and permanent cultivation of land (*Inst.* II. i. 30, 31). Always, the underlying justification of property entails an obligation on property-owners to supply necessities even to those who have nothing to give in exchange; 'for human necessity doth also infer this; but it must be a real and not a feigned necessity' (*Inst.* II. i. 6). I would suggest that Locke presses too far the theory that always it is labour which confers a title to property (see *L.* II. v); thus he is led into the absurdity of suggesting that a picked apple has been improved by expenditure of labour[6] (*L.* II. v. 28). On this point, Stair holds back. 'Specification by industry' indeed justifies *permanence* of ownership, for men are entitled freely to hold the results of improvements they freely make. But not everything owned has been in that sense improved. The right to life, without anything more, sufficiently justifies property taken into possession for use and consumption quite apart from any expenditure of labour. By the same token there is always a debt of justice upon the haves in favour of the have-nots. In the eighteenth century

---

[6] My colleagues Zenon Bankowski and T. S. Midgley object that it is the act of picking an apple which transforms it from that which would rot on its branch to that which is available for eating. I agree, but observe that one should not confuse a necessary condition of one's eating that which has value because already edible (a ripe apple) with the value which an edible thing has in virtue of being edible, to wit, being a ripe apple. Certainly, going out searching for wild apples, picking them, and bringing them back to one's habitation does add to the value one puts on the apples brought home as against apples still on their trees. But the fact that people rationally value their labour does not make it the only thing they value or the only source of value. For a root and branch confutation of the 'labour theory of value' in its developed Marxian form, see Robert Nozick, *Anarchy, State, and Utopia* (Oxford, 1974), pp. 256–62; I am not sure that Nozick sufficiently realizes that he thereby cuts off the Lockean branch on which his own theory of rights rests.

Thomas Reid made the same point[7] in correction of both Locke and Hume.

So much for property, but what of the second problem I mentioned a moment ago; that of the justification of political authority, or political power (as Locke put it)? One can sketch in two sentences Locke's well-known thesis on this point (*L.* II. vii. 87–94; II. viii, etc.). Although men have rights in nature they can enjoy them but insecurely, for each must defend his own right, and punishment or reparation for wrongs done can proceed only in a haphazard and anarchic way. To remedy this insecurity men contract together to form a civil society and to entrust to some of their number the adjudication of infringements of right, the enactment of legislation to clarify and declare natural law and to promote the common good, and the execution of laws made.

I cannot here forbear from giving two long quotations from Stair to drive home again my point as to the striking similarity of basic doctrine:

[I]f the law of nature and of reason were equally known to all men, or that the dispensers thereof could be found so knowing and so just, as men would and ought to have full confidence and quietness in their sentences, it would not only be a folly, but a fault, to admit of any other law. But the prime interest of men being to enjoy their rights, not only in safety and security, but in confidence and quietness of mind, that they may clearly know what is their right, and may securely enjoy the same; therefore human laws are added, not to take away the law of nature and reason, but some of the effects thereof, which are in our power . . . (*Inst.* I. i. 15).

[N]ations of old submitted to their princes, choosing rather to refer their interests and differences to the determination of their sovereigns, than that everyone should be a judge to himself, and should take and hold by force, what he conceived to be his right, without any superior to himself to be judge to appeal to, and thereby live in perpetual war. Whence government necessarily implies in the very being thereof a yielding and submitting to the determination of the sovereign authority in the differences of the people, though one or either party should conceive themselves injured; that thereby private opinion may give place to public authority, although they had natural power sufficient to withstand the same. Otherwise they behoved to dissolve

[7] See Thomas Reid, *Essays on the Active Powers* (Edinburgh, 1788), Essay V, ch. 5.

authority and society, and return to the sovereignty of their private
judgment and their natural force, from which they did flee unto the
sanctuary of government; which, though it may sometimes err, yet
can be nothing like to those continual errors, when everyone owns
himself as a sovereign judge in his own cause (*Inst.* I. i. 16).

What is common to both positions is that the existence of
political power and positive law depends on consent. The insecurity of rights in the state of nature gives men reason to agree
on establishing governments and accepting their authority.
They have so agreed, and their agreement alone constitutes the
obligation of respect for governments and positive laws. That
agreement *alone* constitutes this obligation follows necessarily
from the shared theory of obligation which I enunciated earlier:
obligations arise either by the will of God or by the will of man.
The natural equality and freedom of man entails that none has
that superiority over another which God has over man, therefore none can be obligated but by his own will, therefore rightful
political superiority of one over another can arise only by voluntary consent of the subject. Political obligation must therefore
be a species of conventional obligation, in Stair's sense, dependent on a contract among the members of a community.

It could be objected that the line drawn between obediential
and conventional obligations is bogus. Stair tells us that 'there
is nothing more natural than to stand to the faith of our pactions'
(*Inst.* I. i. 21). If that be so, then surely it is reasonable to
suppose that God requires men to stand to the faith of their
pactions, and therefore that keeping faith is an obediential
obligation.

That is so, but the full account of that would be that God wills
that whatever commitments men of their free will undertake,
those commitments they must keep. So although it would be
wrong within the theory to say that conventional obligations are
independent of the will of God, they are unlike 'obediential
obligations' in that their particular existence and content for
each of us is also and necessarily dependent on our own will.
The objection then requires only a clarification of, not an
abandonment of, the theory. It could be added that currently
fashionable theories of promising such as John Searle's[8] exhibit

---

[8] See John Searle, *Speech Acts* (Cambridge, 1966). I do not myself agree with Searle,
for reasons stated in ch. 10 below.

an exact analogy of structure to this theory. There is postulated a social rule that whenever men say things intending to undertake an obligation by saying them, they are then subjected to the obligation they undertake, and ought to fulfil it. Substitute 'divine rule' for 'social rule', and Searle, Stair, and Locke become indistinguishable.

Be that as it may, we can at least conclude that Locke and Stair have—indeed share—a theory which is intelligible and self-consistent, and which derives political obligation from the free consent of men who have reason to consent to establishing civil government because of the insecurity of natural society.

Now I wish to advert to an interesting difference between them. Locke, as we all know, derives from this a specific theory as to the extent of governmental powers and the rights of subjects faced with an abuse of power (see esp. *L.* II. xix). The social compact imposes a strict constraint (what Robert Nozick calls a 'side-constraint'[9]) on governments. Since they are to secure, clarify, and protect natural rights, and to promote public goods only so far as consistent with respect for rights, no act of government which violates any right of anyone's is valid. Whenever a subject's right is invaded by government he has the right to resist, the right of 'appeal to Heaven' (*L.* II. xiv. 168). As he admits, this may not be of much use to individuals, except when a majority is oppressed; because only in the latter case is the subject's resistance likely to be effectual. But it would be rightful even where it would not or could not be effectual. In this matter his position is extremely close to George Buchanan's.

Stair's is a more cautious and guarded doctrine. The whole point of having positive law is that we are by our weakness and depravity of will incapable of living by the perfect standard of equity or natural law (the terms are, for him, exact equivalents). Motivated by our perception of what perfect justice demands, we set up systems of positive law which look not *in aequo* but *in bono* or *in utili* (*Inst.* I. i. 18)—the best we can make of things, rather than the ideal. That, indeed, is what we agree to in agreeing to have human governments and positive laws. We agree, that, for the sake of a workable system, not at all our natural obligations shall be judicially cognizable or enforce-

---

[9] See Nozick, *Anarchy, State, and Utopia*, pp. 28–30.

able—e.g. obligations of gratitude, and promissory obligations insufficiently supported by written evidence; it is also the case, thinks Stair, that for public convenience we can depart from equity, as when we introduce primogeniture to preserve landed estates as reasonably large units. He even holds that the particular customs and 'hardness of heart' of particular nations may necessitate departures from the ideal standard. God himself set the example when in the law of Moses he permitted a regulated form of divorce and polygamy *faute de mieux* (*Inst.* I. i. 15).

The implication derivable from this, though nowhere expressly drawn by Stair, is that a strict side-constraint view of natural rights would be untenable. If we agree to use positive law to do the best we can to achieve justice and security of rights, we may find that sometimes the best arrangements actually possible in given social circumstances leave some rights unsatisfied or unprotected. Locke in no way contemplates that.

There is a real, obvious, and important difference between a theory such as Locke's which envisages natural rights (derived from natural law) as imposing absolute constraints and limits on positive law and the exercise of political power, and a theory such as Stair's which posits natural law and the rights constituted thereby as setting an ideal aspirational standard for positive law. Yet the difference lies not in the basic premises of the two arguments, for they are substantially the same. The difference, let us observe, arises from a different interpretation of facts (or alleged facts). The whole issue resolves around the question *what did men actually agree to* in agreeing to enter civil society?

But the moment we see that that is a point of possible and indeed actual disagreement, at that moment we see what may be presented as the basic weakness of this approach to the problem of political obligation. Unless it is certain what people agreed to it is not certain what are the contents and limits of political obligation; but it is not certain what they agreed to, or indeed whether they ever actually agreed to anything. Which is just what Hume, Bentham, *et al.* pointed out[10] in their root and

---

[10] Citations below, nn. 11–13.

branch rejection of the whole idea of the social contract as a pointless philosophical myth.

III. THE QUESTION OF LAW, OBLIGATION AND CONSENT

The difficulty about contractarian arguments on the question of political obligation, as the second section has shown, is that writers such as Stair and Locke, who share similar premisses, may yet come to different conclusions through different views as to the content of a social contract. If such differences of view are not open to empirical resolution (and they are not), the argument from the contract gets us nowhere. In that case it is necessary either to reinterpret the argument as a non-empirical one, or to reconsider the prior steps of the argument and see where they might lead us. In this third section I shall therefore (a) reconsider the argument about the social contract, and criticize some contemporary interpretations of it; (b) discuss the view that there are rights independent of positive law which it is the proper function of positive law to protect; and (c) conclude by considering how the issue of political obligation relates to these two prior topics.

(a) The social contract

It is perhaps all too easy for us nowadays to reject out of hand the idea that there ever was any agreement to establish any society. Hume,[11] Smith,[12] and Bentham,[13] and others have

---

[11] David Hume, *A Treatise of Human Nature* bk. III, pt. ii, § 7. Hume's argument is summarized later in the present chapter.

[12] Adam Smith, *Lectures on Jurisprudence* (ed. R. L. Meek, D. D. Raphael, and P. G. Stein), Oxford, 1978), pp. 402–3; ' [T]he doctrine of an original contract is peculiar to Great Britain, yet government takes place where it was never thought of, which is even the case with the greater part of people in this country. Ask a common porter . . . why he obeys the civil magistrate . . . you will never hear him mention a contract as the foundation of his obedience.' Smith makes two further objections, based on the incoherence of the doctrine compared with actual legal institutions. Cf. his *Wealth of Nations* bk. V, ch. 1, p. 2, 'Of the Expense of Justice', 3rd para.: 'Civil government supposes a certain subordination. But . . . the necessity of civil government gradually grows up with the acquisition of valuable property . . .', etc.

[13] Jeremy Bentham, *A Fragment on Government* (ed. W. Harrison, Oxford, 1948), ch. I, paras. 36–48; at para. 48: 'I was in hopes . . . that this chimera had been effectually demolished by Mr. Hume . . . The indestructible prerogatives of mankind have no need to be supported upon the sandy foundation of a fiction.'

poured too much scorn on the idea for it to survive. But as against that, we must take note of Buchanan's argument that the king in taking his coronation oath binds himself to govern according to the established law for the public good. We must note also his discussion of the elective character of the early Scottish monarchy, and its transmutation in the time of Kenneth III to a hereditary system upon condition that the monarch be subject to the law as agreed by the people (Buchanan, sections LIII–LV).

We should consider also Stair's remark that 'nations of old submitted to their princes choosing rather to refer their interests and differences to the determination of their sovereigns, than that everyone should be a judge to himself . . .' (*Inst.* I. I. 161). When we consider the spread of the feudal system in Western Europe, especially in places like Scotland where it arrived otherwise than by conquest, that has the ring of embellished truth rather than rhetorical fantasy. As I understand it, the feudal system did develop precisely by a kind of contractual arrangement whereby a holder of land agreed to hold it 'of' some 'superior' and to render him service for it, the superior in turn agreeing to act as protector of the vassal and judge between him and his peers, the rights and duties of parties being determined by customary law. The tenants in chief, who under this arrangement held, or were deemed to hold, their land of the king directly, in turn stood in a like relation to their vassals, and so on. In the case of free men at least, the status relationships of feudal society, and the access to property which they regulated and on which they depended, were established by 'status contracts' renewed in each generation, formally enacted in the very processes of infeftment (enfeoffment) in lands.[14]

In recalling that, we should recall also Locke's argument about the consent which subjects an individual to a society and its law (*L.* II. viii. 119–21). After the original compact, individuals, he says, must still subject themselves voluntarily to society. This they may do either by express consent or by tacit consent. In what, then, does tacit consent consist? His answer is that it consists in any conscious and willing enjoyment of

---

[14] A most illuminating recent work on all this is S. F. C. Milsom's *The Legal Basis of English Feudalism* (Cambridge, 1976).

property belonging to the society. How does 'property' come to belong to a society? His answer is that whenever at any time a person enters into a society he necessarily brings his property—held by natural right—in with him, and enjoys it henceforward as of civil right. So until the society is dissolved that property henceforward belongs to that society and can be held only by someone who subjects himself to the laws and government of that society. Or, rather, whoever holds it necessarily gives tacit consent to those laws so long as he holds it. This general idea of people bringing property into an order of government by a kind of contractual arrangement, and of others who subsequently hold it being bound at least by tacit consent, seems to me to 'fit' better with the forms of feudalism as understood in the seventeenth century than with anything recognizable in 'bourgeois' society.

Explicit consent binds yet more firmly than tacit consent, says Locke, because it binds permanently so long as a society lasts. That in turn should alert us to the real conditions of seventeenth-century society, and to the weight then put on oaths of allegiance and other express submissions to government.

An example associated with Stair will make vivid the point. It was his eldest son, the Master of Stair and later Earl of Stair, who together with King William devised and brought about the massacre of Glencoe.[15] They caused two companies of troops to be quartered on the Macdonalds of Glencoe and after a fortnight gave orders for them to fall upon their hosts and put them to the sword, men, women, and children. This took place on 13 February 1692, and it took place because of the failure of MacIain, Chief of the Clan, to take the oath of allegiance to William and Mary by 31 December 1691—actually, he had taken it five days late. The social contract, one is tempted to say, was for MacIain and his people a contract of adhesion with a heavy penalty clause for failure to adhere timeously.

Among the reasons why MacIain and others delayed was that they regarded themselves as already bound by their oath to James VII; and indeed only when he had given them permission to swear allegiance to the new order did they do so. It is in just

---

[15] For an account of this unhappy event, see John Prebble, *Glencoe* (London, 1966).

such a context as this that people confront Locke's question of whether a king to whom allegiance has been sworn can by misconduct forfeit his right. They confront it as a keen practical question, not an abstract academic one; Locke knew that, though we need constantly to remind ourselves of the point.

(May I digress for one moment to mention an irony to you. Stair senior in writing of the law of nations says this: 'Such also are the laws of hospitality, or the mutual trust betwixt the host and the guest, whom he hath willingly admitted to his house, whereby neither of them can act anything prejudicial to the life or liberty of the other, while in that relation' (*Inst.* I. i. 11). The peculiar infamy of the massacre devised by his son and his king was that it was carried out in defiance of these very laws. We may doubt whether the father approved of the son's actions.)

But I must apologize for that digression. The point I was making was a simple one: that so far from being pure fiction, the idea of securing people's express allegiance to governments by oaths and promises had a definite political point in the seventeenth century. Let me add that it had greatest political point precisely in relation to the more hierarchical and feudal or quasi-feudal elements in the society. In the Highlands, for example, oaths of allegiance by a relatively small number of people—the chiefs—could reasonably be deemed to secure the loyalty of whole tracts of countryside. For the inhabitants in turn owed to the chiefs an allegiance whose voluntary character was surely not wholly mythical, though dependent indeed on a form of traditional domination in the Weberian sense. The converse of that can be found in Buchanan's assertion, quoted earlier, that the king, by taking an oath 'in the presence of our leading men' thereby engages himself in favour of the whole nation—presumably because of the relation which in turn obtains between them and the lesser man.

The point of these remarks (which I admit to making somewhat tentatively) is to cast doubt on one interpretation of social contract doctrine which has a certain present popularity. The interpretation I have in mind suggests that the social contract doctrine can only be read as an idealized embodiment of an emerging bourgeois ideology, the whole point of which is to represent human beings as free and equal under and before the law, their social relations being essentially contractual relations fixed in the dealings of the market-place. Human beings are as it were transformed into legal persons each with his own property to bring into exchange relations with every other. The social contract is then simply an idealized representation of this order which expresses in terms of the first constitution of every society a specific truth about the concrete social relations of bourgeois society.

The most radical version of this thesis is found or hinted at in the writings of the Russian Marxist legal theorist E. B. Pashukanis,[16] which suggest that the very concepts of law and of legal relations are either specific to bourgeois society, or at least reach their highest and purest expression in such a society.

But if I am right in what I have just been suggesting, that thesis cannot hold, certainly not without substantial amendment. The social contract even in the seventeenth century is, if anything, an archaic doctrine which gains credibility from the traditional and feudal interpretations of social order, rather than looking forward to the emergent order of bourgeois or commercial society. Indeed, it is the high priests of commercial society, such as Hume, Bentham, and above all Adam Smith who pour most scorn on the theory. The question should not be whether social arrangements are ever contractual, but whether they always are. And, consequently, whether there can be political obligation in the absence of contracts.

One might add that although what has been said casts doubt primarily and directly on left-wing interpretations of liberal political and legal theory, the same argument at least shines a warning light in the direction of contemporary liberals such as Rawls who think it profitable to revive contractarian arguments in the interests of revamped liberal theories of justice, in a manner considered in the next chapter.

(b) *Rights independent of positive law?*

All that said, let me return to the central weakness of contract theory as expounded by Stair and Locke. We found that they

[16] E. B. Pashukanis, *The General Theory of Law and Marxism* (Moscow, 1925), tr. D. I. Babb in J. N. Hazard (ed.), *Soviet Legal Philosophy* (New York, 1951); or see the more recent version, *Law and Marxism: A General Theory* (ed. C. Arthur, tr. B. Einhorn, London, 1978). T. S. Midgley, in his Edinburgh Ph.D. thesis, 'The Language of Equality' (1978), first drew my attention to the importance of Pashukanis's view on this point.

disagree over the question of what exactly men have agreed to. The disagreement, though apparently a disagreement of fact, is irresoluble by appeal to factual evidence, because we do not know to what precisely, if anything, people have agreed.

What is more, the arguments offered by Stair and Locke address themselves to a question other than that factual one. They address themselves instead to the issue, 'What forms of government have people good reason to agree to?', or indeed 'Why have people reason to agree to the institution of governments and positive laws at all?' And on this point Stair and Locke are at one. Instituted governments are for securing observance of laws and rights, not that there would be no law and no rights in the absence of instituted governments, but that there would be no security in them if each person relied only on the sovereignty of his own private judgment.

We have to observe and underline the point that even within the rationalist theory of natural law, our authors insist on the possibility that men may misapprehend, or give conflicting interpretations to, the natural law; and that men may fail to be, or to be trusted as, impartial interpreters of their own rights. Weakness of reason and depravity of will therefore make the state of nature insecure. Governments are accordingly introduced by agreement to secure law and rights, not to subvert them.

As David Hume in effect pointed out, this is a very good argument which, however, so far from establishing the hypothesis of an express contract, renders it redundant.[17] If it is the case that there is good reason to agree to have governments and judicatures on the grounds suggested by such as Locke and Stair, then it is simply the case that there is good reason to have governments and judicatures. The alleged agreement is irrelevant, because it is alleged on the basis of reasons for having these institutions which hold good independently of any express agreement or contract. The reason why it is good to have such institutions is the utility they serve, and while that utility does give us reason to assent to their existence such assent is necessary neither to explaining nor to justifying their origins.

But then, we might ask, is their utility best or even intelligibly

[17] *Treatise of Human Nature*, III. ii. 7.

explained in terms of securing rights which are postulated as existing independently of formally enacted positive laws and formally instituted judicatures? Some, such as Bentham,[18] reject that proposition as unintelligible and mischievous: no positive laws, no rights, Bentham tells us. Others, such as Hume, in effect accept the proposition that there can be rights independently of what Bentham would recognize as positive law, but account for such rights on grounds other than the rationalist interpretation of natural law. (Hume's interpretation of rights, especially property rights, and his definition of justice as an artificial virtue, both rest upon a theory about the evolution of conventional norms among human beings. That is a long way from Bentham's view.)

One proposition of which I myself have no doubt at all is that we can intelligibly make assertions about the moral rights of human beings independently of any system of positive law. Such assertions depend upon the moral and political principles to which we subscribe. It is of course the case that logical and epistemological status of assertions of moral and political principles is controversial. Controversy over that is the central controversy in meta-ethics, and lies beyond the compass of the topics dealt with in this book. To say but one thing about it, I am for my part sure that Stair's and Locke's view that principles of right are deliverances of reason is an untenable one, and that a tenable theory has to take account of Hume's objections to rationalism and at least draw on his own theory.

But what matters for present purposes is that on any view of the epistemological standing of moral and political principles, their content is also controversial. Even rationalists accept that. It is in addition true that in some degree each person who tries to expound or elaborate a theory of rights is in his exposition and elaboration affected but not wholly determined by the social and economic system to which he belongs and which is the necessary background to his reflections.

Now certainly Locke's particular theory of rights is distinctly and characteristically a bourgeois or proto-bourgeois one. Of course his theory of property, and his subsumption of all human

---

[18] See Jeremy Bentham, *Anarchical Fallacies*, in vol. II of *The Works of Jeremy Bentham* (ed. J. Bowring, Edinburgh, 1843). Cf. W. Twining, 'The Contemporary Significance of Bentham's Anarchical Fallacies', 61 *Archiv für Rechts- und Sozialphilosophie* (1975) 325.

rights within the category of property, belong classically to what C. B. MacPherson calls 'Possessive Individualism'.[19] The same can as well, perhaps even more firmly, be said of Stair's view[20] that positive law enables men to 'make up societies . . . that they may . . . defend one another, and procure to one another their rights; and also to set clear limits to every man's property; and to maintain traffic and commerce among themselves and with others. So that the three principles of positive law may be [summarized as] society, property, and commerce' (*Inst.* I. i. 18). These are indeed characteristically 'bourgeois' conceptions of right. But it would be the grossest fallacy to argue that therefore 'right' is a bourgeois concept.

Formally speaking, as I argue at length in ch. 8, the concept of 'rights' is definable with reference to a specific type of moral principle. Principles of the relevant type identify goods which are susceptible of enjoyment by individuals severally and which ought to be secured to each individual of a given class. Principles of human rights or natural rights specify goods which ought to be secured to every human being as such. That it is irresolubly controversial what rights people have and ought to be accorded is a logical consequence of the controversial character of substantive moral and political principles. It is not a consequence either of the emptiness of the concept of 'rights', still less of its exclusive appropriateness to one particular brand of political and legal philosophy or ideology. Accordingly, no one with pretensions to be taken seriously as a prescriptive political or legal theorist can dodge the issue of what rights people have and ought to be accorded.

For just that reason it is open to me to disagree with Locke or Stair over the substantive question of what rights people have, without disagreeing over the point which they make about the practical necessity of governmental agencies to establish a particular governing conception of rights and to protect and secure at least those rights. I disagree with them on the point of

---

[19] C. B. MacPherson, *The Political Theory of Possessive Individualism* (Oxford, 1962).

[20] My colleagues T. S. Midgley and Professor W. A. J. Watson independently suggested to me that the reference in Stair to 'commerce' is simply an echo of the traditional view about *ius gentium*. Perhaps so. But it seems to me that Stair's deliberate, and rather successful, attempt to *rationalize* Scots law ties in with his view that law is *inter alia* for securing property and facilitating commerce.

substance, but I do accept the argument. I also disagree with them in their interpretation of the simply rational character of moral principles, which their theory justified them in calling principles of 'natural law'. But that obliges me *a fortiori* to accept the argument about the particular utility of positive law and instituted government, for my position even more than theirs entails an admission of the controversial character of principles of right. And that entails a necessity to have some method of authoritatively determining common rules of law and authoritatively determining disputes of right among the members of a society.

The conclusion which I reach accordingly exhibits strong elements of agreement with the theories I have reviewed. Government under announced laws as distinct from arbitrary and despotic rule is worth having and worthy of assent. It is so, because it is a condition of the reasonably secure enjoyment of rights. What particular rights are secured will of course depend upon the prevailing dominant conception of rights and the right, and none of us has a guarantee that his own conception will prevail.

To all this, discussion about whether we have governments because we or our ancestors agreed to form a society, or whether all or any of us has explicitly or implicitly adhered to such a compact, is quite irrelevant. Even if it were true, as I suggested, that feudal societies could more plausibly be represented in 'social contract' terms than could modern ones, it would not follow that the terms of the contract were fair, nor the bargaining positions of the parties equal. It would not follow that we or anyone else living now would be bound by the terms of any compacts historically established even if we could prove what their terms were or that they really did exist.

(c) *Political obligation and its limits*

What then can be said about the obligatoriness or binding quality of law, about political obligation? Without some express or tacit contract we can hardly claim that there is any obligation to obey the law, at least not a formal conventional obligation. Even if I were right in my conclusion of a moment ago that there is good reason to have and assent to government under law, that by no means entails that you or I morally owe it to each other or anyone else, or are under some mutual obligation, to respect and observe the law. That we have good reason to respect and observe the law at most entails that we ought to do so, not that we have an obligation to do so.[21] But remember what the good reason was. Whatever rights we conceive people ideally to have, their actual enjoyment of any can be secured only by government under law. Yet if people do have any rights, each of us has an obligation to do whatever is necessary to respect these rights in others. In terms of the Stair classification, that is an obediential obligation, not a conventional one. Where there is government under law, there is that which is a necessary guarantee of the security of any rights; and accordingly to that extent each owes it to every other to respect the law, even if not down to the particular minutiae of every rule and regulation.

Furthermore, there is surely something in Locke's argument from tacit consent, albeit subject to significant revision. Not so much or not only by enjoying property in the specific sense, but simply by taking willing advantage of the personal, civil, and political rights which a legal system offers, a person does I would suggest become engaged in favour of others to respect their enjoyment of those same rights. What he or she knowingly enjoys depends on their voluntary acts and forebearances: to them in turn he or she owes similar acts and forebearances. To sustain such a proposition, there is no need to impute to the person in question any express or implied will or intention to undertake such an obligation. The principle at stake is more like that of personal bar or estoppel: no one is entitled to take willing advantage of an arrangement and then subsequently to repudiate the arrangement when it operates in favour of others, the burden now falling on the originally benefited party. You may not both approbate and reprobate, as the Scots lawyers say. The obligation here is not a formal conventional one, though it is generically similar to that class of obligations.

If I left the point there, it could well be objected that the conception of political obligation which I am sketching is too stringent as sketched so far. I am suggesting that there are two independent grounds for such obligation. But suppose that the

[21] For a most powerful analysis of 'obligation' and 'ought', see Alan R. White, *Modal Thinking* (Oxford, 1975), chs. 9, 10; but cf. MacCormick, *H. L. A. Hart* (London, 1981), ch. 5.

prevailing conception of rights is from your point of view or mine a misconception. The problem would be perhaps particularly acute for those who had and enjoyed certain rights at the expense of others who were unjustly denied them. Surely by no argument can anyone be under a moral obligation to respect a system which perpetrates injustice to others? Can indeed those others be under any obligation to respect a system which causes them to labour under injustice?

Locke's position, it may be said, has the merit of clarity in this regard. It sets a clear limit to political obligation. Political obligation is dissolved in favour of anyone whose rights are unjustly invaded or denied by government.

But is this not a self-defeating clarity? If, as admitted even by such as Locke and Stair, and *a fortiori* by such as me, issues concerning rights are intrinsically controversial,[22] there is nothing more certain than that in any ordered society some people and perhaps many people will find their rights as they conceive them unsatisfied.

Accordingly, a Lockean view on the limits of political obligation is itself inconsistent with the argument already adopted from the theory as to the good reasons for having instituted governments at all. We appear to be in something of an impasse.

My way out of the impasse lies along the lines implied by Stair's argument on the very point on which he diverges from Locke. The point of having positive law as he saw it is precisely that human imperfection makes achievement of a perfect order of justice impossible among mere humans. We have to do the best we can in the knowledge that we cannot secure the ideal. That necessitates a choice for each of us between on the one hand demanding full satisfaction of our own conception of ideal justice, the consequence of which is descent or perhaps reversion into some kind of anarchy, and on the other hand acquiescing in arrangements which will inevitably fall short of our own ideal.

And that, as I see it, is how it is. That is precisely the choice we have. The mere fact that a legal order secures only a partial or imperfect protection of the rights we conceive people to have

[22] For a general discussion of the notion of controversy and of the controversial character of political questions, see A. J. Milne, *Political Controversy* (Durham University Inaugural Lecture, 1977).

does not justify us in attempting to topple the whole edifice. Among the reasons why this is so is the rather obvious truth that the outcome of successful revolutionary action is all too rarely a more satisfactory securing of the rights in whose name the flag of revolution was hoisted than obtained in the status quo ante.

But in the nature of the case, that argument holds good only on the hypothesis that the order which the citizen confronts is genuinely a case of government under law as distinct from purely arbitrary and despotic rule. And by that I mean at least that the system is animated by some conception of rights and some genuine effort to secure in practice the announced conception of rights.

What is more, I for one would set certain minimum criteria derived from my own conception of rights and of justice. Most basic is the requirement of equal respect for all human beings as such, as manifested in the equal protection for all citizens of what I take to be the most basic human rights, most obviously of all, the right to life. In addition to that, the very argument concerning the controversial quality of rights, which leads me to require toleration of some degree of perceived injustice, equally leads me to require of the system that it does not suppress controversy. The right to act and speak and organize politically in ways which are consistent with others having and exercising the same right seems to me fundamental. As to what forms of political and economic system are best consistent with these basic requirements, and/or preferable on other grounds, I have of course my own views. But in just this area of controversy it becomes pointless to insist on satisfaction of one's own conception of rights or of justice as a condition of acknowledging any political obligation.

And so I find myself in a position rather like Stair's; beyond my basic minimum I subscribe to a position which Robert Nozick characterizes as a 'utilitarianism of rights' rather than the 'side-constraint' view which he holds himself and ascribes to Locke.[23] I am not likely to find any system of government under which I am likely to live ideal in its satisfaction of my rights or other people's as I conceive them. But there are at least some, including the one under which I do live, which are far

[23] *Anarchy, State, and Utopia*, p. 28.

better than anything likely to be procured by revolutionary action[24]—better, judged by the standard of the non-positive rights which I think should be and can only be effectively protected by positive law. Since important rights of other people are secured and protected by the system, I owe them an obligation to respect the system at least to the extent to which it does secure their rights, quite independently of any voluntary act, undertaking, or other commitment of mine. Since I do willingly accept the protection afforded me by the law and exercise the liberty which it secures me, to those others whose law-abiding acts and forbearances I rely on I owe it to abide by the law in their favour myself.[25] I assert the same obligation of those who are in like case in respect of this or similar systems which satisfy at least my minimum requirements.

---

[24] By 'revolutionary action' I mean strictly what Locke has in mind in relation to the 'appeal to Heaven', that is, the use of force in an attempt to overthrow an established order or government. Attempts to procure 'revolution' in other senses, e.g. to bring about thoroughgoing social and political change through established political processes, are a different matter. T. S. Midgley suggested to me that my 'remarks about revolution are not sufficient reason for passing over the achievements of revolutionary thought (bourgeois and Marxist)'. I agree with him.

[25] This part of my thesis closely parallels and owes much to H. L. A. Hart's argument for obligation arising from 'mutuality of restrictions'. See his 'Are there any Natural Rights?', 64 *Philos. Rev.* (1955) 175–91.

5.
JUSTICE: AN UN-ORIGINAL
POSITION

HUMAN societies are not voluntary associations. At least so far
as concerns national societies and states, most human beings do
not have a choice which one they will belong to, nor what
shall be the law and the constitution of that to which they do
belong; especially, their belonging to a given state is not conditional upon their assenting to the basic structure of its organization. Someone who is born into a given state has obviously no
choice, no opportunity to stipulate conditions upon which he
will accept citizenship. Choice can perhaps be exercised later,
when one is an adult, when one may find oneself free to depart
from one's native state and to take up residence elsewhere with
a view to naturalization as a citizen of the state of one's choice.
But in that latter situation one is in a weak position to set
conditions for one's joining the chosen society. One accepts the
constitution and the laws as they are, or one does not acquire
citizenship. What is more, somebody who is thinking of
changing his citizenship has an appreciably more restricted
range of models open to him than someone thinking of changing
his car; and by contrast with that situation, he does not have the
option of going without if none appeals to him.

That human societies are not voluntary associations is a quite
general truth, embracing the most libertarian of democracies
and the most oppressive of autocracies, though of course there
are marked and significant differences as to the degree to which
in the former the individual citizen has the opportunity of
securing that account is taken of his wishes and desires in the
framing of laws, from the highest reaches of constitutional law
to the lowest trivialities of parking regulations. Nobody's
original citizenship is acquired by choice; subsequent changes
of citizenship are open only to a minority, and even those who
might change but deliberately choose not to do so may be
moved by considerations other than a conviction that their
present national society is, or can practically be made to be, a

perfectly constituted and wholly ideal form of human community.

Men are not born free; yet they are not everywhere wholly in chains; and thus a capital question for the philosophy of law in its critical, if not its analytical, modes, is that of attempting to settle what are the forms of social organization which deserve approval as just and well fitted to the human condition and the human situation. To answer the question is to advance a theory of justice.

One approach to answering that question, an approach which is not without certain obvious attractiveness, and which the work of John Rawls[1] has made important for contemporary thought, is to set up a counterfactual hypothesis, to imagine a situation quite different from that which actually obtains anywhere. The supposition is that we should conceive of a situation in which a society is to be formed by free and mutually independent individuals, as equal in rank, in propertylessness, in status and power as men belonging to no organized society must be, yet not ignorant of the advantages which social collaboration may bring upon beings who find themselves in a world with a sufficiency yet no superabundance of natural resources, their physical and mental capabilities being similar though subject to variation, and their collective being vastly greater than their individual ingenuity, resourcefulness, and strength. Entertaining that supposition, we then ask: 'To what form of coercive social organization would these people in that "original position"[2] assent?' The answer which we give may then be taken as a blueprint, as a critical scheme for the appraisal of our existing involuntary societies, as a pattern for the amendment of our actual states and their laws so that they shall be worthy of the universal and voluntary assent of citizens equal in freedom and equal in human dignity; *worthy* of such assent from all, even though actual assent may not be always given at all times by all citizens, blinded as they may from time to time be by greed, passion, or self-interest.

It is not difficult to conceive of objections to that way of tackling the problem. Suppose that two-thirds of the group who

---

[1] J. Rawls, *A Theory of Justice* (Cambridge, Mass., and Oxford, 1971 and 1972).
[2] Rawl's expression, see ibid., pp. 17–22.

come together have white skins and one-third have black skins. May the larger group not agree to a form of society permanently disadvantageous to the minority? Suppose that there are equal numbers of men and of women, but the men know themselves to be collectively greater in physical strength, as they believe themselves to be in intellectual prowess, than the women. May they not set up a society which permanently favours their interests the more? (Do not our actual societies sadly show forth the intrinsic probability of that?) Suppose that a small group of the most intelligent and articulate succeed in prevailing upon the rest to accept a system which will confer excessive advantages on intelligent and articulate people. It is at least highly questionable whether societies having such characteristics could be approved as just, though there is concrete evidence that they might be viable.

That objection is not, however, conclusive. There are two conditions upon which it might be met: first, demand complete unanimity,[3] not mere majority agreement. But that will not be sufficient to prevent the clever from tricking the less clever into unanimous acceptance of a plan disadvantageous to themselves, and small minorities—Celts, perhaps, for the sake of argument—may be sufficiently aware of the advantages of social collaboration to accept a compromise under which they are relatively disadvantaged as a group rather than excluded altogether. Unanimity being therefore insufficient in itself, we must add the second: let us postulate that the parties in the 'original position' are in fact unaware of their own specific characteristics—colour, race, sex, religious or political convictions, degree of intelligence and physical strength, and so on. They know that they are human beings to whom such characteristics belong, but not what particular characteristics they themselves have, nor in what measure.

At the risk of having moved from an imaginary but imaginable to a fantastic and unimaginable situation, we have met the objection. People forming a society behind a 'veil of ignorance'[4] as to their own characteristics as individuals would not know how to favour themselves unfairly at the expense of others. To

---

[3] As Rawls does; see ibid., pp. 122 ff., 139 ff.
[4] Rawls's expression again; the idea behind it is as summarized here; see ibid., pp. 12, 18–19, 136–42.

agree to a system which allowed for wide variations in fortune or social position and power would be to take a great gamble. One might be lucky, and find oneself very well off, or unlucky and find oneself very badly off. Perhaps people might in those circumstances prefer to settle for some system which allows for only small differentials in wealth and power—or for none?

But again, it could be suggested that the risk is not so enormous. For once the society has been formed as agreed, we move out from behind our 'veil of ignorance', and can we not then change matters if it turns out that we have agreed to something horribly disadvantagous to ourselves? Once I find that I have the advantage of being of the male sex, can I not get together with other men equally safe in the same knowledge and subject women to conditions which would have been unacceptable to me when I did not know to which sex I belonged?

If we allow that, we are back to the old objection that whatever our imagined convention might secure in the way of viability of social arrangements, it will not necessarily secure justice—not if we let people change the rules as agreed once we let them out from behind the 'veil of ignorance'. There is a simple answer to that. We are the masters of our own experiment, so we can simply stipulate that there is to be no such changing of the rules, not for the purposes of this experiment. Let it be recalled that the object of the experiment is to find what would be the ordering of a just society, in which case it is quite irrelevant that some men may wilfully depart from justice in bending their own societies to their own advantage. Indeed, that is the very fact which makes it necessary to formulate principles of justice on which to base a permanent and vigilant criticism of the actual practices and institutions of our own societies. Let us therefore stipulate that the parties in the 'original position' are to frame fundamental principles for the organization of their society on the footing that they commit themselves to them unanimously and in perpetuity, subject to no amendment once the 'veil of ignorance' is removed and an actual society formed.[5] Let these principles be universal in their application and eminently general in their terms, and let it be supposed that there can be no going back on them.

[5] See ibid., pp. 136–42.

What then would be the relevance of such experimentally, or, to speak more truly, hypothetically derived principles for the actual concrete societies in which we live, which as has been said are by no means voluntary associations formed by agreement among free and equal human beings each unbiased by considerations of his or her own individual or class advantage? The argument which we have to confront is the argument that principles so derived would be principles definitive of a conception of justice worthy of the assent of all human beings as free and rational moral agents, and consistent with the mutual respect for each other's persons which is incumbent upon such beings. This is in its essentials precisely the argument advanced by John Rawls in *A Theory of Justice*. It is an argument which he rightly acknowledges to be similar in its premises to the arguments of Kant and Rousseau, before whom it was prefigured in rather different form in the work of Locke, of Hobbes, of Grotius, and of others.

Before turning to assess the argument and its fruits, I must re-emphasize the hypothetical character of the social contract envisaged. Here there is no theory as to the origins of civil society, nor any assertion of political obligation founded upon some contract supposed to have been framed in the past among the founders of a society. The argument is not explanatory nor historical; it is critical and hypothetical. Its conclusions purport to show not how any society was formed but how every society might be reformed. 'Justice is the first virtue of social institutions as truth is of systems of thought.'[6] Justice requires that like advantages and disadvantages accrue to all who find themselves in like circumstances, and that as between those who are in different circumstances there should be no arbitrary differences in the advantages and disadvantages afforded and allotted by society. But that formal concept requires to be filled out with a substantive conception[7] of justice telling us what are to constitute like circumstances, and when inequalities are to be rejected as arbitrary. To frame such a conception is to formulate principles, critical principles for evaluating and justifying or rejecting the legal and economic frameworks and practices of

---

[6] Ibid., p. 3.
[7] For this useful distinction of terminology as between 'the concept' of justice and particular 'conceptions' of justice, see ibid., pp. 5–6.

concrete states and societies. Can we, as Rawls and his lineal ancestors claim, expound such principles convincingly in any possible form?

There was one crucial point in the argument in the form in which I put it (whether or not that correctly represents Rawls's own argument need not detain us if the argument is of interest in its own right), a point which almost seemed to reduce the hypothetical contract from the realm of the imaginary to the realm of the fantastic, and that point needs further consideration. That was the point at which we considered the possibility of an unfair agreement being made, for example in the interests of men as against women, to exclude which possibility I introduced, using Rawls's words, the idea of a 'veil of ignorance' to meet the objection. But even if this is not held to be merely fantastical, does it not involve a fundamental logical fallacy: that of *petitio principii*? The only reason for modifying the 'original position' in this way by introducing the 'veil of ignorance' is that otherwise the principles derived from the hypothetical contract may allow for, or even foster, obvious unfairness, whether it be in favour of white people over black people, men over women, clever over stupid, strong over weak, healthy over sick, or (in each case) vice versa. So it is to obviate obvious unfairness, not any ground of intrinsic plausibility (far from it), that we introduce the idea of people making a contract to form a society on the basis of total ignorance (experimentally postulated) of their own individual characteristics. Are we not then simply assuming what we set out to prove, namely what constitutes obvious unfairness? If the contractarian argument is implausible without the 'veil of ignorance', and question begging with it, what is its worth? We may observe, further, that precisely the same reason justified introducing the stipulation that the agreement must be conceived as yielding general principles of universal application whose acceptance is to be binding in perpetuity. So precisely the same logical criticism may be made of this as of the preceding stipulation.

There is, however, a possible answer to this criticism. It is certainly true that the use of the hypothetical contract must presuppose certain views upon justice. Let me take, for instance, the view that just decisions are dependent upon the impartiality of the decision-maker. I am not likely to be a fair judge of the question whether I am the best qualified candidate for a job which I wish to obtain in competition with other people: even less am I likely to be thought so by the other candidates if perchance I should in fact be entrusted with deciding on the appointment. What is needed is somebody who can assess and evaluate the qualifications of each of the competing candidates solely by reference to criteria relevant to the job itself, and who can assess them impartially without favour to any of the candidates based on any grounds other than the criteria provided by the job-description and the functions to be performed by the person appointed. We may observe that this is a formal requirement understandable by reference to the formal concept of justice, that like cases must be treated alike and any arbitrary differences of treatment rejected, which in turn entails that decisions must be made only in accordance with principles conceived to be of universal application.

I know of no way in which someone who accepts the value of impartiality in decision-making can demonstrate to somebody who rejects it that he is mistaken and ought to change his opinion. Thrasymachus may always remains unmoved by the eloquence and argumentative skills of Socrates. The argument to which I am always driven back is that of Hume,[8] or something like it: if I contemplate the condition of a society in which the principle of impartiality is observed by contrast with one in which it is not, I cannot myself say other than that the former is one which is infinitely more appealing to me, and must be so to anyone whose frame of mind is anything like mine. But that argument falls a long way short of being logically compelling, and it may not even be very persuasive in terms of psychology, for all I know. To say that somebody who rejects it has no idea of justice is obviously appealing—but has all the appearance of an attempt to use a stipulative definition to silence an opponent, and why should my opponent accept my definition any more than the argument whose inconclusiveness led me to assert it?

Be that as it may, even if the value of impartiality is not conclusively demonstrable, it is widely accepted, and there is

---

[8] Expressed with particular clarity in the *Enquiries concerning Human Understanding and concerning the Principles of Morals* (ed. L. A. Selby-Bigge and P. H. Nidditch, 3rd edn., Oxford, 1975).

therefore real value in asking what follows from accepting it; it is especially valuable if we wish to transcend particular examples like that of selection of one out of competing candidates for an attractive job and to proceed to more general and momentous questions about the good and just ordering of societies. If I have understood him correctly, Rawls, in suggesting the use of a hypothetical social contract formed by individuals behind a 'veil of ignorance' as a method of formulating principles of justice, is aiming to do no more and no less than to provide a way of working out the requirements which follow from acceptance of such a requirement as that of impartiality. So he does not beg the question. He does not assume the value of impartiality in order to prove it. He assumes the value of impartiality and then uses the device of the hypothetical contract in order to test out its implications in the context of an attempt to frame principles for the framing or the criticism of laws and other social and economic institutions. His argument plainly cannot then show us that (or whether) we ought to be impartial; what it can perhaps do is show to what a belief in impartiality would commit us if we really took it seriously in relation to the basic constitution and organization of our societies.

I think it is correct reading of his work to say that Rawls intends no more than that—he does at one point expressly state that the hypothetical contract is simply an argumentative tool which can be used to 'make vivid'[9] what the implications of the constraints are, e.g. concerning impartiality, which are commonly accepted in arguments about justice in practical contexts. But whether or not it is correct to impute that view to Rawls, it seems clear from the present argument that the use of a hypothetical social contract as Rawls uses it to elaborate a theory of justice cannot but depend upon presuppositions, including presuppositions about basic requirements of justice, which are not themselves derivable from (because they are logically prior to) the contractarian argument.

Indeed it can well be said, and has been said, that an obvious truth about any contractarian argument is that one can only get out of it the logical consequences of what one has initially put

<hr/>

[9] Rawls, *Theory of Justice*, p. 18.

into it [10] in stipulating the circumstances and characteristics of the parties envisaged as making the initial compact to form an entirely new society. The idea, put in broad and crude terms, is something like this: a social arrangement would be just if all the parties affected by it have the opportunity of participating in the design of the arrangement, but only if each is impartial in weighing his own interests and the interests of others, and only if some subgroups do not gang up to further their own interest at the expense of the others. Each person, having interests of his own to secure and to pursue, must be given an opportunity to secure and pursue them to the extent that is fair, given the interests which others wish to secure and to pursue, and the one way to settle the problem of fairness and balance is to try to find out a system which all could agree to if each gave due weight to the interest of others. Since, for a variety of reasons, actual societies have not been and could not be established by such a procedure, we have to resort to intellectual experimentation to find out what would result in ideal conditions from such a negotiation, and by appropriately designing a hypothetical model we can find out what would be the result, writing in such notions as that of the 'veil of ignorance' as a proxy for the principle of impartiality. But already we have written in the notion that what is crucial to a just ordering of society is that each person should be free to pursue whatever interests he has, of whatever kind, subject only to constraints agreement to which is required in order that every other person should be free to pursue whatever interests he has, subject only to the like constraint. The use of the model in effect writes this into the intial programme, and must again be reflected in the result— there can here be no discrimination between different objects of human interest in terms of their intrinsic worth, [11] nor can there be any allowance for notions such as that the Marxist one of false consciousness in terms of which people may mistake their real interests and pursue false ends by reason of such a mistake. What we are in effect writing in is the classical liberal presumption that people are ordinarily the best judges of their own interests and ought always to be treated as being such.

[10] This point is essentially derived from B. Barry, *The Liberal Theory of Justice* (Oxford, 1973), p. 22.
[11] Cf. ibid., pp. 20–6.

What is more, because the model postulates hypothetical people making an agreement in circumstances (including the 'veil of ignorance') in which no actual human beings can ever be placed, we have to decide what characteristics they are to be deemed as having in order that we may calculate what principles they would choose as the basic principles of social organization. Not merely do we in effect write in certain basic principles such as that of impartiality; we must also ascribe to them general characteristics—such as that of having interests which they desire to pursue, and knowing what their own interests are. We have to ascribe to them some degree of knowledge of the general facts of human nature and the human situation as revealed to us by the natural and social sciences— subject to all the imperfections and controversies of and over contemporary knowledge in those fields. Only by ascribing to them some such knowledge will we be able to reach any conclusions at all as to the agreement our hypothetical people will reach; but to ascribe to them any particular knowledge is to take some position on contentious questions, and the position one takes will in turn, and necessarily, contribute to the result one obtains from the experiment. Not merely must one ascribe to one's hypothetical co-contractors knowledge about the world and the place within it of men as social animals; one must have some view on matters of motivation, and must ascribe some motivational attitudes to the parties—for example, attitudes to taking risks.

Here I touch upon a theme which has been much elaborated by critics of Rawls's work. Among the results which Rawls derives from his own hypothetical contract is that people in the 'original position' would of necessity accept that there must be the most complete freedom of religious, moral, and political belief and practice as is consistent with each having equal freedom in these matters. His reasoning is that people who know what it is to have, e.g. religious convictions, but who do not know what religious convictions they themselves have (because of the 'veil of ignorance') would necessarily insist upon a principle of religious freedom and tolerance rather than accept any principle as to the establishment of a single official religion. They would do so because they would be unwilling to risk finding themselves in a persecuted minority if it turned out that their religious group was a minority in the society to which they actually belonged.

Rawls's conclusion that religious tolerance is a requirement of justice is one to which I personally am happy to assent. But what is obvious is that its deduction from the hypothetical contract is entirely dependent on the characteristics ascribed to the hypothetical parties, for example on their attitude to gambling and risk-taking. Ascription of different characteristics would result in different conclusions—it is not inconceivable that we should so adjust the hypothesis that the parties would prefer a principle of establishment of religion under which those whose religious position happened in fact to be orthodox would have the comfort and psychological security of practising their faith in conditions in which dissent was not tolerated while those who held dissenting faiths would have the satisfaction of martyrdom in the cause of the faith held by them in turn. For many who have held firm religious convictions those alternatives have in fact proved more attractive than the liberalism which Rawls deduces from his favoured premises.[12]

As is obvious, this is a vein of argument which one could pursue at very great length. But it has now been pursued far enough to enable us to consider whether the resuscitation of the Kantian idea of a hypothetical social contract is of any substantial value in attempting to elucidate principles of social organization definitive of an acceptable conception of social justice.[13] The most recent part of the discussion may prompt the reflection that so far from elucidating debate upon these difficult and fundamental questions, the effect may rather be to obscure points of contention by concealing them within the explicit or implicit premises established by the characterization of the original position and the parties who find themselves in that position and who seek to establish a society by unanimous agreement.

For my own part, that is a criticism of Rawls's attempt to establish his own principles of 'justice as fairness' which I have

---

[12] On the matters discussed in this and the preceding paragraph, cf. ibid., pp. 121–4. See also MacCormick, 'Justice According to Rawls', 89 LQR (1973) 393 at 408–12.

[13] For criticism of the use of this form of argument, as distinct from the principles derived from it, see D. D. Raphael, 'The Standard of Morals' (Presidential Address to the Aristotelian Society), XCVI *Proc. Arist. Soc.* (1974–5) 1. Cf. Barry, *Liberal Theory*, ch. 11.

come to reject. Despite accepting it as indubitably true that the principles derived are entirely determined by the premises one establishes in choosing how to set out the 'original position', I find the Rawlsian argumentative procedure an interesting one; indeed I find it so precisely because that is the case. It provides a convenient method for testing the implications of adhering to certain factual views about the essential nature of human beings as social animals and to certain broad principles of formal and procedural justice, together with the ideal that human societies should be such that all their members would be able willingly to consent to their organization as free and rational moral agents. The implications of holding to specified premises of that sort can be tested precisely by considering the substantive principles which would be derived from them in the negotiation of a hypothetical social contract. What is more, one can use the procedure as a way of testing the rival merits of competing social principles, by considering what variations in the premises would lead to acceptance of one or another of rival principles. For example, if utilitarianism is consistent with the possibility of very considerable differentials in the matter of individual wealth or power, one might find it necessary to impute to human beings a very great readiness to take the risk of extreme wealth or extreme poverty, necessary, that is, in order to be able to derive acceptance of the (or a) utilitarian principle from the negotiations in the 'original position'. If ascription of such a characteristic is implausible, to that extent doubt is cast upon the acceptibility of utiltarianism.

Yet is it really true that one's acceptance of a given conception of justice is best tested by considering its derivability, and the possible modes of its derivation, from some hypothetical contract? I cannot believe that the answer to that question should be 'Yes'. The ultimate test of any moral theory surely is critical evaluation of the principles which it propounds as substantive principles of conduct, whether principles of distributive justice, or principles relating to some other sector of morality (I take it as true that questions of justice do not exhaust the whole range of possible moral questions). A set of principles of justice is in effect a sort of manual of instructions for shaping the laws and institutions of society, and competing conceptions of justice are thus in effect manuals whose adoption will yield different laws and institutions, different forms of society. By their fruits they shall be known. The ultimate tests by which anyone can evaluate any conception of justice are, I submit, twofold: first, that of coherence and consistency—are the principles self-consistent and free from contradictions or antinomies internal to themselves, and are they in the same sense consistent with the constellation of other principles to which I subscribe?—and secondly, do I assent to the idea of my society's being reshaped as the 'manual' would require it to be reshaped? Would I so assent whatever position I were assigned in that conceived society?[14]

Of course, this too involves an effort of the imagination, to the extent that one's attempt is to visualize the world as it would be if the principles under consideration were put into effect. But the world is such that more practical tests can take place, in so far as there are processes for changing laws and institutions. To be committed to a given conception of justice is to be committed to trying to procure such change; to the extent that change occurs it can be evaluated in concrete and not merely in abstract form. The question shifts from the question 'Would I accept this realized form of society for myself and for all my fellow citizens, each of whose humanity I am obliged to respect?' By my view of rationality, rational commitment to any conception of justice requires such continuous revaluation of one's principles to the extent that they are put into concrete effect. I do not believe in final blueprints, but rather in a permanent effort to articulate the principles by which one conceives oneself to be acting, and in a permanent disposition to criticize them in the light of what results from putting them into effect, and to amend principles and practice in the light of the critique of their effects.[15] Therefore, while defending the value of Rawls's argumentative procedure for some purposes, I nevertheless say of it as of other forms of hypothetical reasoning that the ultimate test is that of criticizing the results derived from it. If a legal model were to be sought for the process, I would look

---

[14] The business of assessing principles by reference to the tests of coherence and consistency and by reference to the consequences of their adoption is fully discussed in my *Legal Reasoning and Legal Theory* (Oxford, 1978).

[15] Barry puts a similar point: *Liberal Theory*, p. 121, and cf. R. M. Hare, *Freedom and Reason* (Oxford, 1963).

not to the concept of contract, but to the practice of critical reasoning characteristic of the justification of legal decisions.

And so by a long road I come at last to the crucial point; to the point of stating and considering the principles advanced by Rawls. Here I shall confine myself to his 'special conception' of justice, which is an elaboration of a more general conception and which he regards as being appropriate only to relatively developed societies, in the economic sense.[16] To state the governing principles of the 'special conception', they are as follows:

First Principle. Each person is to have an equal right to the most extensive total system of equal basic liberties compatible with a similar system of liberty for all.[17] (The basic liberties he lists include 'political liberty (the right to vote and to be eligible for public office) together with freedom of speech and assembly; liberty of conscience and freedom of thought; freedom of the person along with the right to hold (personal) property; and freedom from arbitrary arrest and seizure as defined by the concept of the rule of law'.)[18]

Second Principle. Social and economic inequalities are to be arranged so that they are both: (a) to the greatest advantage of the least advantaged, consistent with the just savings principle, and (b) attached to offices and positions open to all under the conditions of fair equality of opportunity.[19]

These two principles are placed by Rawls in what he calls an order of 'lexical' priority;[20] by that he means that in any given situation the requirements of the first must be fully met before the second comes into play—and, in a manner too complex to explain here, a similar priority holds in relation to the internal elements of the second. So, in any conflict between economic efficiency and a claim of liberty justified by the first principle, such a claim of liberty must prevail. Moreover, any increased economic advantage to the worst off groups in society which would conflict with their own, or others', liberty as defined

[16] For this distinction, see *Theory of Justice*, p. 303; discussed in Barry, *Liberal Theory*, ch. 7.
[17] Ibid., p. 302.
[18] Ibid., p. 61.
[19] Ibid., p. 302.
[20] Ibid., pp. 42–4; discussed in MacCormick, 'Justice According to Rawls', pp. 414–15.

under the first principle would be ruled out even if it would otherwise fit in with the criteria posed in the second principle.

The first principle, the principle of equal liberty, is subjected to one qualification not stated by Rawls in the summary which I quoted above. For he states that in one circumstance a scheme of liberties which distributes liberties unequally may be just. That circumstance is if a grant of greater liberty to some group is acceptable to all those who have the lesser liberty as a means of further securing their scheme of liberties (liberty can be restricted only for the sake of liberty).[21] A relevant case is perhaps presented by the immunities and privileges, e.g. in relation to defamatory statements, enjoyed by legislators in most democratic legislatures, at any rate so far as concerns their utterances made in the deliberations of the legislature.

When I apply my kind of test, I have no difficulty in accepting this principle as proposed by Rawls, though of course it is very vague and might give rise to much controversy as to its proper application. I accept it if for no other reason than that continuing critical revaluation of social principles requires the greatest possible freedom. There is perhaps a potential criticism that liberty is a value distinct from justice, and that the maximization of liberty, even if it does not conflict with justice, is a policy distinct from the promotion of justice, concerned as that is with the elimination of arbitrary differentials between people. On the other hand, it might be argued that everyone values liberty in some respects, though not each to the same degree nor in the same respects as every other. Therefore any system of laws and institutions which curtails liberty in other ways than are essential to achieve a maximal overall scheme of liberty will in fact bear harder on some than on others, in circumstances where the sole difference is the activities which one rather than another wishes to pursue freely. Thus, justice requires not merely equality in respect of such liberty as is granted, but maximization of the range of the total regime or constellation of liberties, as a measure which practically secures equality between people with differing tastes, interests, and desires to pursue.

Some will say that in a society in which there are gross

---

[21] Rawls, *Theory of Justice*, p. 302.

inequalities, mere equality in formal legal liberties, so far from being a requirement of justice, may merely be a mask for real injustices. The poor and the rich alike are permitted to propagate whatever views they wish through publication of newspapers under a guarantee of freedom of the press—but it just so happens that the poor cannot afford to run newspapers to propagate their views. That is an opinion which seems to me to be eminently justified, and of which Rawls takes account in terms of a distinction between the existence of freedom and its *worth*[22] to an individual upon whom some formal freedom of action is conferred. On the ground that the priority of liberty is defensible only when circumstances are such that legal liberties have substantial worth to all citizens, he restricts his 'special conception of justice' to societies enjoying advanced economies in which even the worst off are (or can be, given just arrangements) relatively well off.[23]

But that brings us to the question of the acceptability of the second of Rawls's principles stated above. There is on the face of it something odd about a principle of justice which appears to advocate the existence of inequalities, as though the object were to procure rather than to diminish social and economic inequalities. To present it as a requirement of justice that 'social and economic inequalities are to be so arranged that they are to the greatest advantage of the least advantaged' is at least to appear to be primarily concerned with the advocacy of inequality. Far preferable from this point of view is Rawls's statement of the 'general conception' from which the 'special conception' is elaborated, and which he states thus: 'All social primary goods—liberty and opportunity, income and wealth, and the bases of self-respect—are to be distributed equally unless an unequal distribution of any or all of these goods is to the advantage of the least favoured.[24]

What that more general formulation makes clear, is that the basic idea is to secure equality as between all citizens, except where there is some specific justifying reason for so organizing legal and social institutions that inequalities may arise or exist

[22] Ibid., pp. 204 ff.

[23] Ibid., pp. 151–2; Barry makes rather heavy weather of this point in *Liberal Theory*, ch. 7.

[24] *Theory of Justice*, p. 62.

within their framework. What is more, it is clearly stated that there is to be one and only one specific justifying reason for the toleration of inequalities, namely that they maximize the well-being of the least favoured under such arrangements. The Prime Minister of a state has more power than his fellow citizens, but is this inequality of power unjust?[25] By Rawls's thesis, it is unjust unless it can be shown that those who have less power, and especially those who have the least power, are better off under a constitution which confers that degree of power on a head of government than they would be in any possible alternative arrangement. And that argument goes in the same way for other forms of inequality, all of which must be justifiable by that test or rejected as unjust. Thus in economic matters, differences of individual income and wealth must be restricted to that minimum which secures the existence of a system which secures to the poorest members of a community a standard of living better than could be achieved by any alternative scheme of distribution, judged in the long term.

All this is, as the 'second principle' quoted makes clear, subject to two qualifications. The first arises from the obligation of any given generation to successor generations in the matter of conservation of resources and investment for the future. One way to make the present generation immediately better off is to give them the seed-corn to eat, but the consequences of doing so are catastrophic for successor generations. To cover this risk Rawls advocates a just savings principle, under which invest-ment is to be pursued to the extent acceptable to the least fortunate of the present generation in view of the advantages which it will confer on the least fortunate of the next. That should be taken as meaning that no generation has a right so to consume resources that their successors are put in a worse position, and that each has a duty to make some provision towards improving their successors' lot, the extent of the duty being determined by the degree of 'slack' which the poorest of the present generation could be reasonably expected to allow for their own children and grandchildren.[26]

[25] For a rather different illustrative example worked out at greater length, see MacCormick, 'Justice According to Rawls', pp. 401–2.

[26] On 'just savings' see *Theory of Justice*, pp. 284–93; contrary to Rawls's view, I see no reason to think that justice in matters of conservation and investment is forward-looking only—see MacCormick, op. cit., p. 405.

The second qualification is that concerning 'fair equality of opportunity'. While inequalities are not unjust if they arise from schemes which confer the greatest available advantage on the least favoured, they become unjust if unequally favoured positions are the closed preserve of a restricted group, class, caste, or whatever identified by criteria other than their specific fitness for the social tasks to which the advantages in question accrue. The system must make such positions open to all simply on the basis of talent, ability, and fitness for the job; and must do so in conditions of fairness to all, which means that educational and other provision must be made to secure that every person is given the best possible chance of developing his or her talents, gifts, and abilities to the full.

That gives the clue to the grounds for Rawls's belief that inequalities can sometimes be justified as being in the best interests of those least favoured by the regime allowing for inequality. Society being a collaborative enterprise capable of securing for all advantages which none could secure alone, division of functions and division of labour increases the capacity of a society to confer benefits on its members. The more it can be secured that people are called to the functions which their native abilities best fit them to perform (and fit them to perform best), the greater the general advantage. But such advantages are not worth pursuing at the price of great inequalities, and the best equilibrium is when only such inequalities are permitted as are either intrinsic to the performance of a function (prime-ministerial powers) or essential as incentives to secure the attraction of individuals to those jobs which they are best fitted to perform (high pay for doctors might be an example), in circumstances in which the performance of those tasks at all, and their performance by the best qualified people, secures the greatest possible benefits to those who benefit least from the overall scheme.[27]

How inegalitarian a society does this envisage? That seems to me to depend essentially on questions of fact. In a society whose members were imbued with a sense of justice and a common acceptance of principles like Rawls's as defining the content of

---

[27] Barry (*Liberal Theory*, p. 51) refers to Rawls as favouring meritocracy; but Rawls denies this, in my opinion with justification—see MacCormick, 'Justice According to Rawls', pp. 406–8.

that sense of justice, and in which a conscious effort was made to reduce inequalities to such a point of equilibrium as that envisaged, differentials, and especially differential incomes provided as incentive payments, might well be quite small. Especially would this be so if, as he claims, such a society would embody the idea of fraternalism in a common sense that everybody's abilities were being consciously used with a view to furthering the advantage of all.

There are certainly formidable difficulties in calculating how to apply the principle, as perhaps the last paragraph indicates; and Dr Barry has shown that powerful criticisms may be made of Rawls's own suggestions about practical methods of applying it.[28] But subject to all such difficulties in trying to imagine its application, I am bound to say that I find myself in substantial assent to the proposition that we should so adjust our legal,· economic, and social systems as to secure that they allow for no inequalities save those which advance best the lot of those who enjoy the lower positions on the existing scales of inequality. If in the end that should lead us to discover their total eliminability, I should be none the sadder for that.

As I said at the outset, human societies are not voluntary associations, and can never be entirely so. But if they were developed along the lines suggested by Rawls on the basis of this hypothetical social contract, they would become more and more worthy of the consent of all their members, and thus approximate more and more to being voluntary associations. One cannot say this with the certainty of absolute conviction, but the proposition is worth considering seriously.

[28] *Liberal Theory*, ch. 5. See ibid., p. 50: 'Surely not since Locke's theory of property have such potentially radical premises been used as the foundation for something so little disturbing to the *status quo*!' But the premises are certainly open to a more radical reading, which is what I have given them here.

6.
LAW AND ECONOMICS:
ADAM SMITH'S ANALYSIS

I. PROLOGUE

So FIRM has been the grip of Bentham and Austin on the British juristic imagination that jurists have all too rarely considered their predecessors. From Bentham's and Austin's mixture of rigorous conceptual analysis and implausibly simplistic utilitarianism, we have sifted out the analytical element, and our dominant jurisprudential tradition has concentrated on perfecting and re-arguing analytical schemes. That is not to be regretted in itself, since rigorous analysis is an essential groundwork for any worthwhile philosophical effort. It should, however, be deplored that we have failed to give adequate attention to what went before Bentham in eighteenth-century legal theory. In particular, the writings of the Scottish Enlightenment and the later seventeenth century—by jurists such as Stair, Erskine, Bankton, Kames, and John Millar, and by philosophers such as Francis Hutcheson, David Hume, Adam Ferguson, Thomas Reid, and Dugald Stewart—elaborate themes which should have been developed, not neglected.

The disputes over natural law and rationality in ethics among the Scottish moralists were carried on at a level to which Benthamite moralizing on the basis of a merely asserted principle of utility never aspired; and the attempts of the Scottish moralists to account for the historical development of legal orders within theories of economy and society has been altogether too much neglected since then—it has been left to sociologists such as William C. Lehmann to renew our interests in their theories.

It is within that general intellectual context that we must place Adam Smith as a theorist of law. Smith succeeded Francis Hutcheson as professor of moral philosophy at Glasgow in 1750 at the age of twenty-seven. He followed the contemporary understanding of the tasks of his office by giving a series of lectures on natural theology, ethics, jurisprudence, and political economy. His course on ethics was worked up for publication in 1759 under the title of *The Theory of Moral Sentiments*. The work on political economy led to the publication of *The Wealth of Nations* in 1776, thirteen years after his resignation from the Glasgow chair. He continued working on other themes, but shortly before his death in 1790 he gave orders for the destruction of all of his manuscripts save a few essays entrusted to his executors for publication.

In 1896, however, Professor Edwin Cannan discovered and edited a remarkably full set of student's notes from Smith's 'Lectures on Justice, Police, Revenue and Arms', being none other than the lectures on jurisprudence—of which presumably the more developed manuscript by Smith had been destroyed in 1790. Almost twenty years ago Professor Lothian of Aberdeen discovered another more complete set of notes from the same course of lectures, apparently belonging to an earlier year. The recent publication of this version of Smith's *Lectures on Jurisprudence*, under the joint editorship of Professors R. L. Meek, D. D. Raphael, and P. G. Stein, will doubtless occasion a revival of interest in this aspect of Smith's work—together, it may be hoped, with a revival of interest in the legal theories of the eighteenth century generally.

It was from the topics covered in those parts of the lectures dealing with police, revenue, and arms that the themes of *The Wealth of Nations* derived. The relevance of 'revenue' is obvious, but it needs to be recalled that for Smith 'police' had nothing much to do with the gentlemen in blue. 'Police', Smith said, 'is the second general division of jurisprudence' The name is French and is originally derived from the Greek *politeia*, which, though properly signifying the policy of civil government, came to mean only the regulation of the inferior parts of government, *viz.*, cleanliness, security, and cheapness or plenty. Smith dealt with cleanliness and security fairly summarily before proceeding to the theme of cheapness or plenty in Division II of Part II of the lectures. There we find much of the theorizing of *The Wealth of Nations* already present in embryo. 'Arms' were dealt with in *The Wealth of Nations* under 'Expenses of the Sovereign'.[1]

In these days of interdisciplinary endeavour, it is pleasing to discover that the origins of economics were so firmly located by the inventor of the dismal science within the second general division of jurisprudence, namely, 'police'. It is time now for jurisprudents to enquire and discover what economics has now to offer for the understanding of law. Where would be a better place to start than by an enquiry into what Adam Smith himself had to offer?

In what follows I lay no great claim to originality; I have been much influenced by works of colleagues such as Professor T. D. Campbell, Professor Andrew Skinner, Professor P. G. Stein, and Mr. G. L. Davidson.[2] In particular, my account of what Smith has to say owes a great deal to Skinner's essay, 'Adam Smith on Law and Government'. To some extent, one is faced with the task of reconstructing themes out of lectures which he had hoped would never be published. In that, I merely follow where others have led.

II. NATURAL RIGHTS AND POSITIVE LAW

One of the most fascinating things about Adam Smith is the way in which he combined, as the basic elements of the economy of different forms of human society, a theory of natural rights with a theory of the social development of laws and legal institutions. His lectures on justice begin with the confident

---

[1] A. Smith, *An Inquiry into the Nature and Causes of the Wealth of Nations* bk. V, ch. 1, pt. 1 (Glasgow edn., ed. R. H. Campbell, A. S. Skinner, and W. B. Todd, Oxford, 1976; 1st edn. 1776).

[2] T. D. Campbell, *Adam Smith's Science of Morals* (London, 1971); Andrew Skinner, 'Adam Smith on Law and Government', *Perspectives in Jurisprudence* (ed. E. Attwooll, Glasgow, 1977), ch. 11; P. G. Stein, 'Legal Thought in 18th Century Scotland', 1957 *Jur. Rev.* 1; id., 'The General Notions of Contract and Property in 18th Century Scottish Thought', 1963 *Jur. Rev.* 1; id., 'Law and Society in 18th Century Scottish Thought', *Scotland in the Age of Improvement* (ed. N. T. Phillipson and R. Mitchison, Edinburgh, 1970), ch. 7; id., 'Rights and Relativism in Adam Smith' (unpublished, 1975); G. L. Davidson, *Adam Smith's Lectures on Justice* (University of Cambridge LLB dissertation, 1974).

assertion that 'The end of justice is to secure from injury'.[3] Human beings may be injured in several respects; namely, as human beings *simplicitier*, as members of families, and as members of states. Taking the first of these categories as the principal one, which indeed it was for Smith, he tells us that a human being 'may be injured in his body reputation or estate'.[4] Smith draws an important distinction between injuries to body and reputation and injuries to estate. 'These rights which a man has to the preservation of his body and reputation from injury are called natural, or as the civilians express them *iura hominum naturalia*'.[5] Injuries to a person's estate are different, in the sense that 'his rights to his estate are called acquired or *iura adventitia*, and are of two kinds, real and personal'.[6]

In drawing these distinctions, Smith was, of course, anything but original. As befitted a professor of moral philosophy giving lectures on justice, police, revenue, and arms, he was simply expounding some distinctions common among civilian writers of the period. It was no doubt his good fortune to have been reared in the civilian tradition of the Scottish universities, a tradition which by contrast to that prevailing in contemporary English legal education secured a systematic and principled approach to tasks of legal description and analysis. But if the schema was unoriginal, the use to which Smith put it was far from unoriginal. Looking to his moral philosophy as expressed in the *Theory of Moral Sentiments*,[7] we find a particularly interesting account of what constitutes an injury; if we look to his political economy, which was already developing in the lectures on justice, police, revenue, and arms, we find one of the most interesting expositions anywhere of the correlations between conceptions of injury and forms of society.

First, I shall deal briefly with his general notion of injury. As is well known, Smith's general account of our moral perceptions advanced in the *Theory of Moral Sentiments* is based on the idea of

[3] A. Smith, *Lectures on Jurisprudence* (Glasgow edn., ed. R. Meek, P. G. Stein, and D. D. Raphael, Oxford, 1978), pp. 397–9; or see id., *Lectures on Justice, Police, Revenue and Arms* (ed. E. Cannan, Oxford, 1896), pp. 3–4.

[4] Ibid.

[5] Ibid.

[6] Ibid.

[7] A. Smith, *The Theory of Moral Sentiments* (Glasgow edn., ed. D. D. Raphael and A. L. Macfie, Oxford, 1976; 1st edn. 1759).

the 'impartial spectator'.[8] Of the actions which human beings may take in relation to each other, some cause pain and distress. The person who suffers pain, distress, or other harm from the action of another human being has a natural inclination to resent it, all the more so if he sees that the harmful act was intentional, and was intended to be harmful. Human beings have the capacity for sympathy (or, as we might say, empathy) with each other. Someone who observes a harmful act intentionally being done by one person to another, can enter by sympathy into the feelings of the victim, and can in some degree, though not as acutely as the victim, share in the sense of resentment. But of course, this depends equally on being able to enter into and understand the motives of the attacker. If, for example, it should turn out that the attacker is retaliating against harm previously done, this may lead the spectator to share in the resentment of the attacker and to regard the attack as justified rather than to enter sympathetically into the resentment of the victim. Of course, if the spectator happens to be someone who is already 'on the side of' either the attacker or the victim, this will render his approbation or disapprobation of the action no less partial than that of the party whose side he takes.

Since morality is based on a common sense of propriety and impropriety among human beings, the common position can be found only by reference to the position of an impartial spectator; that is, one who is not predisposed to take the side of either of the parties. What is more, the worth of an impartial spectator's judgment is dependent on the degree of his knowledge, and we can never have perfect knowledge of the actions, intentions, and motivations of other human beings. We can, however, have or acquire a relatively good understanding of our own intentions and motivations. The extent to which human beings possess a fully developed moral judgment depends on their, as it were, constructing within their breast an ideal impartial spectator who is genuinely impartial in relation to themselves and those with whom they deal, but who is fully informed of the intentions and motivations of the agent, because the impartial spectator shares them. So for each of us, our moral judgments are framed

---

[8] Ibid., pt. II, § iii, ch. 1. See also Campbell, *Science of Morals*; Skinner, 'Law and Government'; and Knud Haakonssen, *The Science of a Legislator: The Natural Jurisprudence of David Hume and Adam Smith* (Cambridge, 1981).

by a reference to this ideal impartial spectator, this 'man within the breast' with whom we can enter into dialogue in moral matters.

Rough and crude as that explanation is, it enables one to understand Smith's idea of an injury. When a person suffers harm that he resents, as the result of the act of another person, and when the impartial spectator can enter into and fully share in the ensuing resentment in degree and kind, or rather, to the extent that the impartial spectator can enter into that resentment, we may say that the harm-causing act was an injury. From the impartial spectator's point of view, an appropriate act of retaliation is then justified, and indeed constitutes a just punishment for the injury. Thence we derive our basic notion of injury, and our notion of justice as the punishment or other correction of injuries. We may observe that this leads to a theory of justice in which justice is necessarily conceived of as being corrective rather than distributive.

In turn, we can make sense of the idea that there are natural rights; there are natural rights to the extent that there are natural injuries. Natural injuries are those which people can suffer, inflict, and rightly resent in any social setting whatsoever. When one person hurts another in his body or his reputation, I do not need to know anything more about the social or economic background in order to know that a wrong or an injury has been done. Though different cultures may take different actions in repression of, retaliation for, or correction of the wrongdoing, we need postulate no substantial degree of cultural relativity in the recognition that a wrong has been done.

In some respects also, Smith is prepared to treat some basic elements of adventitious rights as being in the same sense natural. For example, if someone has taken possession of an ownerless thing, as by killing a wild animal, invasion by another of that possession would be resented, and the resentment would attract the sympathy of the impartial spectator.[9] The same is true for voluntary obligations. If someone knowingly puts another person in a position of relying on him for performance of some act, which for Smith is the essence of promising, then

---

[9] See Smith, *Lectures on Jurisprudence*, p. 459 (Cannan edn. pp. 107–9).

subsequent disappointment of the person who has that reasonable expectation is a wrong in the view of the impartial spectator.[10] Nevertheless, in general terms, although adventitious rights may have in such ways 'natural' foundations, their protection and enforcement, and indeed in some measure their institution, are matters regulated by positive law. Further they are matters that positive law regulates in various ways according to the circumstances, with the regulations being determined chiefly by the mode of economy of a society. This will sufficiently appear in due course. What presently has to be observed is the relationship between Smith's basic theory of positive law and his notion of injury.

So far as concerns the nature of positive law, Smith subscribes to the standard voluntarist notion, later adopted by Benthamite and Austinian 'positivists', that the actual positive law of a state is to be identified with the command of the sovereign.[11] Positive law, as such, emanates from organized institutions of government. But as to its function, the aim of positive law is to secure justice, in the sense of the prevention and repression of injuries.[12] It is not a substitute for what is morally right, but a reinforcement of it. There are at least some circumstances in which people in society will exhibit a tendency to unjustly invade each other's rights, and in which there will not be proper security for the enjoyment of rights. In these circumstances there must be a positive law, not to define, but to secure justice among people. It is when we consider what in Smith's view these circumstances are that require positive law, that we hit upon the sociologically innovative aspect of his theorizing about law.

III. LAW AND ECONOMY IN GENERAL

At this point we must return to the theme of acquired rights. A person's estate is composed of the sum total of his acquired

[10] Ibid., p. 472 (Cannan edn., pp. 130–1).

[11] See Smith, *Theory of Moral Sentiments*, pt. III, ch. 5 para. 6 (Glasgow edn. p. 165): 'All general rules are commonly denominated laws . . . [for example] laws of motion. But those general rules which our moral faculties observe . . . may more justly be denominated such. They have a much greater resemblance to what are properly called laws, those general rules which the sovereign lays down to direct the conduct of his subjects.'

[12] Ibid., pt. II, § ii, ch. 1 (Glasgow edn. pp. 78–82).

rights.[13] These Smith divides into the standard categories of real rights and personal rights. Real rights he subdivides into four kinds, of which the first three are standard: property, servitudes, pledges, and exclusive privileges. Property, Smith analyses in terms of the right to exclusive possession of a thing, together with the power to recover the thing owned from any other possessor whatsoever. Servitudes and pledges (in which term Smith includes mortgages) he analyses in a quite standard way. An exclusive privilege, says Smith, is like 'that of a bookseller to vend a book for a certain number of years, and to hinder any other person from doing it during that period'.[14] I do not know whether Smith's use of the concept of 'exclusive privilege' in this context is original; certainly, it is a brilliant way of characterizing various forms of 'incorporeal property' which have become much more common since Smith's time. Copyright obviously fits the category; as would patents and various forms of statutory monopoly, and even perhaps such things as equity shares. Smith also includes in 'exclusive privilege' the right of an heir who has not yet entered on the inheritance, and suggests that there might be 'natural' rights by way of exclusive privileges; for example where a hunter has started a hare and pursued her for some time and has thus, in Smith's view, a right against all comers to pursue her to the final kill.[15] The identification of this category of rights that are real but incorporeal is clearly of some importance; certainly for Smith, in the light of his political economy, given his views on the undesirable quality of monopolies, the category was important.

Rights under contracts and the right to reparation for damage done by delinquency also belong to the category of acquired rights. Smith would certainly have been anxious to deny in both cases the fashionable contemporary thesis that such rights have no moral foundation; and it is submitted that he would be entirely correct. But he is surely right in also saying that even if the basic right to performance of a promise, to to be free from harm, are in a sense natural, nevertheless the remedial right to compensation for contracts broken or harm done is a creature of positive law.

[13] Smith, *Lectures on Jurisprudence*, pp. 399–401 (Cannan edn. pp. 6–8).
[14] Ibid., p. 400 (Cannan edn. p. 7).
[15] Ibid.

'Acquired rights such as property require more explanation [than natural rights]. Property and civil government very much depend on one another. The preservation of property and the inequality of possession first formed it, and the state of property must always vary with the form of government.'[16] It is the basic thesis of Smith's—that property and civil government, and therefore positive law (which is the creature of civil government), are closely intertwined—which is of the greatest interest to us. He put the same point another way: 'Till there be property there can be no government, the very end of which is to secure wealth and to defend the rich from the poor.'[17] These words, taken from the lectures, are echoed in the section of *The Wealth of Nations* dealing with 'The Expense of Justice'.[18] It was a fundamental tenet of Smith's, which nowadays most people wrongly ascribe to Karl Marx, that forms of government and property relations are mutually interdependent. Positive law is shaped, according to Smith, by the mode of economy of a society. People have not always lived in societies subjected to formal institutionalized magistrates or governments.

Among nations of hunters, as there is scarce any property, or at least none that exceeds the value of two or three days' labour; so there is seldom any established magistrate, or any regular administration of justice. Men who have no property, can injure one another only in their persons or reputations. But when one man kills, wounds, beats or defames another, though he to whom the injury is done suffers, he who does it receives no benefit. It is otherwise with the injuries to property. The benefit of the person who does the injury is often equal to the loss of him who suffers it. Envy, malice, or resentment, are the only passions which can prompt one man to injure another in his person or reputation. But the greater part of men are not very frequently under the influence of these passions; and the very worst of men are so only occasionally.[19]

Smith subscribed to and gave his own version of, though he did not invent, the theory of the 'four stages' of human society.[20]

---

[16] Ibid., p. 401 (Cannan edn. p. 8).
[17] Ibid., p. 404 (Cannan edn. p. 15); cf. *Wealth of Nations*, bk. V, ch. I, pt. 2.
[18] Ibid.
[19] Ibid.
[20] See Smith, *Lectures on Jurisprudence*, pp. 14–15, 459–60 (Cannan edn. p. 107). Mr G. L. Davidson has pointed out to me a passage in Montesquieu, *De L'Esprit des Lois* (bk. 18, ch. 8), which is perhaps the original source of this idea, which was common among writers of the period.

That is, that in the evolution of human societies four main stages are discernible, in terms of the basic features of their economy. There are societies of hunters and fishermen, societies of shepherds, societies of agriculturalists, and commercial societies. In the first of these stages people would own no permanent property; and for that reason, said Smith, they would not require institutionalized magistracies or positive laws. The corollary, which Smith regards as obvious, is that in societies that recognize private property and thus inequality of possessions, there are and must also be laws and regular systems of law enforcement. For once inequality of possession exists, there is the possibility of envy and resentment by the poor of the rich, who accordingly have to secure by some means their possessions against the depredations which are a permanent danger in such circumstances. Not merely does the establishment of property give rise to the risk of invasions of possessions, but it also gives rise to motives for interpersonal violence, assaults on reputation, and all those other wrongs which, as he assures us, would be relatively uncommon among nations of hunters. Governments and positive laws evolve as a means to secure the position of property-owners and check the other modes of wrongdoing that are occasioned by the very existence of property regimes.

Thus it appears that in societies that have evolved beyond the stage of hunting and gathering, positive law is not so much a separate phenomenon brought into existence by the political economy as it is an intrinsic element of such economy. The development of a pastoral economy dependent for its subsistence on the produce of herds leads to an allocation of domesticated animals to individuals or families, and a protection of that allocation by means of enforced laws securing to 'owners' possession of their beasts, their produce, and their progeny. It would not be true to say that the development of a pastoral economy causes the existence of enforced laws of property; rather, the development of a pastoral economy is a development in which an intrinsic part is the recognition and protection of property rights in those things that to such a society represent the essentials of wealth; namely, herds.

A necessary feature of such a development is the existence of inequalities in the possession of the animals that increasingly represent exclusive necessities of life; the population grows beyond the point at which sustenance by hunting and fishing is a possibility, and the pasturage of herds in itself tends to diminish the numbers of wild animals available for hunting by those who would thus choose to subsist. Here we find an explanation of the origins of the subordination of one human being to another; the 'origin of the distinction of ranks' as Smith and his pupil John Millar[21] called it. Those who have not, become dependent on those who have; those who have, can do nothing with their excess produce other than maintain a train of dependants, over whom their power tends to the absolute, since they control the means of life of their dependants. The wealth of those who have gives them authority by giving others reason to accept that authority.

Pasturage itself may give way in turn, albeit extremely gradually, to the development of a settled agricultural system, which again is capable of sustaining a larger population on the same area of ground as a pastoral system. The development of settled agriculture replaces the nomadic system of pasturing when the agriculturists appropriate the pastures of the nomads. Again, the need for force to protect the land that is held is obvious; also obvious are the intrinsic necessary legal developments. Legal recognition must now be given to the possibility of the ownership of land as well as to the ownership of movables, which hitherto has constituted the only property.

In an agricultural economy as well as in a pastoral economy, control of the land, upon which all depend for their subsistence, confers power upon those who control it over those who do not, and places the latter in a condition of dependence on the former. The landlord is necessarily a lord over the people who depend on the land, as well as over the land itself. The establishment and maintenance of such lordship evidently depends on the organization of sufficient force to sustain the position of those at the top, as indeed the history of European feudalism indicates.

However, the very decentralization of power among great territorial magnates which earlier allodial and later feudal property involved created a permanent tension or rivalry

21 See Smith, *Theory of Moral Sentiments*, pt. I, § iii, ch. 2 (Glasgow edn. pp. 50–61); J. Millar, *Of the Origin of the Distinction of Ranks* (4th edn., Edinburgh, 1806), reprinted in W. C. Lehmann, *John Millar of Glasgow* (Cambridge, 1960).

between royal and baronial power. Kings in seeking to establish their position of primacy over the territorial lords, who (after the introduction of feudal tenure in place of allodial) were theoretically their vassals, naturally looked for allies in that struggle. In Europe, said Smith, kings found such allies in the cities.[22] By strengthening the independent rights of the cities, granting monopolies to their tradesmen's and merchant's guilds, kings secured a powerful source of support in the perennial struggles within feudalism. The burgesses, through taxation and other means, in return for their privileges, provided revenue for the king which increasingly enabled him to organize his own armed forces independently of the feudal host and to transcend his original role as, essentially, *primus inter pares.*

At the same time, the growth of the cities erodes feudalism in another way. Cities must trade at least with their own hinterland in order to survive. But that process of trade creates, consolidates, and in due course increases a taste for the manufacturers of the city. In the earliest stages of feudalism, the tenure of land is necessarily and essentially based on mutual personal services—protection and adjudication by the lord in return for services by the tenant, different in kind accordingly as the tenure is 'free' or not; the landlord's interest is best served by maximizing the number of his dependants to the greatest productive capacity for the land. The growth of trade in manufactures gives to the landlord a new outlet for the excess production of his land, namely the purchase of luxury goods. As the taste for these grows, the more there is motivation for a commutation of personal services to money payments. The development of such commutation of services is of course well attested in history. Thus, land-holding over time becomes a means of revenue rather than a basis for status relationships based (at least notionally) on mutuality of services. These developments, extended over a long period of time, and proceeding with local differences and at different paces according to local circumstances 'the contrasts between lowland and highland Scotland, between Scotland and England, between Britain and the Netherlands, were for Smith a source of obvious

---

[22] See Smith, *Wealth of Nations*, bk. III.

contemporary contrasts) constitute the gradual evolution of a commercial form of society out of the preceding feudal and agrarian order.[23]

Such a transformation again, and necessarily, involves or includes a transformation in legal relations. Most obviously, this is marked in a growth in the importance of contractual relations. People who work for their living do so not on the basis of a status relationship with a feudal superior who supplies land or access to the produce of land in return for personal, manorial, or military services. They do so by entering as free persons into contractual relations with those who have work for them to do, the contract being for service by the workman in return for payment by the master. The workman then takes his wages into the market in order to purchase the necessities of life. Labour and the produce of land are assimilated to the commodities produced by tradesmen and manufacturers, circulating in a market regulated by supply and demand. The alienability of property, rather than the right to its possession for use and enjoyment, becomes a key feature of the right of property. Increasingly land itself becomes subject to freedom of alienation, except where this is inhibited by legal means such as the Scots law on entails, which Smith and many of his associates strongly wanted to abolish.[24]

I am not a sufficient historian, economist, or sociologist to make an informed judgment on Smith's general argument, which I have tried to outline here in an admittedly over-compressed form. Neverthless, it does seem to me to have a certain intrinsic plausibility in broad terms, if not in details. It brings sharply to our attention the way in which laws and legal institutions are an inherent part of the economy of a society and must be understood and explained as such, if we wish to proceed beyond purely formal and structural analysis of legal systems considered in the abstract. In that respect, Smith's work has a clear lesson, even today, for both jurists and economists: neither group can regard the other's field of work as alien

---

[23] I am entirely indebted for the account in this and the preceding five paragraphs to Andrew Skinner's essay, 'Adam Smith on Law and Government', which drew to my attention the significance for this purpose of *Wealth of Nations*, bk. III.

[24] Smith said of entails, 'Upon the whole nothing can be more absurd than perpetual entails', *Lectures on Jurisprudence*, p. 70 (Cannan edn. p. 124).

to its own interests and concerns. Economists ought not to treat legal relationships either as indifferent to their questions or as mere background data assumed as invariant elements of the economic landscape. Jurists ought not to regard economic relationships as existing apart from and indifferent to legal relations, for the latter are indeed an intrinsic part of the former.

IV. RATIONALITY OR DETERMINATION

One question which should be considered is how far Smith's general theory is a deterministic one. In my view, it is not in any crude or simple sense an instance of economic determinism. As we saw in the quotation from *The Wealth of Nations*, with which the last section commenced, an important question for Smith is what rational motives people can have for various actions in given circumstances. 'Where there is no property, or at least none that exceeds the value of two or three days' labour, civil government is not so necessary [as where there is "valuable and extensive property"].'[25] This is so because people in these circumstances lack any rational motive to envy or to do violence.

Human beings as rational choosers make choices in given circumstances, and the choices that seem to them rational are genuine choices based on reasons that are genuinely good. It does not follow, of course, that the outcome of individual rational choices, taken in the aggregate, was intended or foreseen by those who made the choices that cumulatively led to the net outcome. Kings may have had (genuinely) good reasons for favouring burgesses; burgesses individually and collectively undoubtedly had good reasons of self-interest for accepting royal favours and making appropriate returns therefor. It does not follow that they chose jointly to transform feudal society into commercial society. To say this is simply to repeat the old and obvious truth that human actions rationally chosen within a certain compass can have unintended outcomes well beyond that compass. Smith was well aware of that as a general tenet

[25] Smith, *Wealth of Nations*, bk. V, ch. 1, pt. 2.

among Enlightenment thinkers, and his own 'Invisible Hand'[26] is, I take it, a particular exemplification of the general idea.

This has important implications for his own work. If Smith was an out-and-out determinist, there would be a more than paradoxical element about much of his own work in *The Wealth of Nations*. If forms of economy necessarily generate their own internal forces that sweep men along regardless of any illusory notions of rationality and choice, there would be little point in writing a book which is not merely descriptive, but it is an important measure prescriptive, advocating legislative and other policies (such as the abolition of statutory monopolies) that are aimed at improving the economic order and producing a more rational basis for a commercial economy.

Smith's overall position seems to be in principle a self-consistent one. The more we know and understand of our own circumstances, the more we can make genuinely rational choices guided by a well-founded view of individual or of collective interests. Therefore we ought to seek to understand our circumstances as well as possible, and ought to make those choices which seem most sensible given our necessarily imperfect, but always improvable, understanding of those circumstances. That Smith does not venture any predictions as to what will happen beyond commercial society is a strength rather than a weakness of his approach, since our capacity to foresee the unintended outcomes of what we now do is in practice and in principle bound to be imperfect. I would venture to suggest that it is a weakness and not a strength of Marx's that he observed no such modesty in his pretended capacity to foresee the future; we are still living with the unintended outcomes of that lack of theoretical modesty.

In any event, we have to take account of Smith's qualified rationalism in ethical as well as technical questions. He was by no means an advocate of the pursuit by each person of his own interest at all costs. He certainly held the view that human beings have natural rights, and that each person's pursuit of

[26] Ibid., bk. IV, ch. 2, p. 456: Every individual in a market 'intends only his own gain, and he is in this, as in many other cases, led by an invisible hand to promote an end which was no part of his intention'. For a discussion of 'invisible hand' explanations, see R. Nozick, *Anarchy, State and Utopia* (Cambridge, Mass., 1974), pp. 18–22, 336–7.

interests is legitimate only when subject to respect for those rights. At one point in *The Theory of Moral Sentiments* he ascribes our knowledge of basic moral rights and duties to the moral norms implanted by God in man's nature.[27] To that extent he belongs within the natural law and not the utilitarian tradition. That each may pursue his own, and that governments ought to pursue the general utility, is not a single simple and overriding principle with Smith, but one which comes into operation only within the area of indifference of the basic moral code.

There is no doubt that Smith believed that the development and growth of commercial society represented 'progress', and that progress was, on the whole, good. First of all, as we have seen, commercial relationships favour the liberty of individuals, and it is right that people be free from bondage. That people who are in bondage will not, in practice, be freed therefrom by their masters on the mere ground of their moral claim to freedom does, however, seem obvious to Smith. It is therefore a merit of the commercial system that it actually gives the slave-owner a good motive (whether perceived by him or not) to grant his slaves their freedom. Free wage-labourers present a better deal overall to a capitalist than slaves, who never have any reason to produce more than guarantees their own subsistence. Free wage-labourers have a motive to maximize production to increase their own income above subsistence level, which in turn also enhances the profits of their capitalist masters.[28] Secondly, and this point follows from the first, a commercial economy is one which from generation to generation encourages the increase of wealth, and thus the general well-being. People in general are simply better off in commercial rather than in agrarian, pastoral, or hunting and fishing societies, even though there is a necessary inequality in the distribution of the resulting wealth.

Smith was, however, if less acutely than Adam Ferguson, well aware of the countervailing disadvantages of commercial society.[29] The division of labour produces among the lower

---

[27] Smith, *Theory of Moral Sentiments*, pt. III, ch. 5, para. 6 (Glasgow edn. p. 165).

[28] On this argument in general, see Smith, *Lectures on Jurisprudence*, pp. 453–4 (Cannan edn. pp. 99–104).

[29] See ibid., pp. 539–50 (Cannan edn. pp. 255–60); cf. A. Ferguson, *Essay on the History of Civil Society* (ed. D. Forbes, Edinburgh, 1966).

classes a diminishing range of experience and of interests. The production line maximizes the production of pins at a severe human cost in terms of the restricted life the operatives enjoy. Children become employable at younger and younger ages, and lose opportunities of education. In addition to depressing the education of the poor, this process weakens family structures and parental authority and contributes to drunkenness and disorder in the towns. The martial ardour of the nation and its capacity to defend itself in time of war is diminished by the same processes. (A graphic illustration of this which much impressed Smith was the capacity of Charles Edward's Highland army to take practically the whole of Britain by storm in 1745 until the return of the professional soldiery from the Continental wars.)

It is difficult to acquit Smith, with hindsight, of a certain complacency in the blandness of his conclusion that despite all these evident defects, commercial society was on the whole genuinely progressive and good. Nevertheless he reached that conclusion, and advocated the rationalization of the laws and the economic practices of his time in order to promote what he took on the whole to be good. This clearly indicates that he did not pretend that the development of societies was the mere product of blind forces of nature independent of rational moral choices by human agents.

V. TWO PARTICULAR AREAS OF SMITH'S JURISPRUDENCE

So far this chapter has dealt in relative generalities; in order to bring it to a close, it may be worth while to take up two particular points that illustrate how Smith's general account forms a setting for illuminating consideration of more particular matters. I shall deal very briefly with aspects of contract and of the administration of justice.

Contract

I have already mentioned Smith's general theory of contractual and other voluntary obligations. 'A promise is a declaration of your desire that the person for whom you promise should depend on you for the performance of it. Of consequence, the promise produces an obligation, and the breach of it, an injury.'[30]

The foundation of contractual obligation thus explained is not culturally relative. However, according to Smith, the importance of contract as an institution certainly is. 'Breach of contract is naturally the slightest of injuries' and in 'rude ages' little regard is paid to it.[31] In the earliest periods of positive law, enforceable contracts would be those which related to matters of great substance, and which had been undertaken in circumstances of great formality—essential to indicate clearly to all parties, despite the 'uncertainty of language', the character of the obligation being undertaken. By tracing the development of Roman law, Smith shows how we can perceive the steady evolution of a less and less formalistic approach to contracting. In contrasting Smith's own commercial society, and 'the ancient state of contracts', Smith said, 'At present almost anything will make a contract obligatory.'[32]

Why should all this be so? Not, says Smith, because of changes in the basic character of people; rather, it happens because of changes in their social and economic circumstances. In his discussion in the *Lectures* on the influence of commerce on manners, he makes the very point that 'probity and punctuality' in the keeping of undertakings is an effect rather than a cause of the development of commerce. He says that for fidelity to their word the Dutch are the most outstanding people in Europe, greatly superior to the English who are slightly superior to the Scots, among whom a distinction exists between the commercial and the 'remote' parts of the country.

This is not at all to be imputed to national character as some pretend. . . . it is far more reducible to self-interest, that general principle which regulates the actions of every man, and which leads men to act in a certain manner from views of advantage. . . . A dealer is afraid of losing his character and is scrupulous in observing every engagement. When a person makes perhaps twenty contracts in a day, he cannot

---

[30] *Lectures on Jurisprudence*, pp. 87, 462 (Cannan edn. p. 131). This view is close to that of Henry Home, Lord Kames, as expressed in *Essays on the Principles of Morality and Natural Religion* (1st edn. Edinburgh, 1751), pt. I, essay II, ch. 6: 'The reliance upon us, produced by our own act, constitutes the obligation.' For a vindication of the reliance theory of promising, see ch. 10 below.

[31] Lectures on Jurisprudence, pp. 87, 472 (Cannan edn. p. 131).

[32] Ibid., p. 473 (Cannan edn. p. 132).

gain so much by endeavouring to impose on his neighbour, as the very appearance of a cheat would make him lose. When people seldom deal with one another, we find that they are somewhat disposed to cheat, because they can gain more by a smart trick than they can lose by the injury which it does their character.[33]

As well as neatly and concretely illustrating the point made at the outset about Smith's ability to combine a theory of natural rights with a theory of the social development of laws and legal institutions, this statement points toward an area of interesting research. The trouble is that, at least for the United States, some of it has already been done. But it is surely a mark of Smith's acuteness that he should have so clearly anticipated such works as those of MacAulay and Ross,[34] in broad outline at least.

The Administration of Justice

On this topic we must look to 'Of the Expense of Justice' from the *Wealth of Nations*.[35] It is in pastoral societies, says Smith, that we first find the beginnings of institutionalized adjudication, albeit in a rudimentary form in which lesser people look to great chieftains distinguished by wealth and power for determination and remedying of injuries. In addition to his position as a military leader, 'his birth and fortune procure him some sort of judicial authority'. So far from being a source of expense to him, however, this is in fact a source of revenue, for 'those who applied to him for justice were always willing to pay for it'.[36] Even in feudal and agrarian societies this persists. As late as the time of Henry II of England, Smith points out, the circuit judges were as much as anything else factors sent out to levy certain types of revenue, and the administration of justice— albeit now through delegates—was as much as anything else a means of procuring revenue. But so long as the giving of 'presents' and the risk of amercements were essential adjuncts

---

[33] ibid., pp. 538–9 (Cannan edn. p. 253).
[34] See, e.g., S. MacAulay, 'Noncontractual Relations in Business: Preliminary Study', 28 *Am. Soc. rev.* (1963) 55; L. Ross, *Settled Out of Court* (Chicago, 1970). Of course, both MacAulay and Ross have covered enormous tracts of ground not contemplated by Smith, but his thoughts seem to point in a direction similar to that of their far more elaborate studies.
[35] *Wealth of Nations*, bk. V, ch. 1, pt. 2.
[36] Ibid.

of litigation, the risk of corruption of justice was inevitably high, and was everywhere realized.[37.]

What led to change in this? Smith's answer is that at some stage in feudal society the expenses of defence become so great that the king could no longer live off his own estates and feudal dues. Taxation becomes a necessity, but the *quid pro quo* generally demanded is that gifts and presents and fees should no longer be accepted or rendered in return for the ajudication of suits. Fixed salaries are appointed to the judges to compensate them for the loss of other income, the salaries being payable out of general revenue from taxation.

This in turn may procure its own mischiefs, for the judges may be unduly exposed to executive pressure. In addition, their income is no longer dependent on their industry and expeditiousness in the conduct of business—unlike the conditions of competition which formerly prevailed, to Smith's characteristic admiration, among the various different royal courts in England. Smith canvasses various ingenious schemes for remedying the former defect, suggesting, by analogy to the then still extant endowment of the Court of Session, that it might be apt to provide courts with certain land or funds, the income of which could sustain them independently of the executive. 'The necessary instability of such a fund seems, however, to render it an improper one for the maintenance of an institution which ought to last forever.'[38]

Smith's preferred solution, which he regards as a remedy for both mischiefs, is to find a system of charging fees for court business, which would be administered independently of the executive and of individual judges. The fees would be payable after the relevant work was done and would be apportioned among judges according to their diligence and expeditiousness in the discharge of business. The French *Parlements*, he points out, operate on a similar footing, and they are, if not convenient as courts of justice, neither suspected nor accused of corruption.

He has already anticipated the objection that this would be a retrogression from the position in which justice is administered gratis:

[37] Ibid.
[38] Ibid.

Justice . . . never was in reality administered gratis in any country. Lawyers and attorneys, at least, must always be paid by the parties; and if they were not, they would perform their duty still worse than they actually perform it. The fees annually paid, to lawyers and attorneys, amount, in every court, to a much greater sum than the salaries of the judges. The circumstance of those salaries being paid by the crown, can nowhere much diminish the necessary expense of a law suit.[39]

The topicality of Smith's concerns can hardly be doubted in view of the considerable present concern about the quality and distribution of legal services in many jurisdictions. The more we are interested in trying to disseminate legal services—not just judicial services—through the community, the more acutely we face the problem of securing the genuine independence of such services and coupling it with proper efficiency—especially to the extent that lawyers' incomes cease to be dependent on client satisfaction.

Quite apart from that, Smith's penetrating observations about the real total expense of the administration of justice being far greater than the apparent exchequer cost should prompt reflection. Much legislation is ostensibly cheap, and may indeed involve no immediate identified public expense at all. But ought we not to enquire far more closely into its real cost in terms of burdens on court time, and its costs to those who have to employ lawyers to guide them through more and more complicated legal mazes, and all the rest of it? If reflection on Smith's work were to lead us to reflect more on the true overall cost of ostensibly beneficial laws, it would be well worth while for that alone. There would be enough research projects concerning this to keep us busy for a good long time.

VI. POSTSCRIPT: THE NEW ECONOMIC ANALYSIS OF LAW

It is, no doubt, obvious that the writing of this chapter was prompted more by an interest in the history of legal and moral philosophy in the eighteenth century than by any pretension to

[39] Ibid.

economic expertise. At the time at which it was first written,[40] I was quite unfamiliar with the contemporary 'Economic Analysis of Law' (EAL for short) put forward by Richard Posner, Ronald Coase, Harold Demsetz,[41] and others.

Having subsequently begun to scratch the surface of that theoretical approach,[42] I ought to add a brief comment about a significant contrast between Smith's approach and that of EAL. The contrast is to Smith's advantage. His theory of 'natural rights' is a moral theory independent of and more fundamental than his analysis of the economic consequences of any legal ascription of rights to individuals. A particular example is his theory of promisees' rights, founded, he says, in the injustice of disappointing people in any matter upon which a promisor has intentionally induced them to rely. The enforcement of promissory or other 'natural' rights is indeed subject to variation according to the degree of economic development of a society, and in any society it has economic consequences relevant to the desirability of given enforcement systems. But such consequences are not the justifying reason for recognizing or upholding the rights themselves.

By contrast, Posner's thesis holds that a given allocation or distribution of *any* rights whatsoever is justifiable only by the criterion of economic efficiency to the end of wealth-maximization. Moreover, if I understand his and Coase's case correctly, such efficiency is established by reference to the optimal outcome of some ideal bargaining procedure.

In so far as such a supposed bargaining procedure is essential to the theory, it appears incoherent. The concept of a 'bargain' requires at least two presuppositions: (a) that a promise has a right to a promised performance (for otherwise there could be no idea of *binding* bargains, i.e. mutual exchanges of binding

---

[40] It was originally written as a paper for a seminar on law and economics in 1977 at the University of York, organized by Professor C. K. Rowley on behalf of the (British) Social Science Research Council.

[41] Posner, *Economic Analysis of Law* (Chicago, 1974); Coase, 'The problem of Social Cost', 3 *Journal of Law and Economics* (1960) 1; Demsetz, 'Wealth Distribution and the Ownership of Rights', 1 *Journal of Legal Studies* (1972) 223; id., 'When does the Rule of Liability Matter?', 1 *Journal of Legal Studies* (1972) 13.

[42] My acquaintance was initially formed through Charles Fried's *Right and Wrong* (Cambridge, Mass., 1978), pp. 86–105, and an unpublished paper given by Dr J. M. Finnis to a seminar in Edinburgh. See also J. W. Harris, *Legal Philosophies* (London, 1981), pp. 42–7, and references therein.

promises); and (b) that persons have rights to security from physical and psychological assaults and acts of coercion, respect for which in any bargaining situation is a precondition of the validity of the bargain struck.

If EAL does rest upon ideal bargains, it presupposes at least these 'natural' rights. If EAL then claims also to justify *these* rights it commits the fallacy of begging the question. If EAL purports to be a complete theory of law, but fails to include in its explanation the rights which it presupposes, it commits the alternative fallacy of *ignoratio elenchi*. In either case, it is obliged to restrict its pretensions to its performance.[43]

A useful restriction might be a reformulation of EAL as a theory of 'adventitious' rights, including the forms of remedial right established by legal systems. This seems conformable to the observation that much of the most striking critical work of economic analysis has been achieved in the area sketched somewhat amateurishly in section v of this chapter.

Be that as it may, Adam Smith's theory of law differs from EAL in that it contains three distinct elements: (a) a theory of justice, that is, a moral theory of the rights the law ought to uphold; (b) an outline of an analytical theory of law, in the unsatisfactory 'sovereign command' mode; and (c) a theory of the economic conditions and consequences of various kinds of legal order. Smith did not suppose, nor is there any reason to suppose, that the first of these can be subordinated to or derived from the third.

---

[43] This argument is, in shortened form, essentially the same as Fried's in *Right and Wrong*, pp. 86–105.

7.
TAKING THE 'RIGHTS THESIS' SERIOUSLY

I. INTRODUCTION 'THE CONSTRUCTIVE MODEL'

N O T the least interesting element in Ronald Dworkin's work[1] is his theory as to the nature of ethical theorizing. This he develops from a discussion[2] of Rawlsian 'reflective equilibrium'. It is the theory that the distinctively moral point of view—morality as against mere mores—is developed by contruction of a consistent and coherent set of principles which most adequately justify and make sense of our intuitive moral judgments. The intuitive judgments we make in particular cases are, in a sense, the data from which moral theory commences. But they are not unquestionable, in the sense that each and every one must be accommodated within the constructed set of principles. We can and should revise our judgments to fit in with the set of principles which best fits the judgments to which we are most strongly committed.

This he calls a 'constructive model' of morality, in contrast to the alternative possible 'natural model', which would postulate that moral principles are not created but discovered by people, being a kind of description of an objective moral reality. If we adhered to the 'natural model' we would not be able to take a high-handed way with troublesome intuitions, as the 'constructive model' authorizes. If these are apperceptions of moral facts, we must stick by them in the hope that we will in the end find the true set of principles which can accommodate all the facts—rather as the natural scientist may not suppress inconvenient data, but must hope that in the long run improvements in scientific theory will enable them to be accommodated within a full understanding.

[1] This essay is presented as a critique of Ronald Dworkin's *Taking Rights Seriously* (London, 1977), cited in this chapter as *TRS*.
[2] *TRS*, ch. 6, esp. pp. 159–68; see also chs. 4 and 5.

The correlation of this view of ethical constructivism with the work of Rawls, and indeed with that of now unfashionable 'intuitionists' such as W. D. Ross, H. A. Prichard, and W. G. Maclagan, is obvious. It gives body to the idea of 'reflective equilibrium', of securing that our judgments match our principles and our principles our judgments. It is also true that it facilitates interesting comparisons between moral argumentation and legal argumentation, and the drawing of analogies further afield in the realms of aesthetics.

In his recent essay, 'No Right Answer'[3] Dworkin has made that further comparison, pointing out that literary criticism can and does go beyond mere textual criticism concerned with the *ipsissima verba* of the author's text. The critic does and should read a novel with a view to constructing a vision of the world created by the author's text. There can be truths about David Copperfield not stated in the very words of *David Copperfield*; so too can a legal system contain genuine answers to problems which no case has yet directly decided. The ultimate unity of legal and moral deliberation, and the possibility of right answers to questions of right, both of which Dworkin's theory envisages, depend on a fundamental unity of method: the method authorized by the constructive model.

It is convenient for the critic that Dworkin should himself have made the literary analogy, since at the present time a constructive review of his work has to be 'constructive' in the Dworkinian sense. *Taking Rights Seriously* has a right to be taken seriously, but it would be only too easy to take it to pieces at the level of textual criticism for inconsistencies and shifts of position. Such are inevitable in a book which collects together pieces published separately over a decade, ordering them according to theme rather than chronologically. In truth, what is remarkable about the performance is not the inconsistencies but the overall consistency and sense of theoretical unity which the work taken as a whole presents. Even so, much more than would be acceptable in the case of a purpose-written monograph, the reader is left to construct a whole view of the 'Dworkinian Theory' out of what seem to him the main points of the position. On the whole, this review will attempt to come to

---

[3] In *Law, Morality, and Society: Essays in Honour of H. L. A. Hart*, ed. P. M. S. Hacker and J. Raz (Oxford, 1977).

terms with Dworkinianism benignly constructed, and air objections to that, rather than nit-pick around the text for internal inconsistency. But some adverse criticism of some textual points is necessary and inevitable.

The key fact about Dworkin is that he is a pre-Benthamite; the perspective of jurisprudence since Bentham with its insistence on the separation of expository and censorial jurisprudence, legal facts and legal values, he finds as inimical to grasping the truth as did the pre-Raphaelites find that other perspective which they abandoned in their painting. Dworkin's stated ambition[4] is to restate legal theory in such terms as reunify exposition and censorship. Legal theory in this programme is not divided from but an intimate part of moral and political theory. As important as anything else in Dworkin's writing are the elements of ethics and politics which he finds essential to the elucidation of laws and rights.

In my judgment the execution does and must fall short of fulfilling the ambition. But the failure, like others before it, is an enormously instructive one, one which has already revised the agenda for legal philosophy, and one in which those who reject the central tenets cannot but find both a challenge, and a host of valuable insights which any view of law, politics, and morality must accommodate or even incorporate. Dworkin has not succeeded in demonstrating (not to me, anyway) that there is no gap between the description of law and the framing of critical principles against which to test the quality of actual laws. But he has succeeded in showing that existing schemata for analysis and description of legal systems are defective, and he has put forward a version of political liberalism which is interesting and provocative as a critical morality for the criticism or justification of laws and legal institutions.

One reason for the failure is that the constructive model will not take the weight which Dworkin puts upon it. The natural model has a certain attraction in that it founds upon a claim that there is in some sense 'an objective "order of values"' (as W. G. Maclagan put it[5]) to which our specific judgments are oriented and which our statements of principle attempt to capture. Such a model can account for differences of moral view

---

[4] *TRS*, pp. ix-xi, 7.
[5] See W. G. Maclagan, *The Theological Frontiers of Ethics* (London, 1961), p. 54.

precisely as differences of view, different ways of looking at the
same thing, the same order of values. The best view is the one
which most fully grasps that objective order. The constructive
model retreats from that assertion, beset as it notoriously is with
epistemological and ontological problems, to the weaker claim
that, as Dworkin puts it: 'Men and women have a responsibility
to fit the particular judgments on which they act into a coherent
program of action, or at least, that officials who exercise power
over other men have that responsibility.' (*TRS*, p. 160.)

This does seem to me a responsibility worth taking seriously,
for what it amounts to is an insistence on rationality in practical
affairs. Whatever be the variations in possible moral positions
which people may have, there are criteria of coherence and
consistency of judgments and principles which can be and
ought to be applied to anything which claims to be a 'moral
position', as distinct from mere gut-reaction or knee-jerk
prejudice. Respect for rationality imposes formal constraints on
practical arguments and on practical theories, theories *for*
action, whether they be moral, political, or legal. Such formal
constraints are not intrinsically different from those which
respect for rationality imposes upon us in speculative matters
such as scientific enquiry.

But ought we in either sphere to observe the constraints
imposed by respect for rationality? There are two possible ways
of answering such a question as that. One way is to say that
rationality is and is perceived by us to be an objective good, to
belong within the 'objective order of values'. The other way is to
offer rationality as a value absolute so far as it goes within a
Weltanschauung, the 'constructive' nature of which one cheerfully
admits, happy in the knowledge that if anyone presents *reasoned*
argument against such a position, he is thereby estopped from
denying the standing of rationality. The latter is certainly the
course which I would take. But then what is one doing? One is
offering to others for their adoption a certain form of life which
for oneself one finds more acceptable than available alternatives. In the last resort the appeal is to what is experienced as
acceptable to this, that, or another human being.

So far from being a weakness, this seems to me to be truly a
strength of what I would understand by the 'constructive
model'. For what we are out to do is to find the way or ways in

which we are to live, and that can only to be found in terms of what we find by experience acceptable to us as beings endowed with passion and will as well as reason. If what Hume called the 'calm passions' are not engaged by such argumentation, it is in the end pointless.

If this be true, one position which cannot be sustained is the position that over and above the various practical theories or systems we may construct, there is some criterion independent of any of them whereby we can judge of one theory or system as better than another. Each of us is committed to the search for what seems to him the best, but it is a delusion to suppose that that which we find to be the best is the best there is for any human being. Only by covertly reverting to the natural model could we sustain that claim.

What has been said of the demands of rationality as a value can in turn be said of anything else, for example justice, fairness, humanity, which one might present as an important practical value; there is no need to repeat the steps of the argument. If the constructive be preferred to the natural model, whatever is good is apprehended and presented as such within the four corners of that which is experienced as the most acceptable practical theory or system one can construct, and none of us can claim to find an Archimedean point beyond any such theory or system whereupon to lever one theory to a position above others as self-evidently or even evidently the best for everyone.

Dworkin's fundamental weakness is a desire to have it both ways. Consider for example the following remark: 'The constructivist model insists on consistenc' with conviction as an independent requirement, flowing not from the assumption that these convictions are accurate reports, but from the different assumption that it is unfair for officials to act except on the basis of a general public theory that will constrain them to consistency, provide a public standard for testing or debating or predicting what they do, and not allow appeals to unique intuitions that might mask prejudice or self-interest in particular cases' (*TRS*, p. 163). What, we must ask, is the status of the said 'different assumption' which the constructivist model makes about the unfairness which would follow from noninsistence on consistency with conviction? Is it a 'unique intuition', or is it a considered judgment within the theory 'constructed' by Dworkin? If the former, is he not a naturalist after all? If the latter, can constructivism quite so blatantly heave itself up by its own bootstraps?

To raise these questions is to dig out the ambiguity which is at the heart of *Taking Rights Seriously*. The kind of unity—unity in substance, not only in method—of law, politics, and morality for which Dworkin argues has hitherto been taken for a hallmark of natural law thought. But in its classical manifestations natural law thought did found on what Dworkin now characterizes as the 'natural model' but which he expressly forswears. He cannot in my judgment make the switch to the 'constructive model' and at the same time assert that unity in substance and method. Especially he cannot sustain the assertion which has set the jurisprudential community by the ears, the assertion that there is after all in any hard case at law a single uniquely right answer to the points at issue between the parties.

It may be that my own argument to this point is one which manifests a failure properly to grasp Dworkin's conception of the constructive model. But even were that so, I would argue that the most credible version of what he calls 'the constructive model' certainly supports the argument I have put. Elsewhere,[6] in analysing the nature of legal arguments, I have tried to show the necessity of the constraints of consistency and coherence in legal argument in a manner which, I discover, chimes closely with Dworkin's account of the constructive model. But in my conception of it, it certainly won't takes us to the length to which Dworkin thinks it will. In the next section of this chapter, I shall test out the Dworkinian theory as to the adjudication of hard cases to show why that seems so.

II. HARD CASES

Dworkin's theory of law has as its nodal point the topic of hard cases and indeed the essay on 'Hard Cases'.[7] The phrase signifies those litigated disputes in which, even apart from any dispute about the facts of the matter, there is a dispute between the parties as to the bearing of the law on whatever facts can be proven. To take an example paralleling one which Dworkin

---

[6] See my *Legal Reasoning and Legal Theory* (Oxford, 1978).
[7] *TRS*, ch. 4.

uses,[8] let us suppose that X's employee has incautiously severed a power cable in the course of road-work operations, the cable being the property of a public utility corporation. Y's factory has lost production because of a resultant failure in the electricity supply. Founding on the legal doctrine that an obligation of reparation is incumbent on one whose careless act causes reasonably foreseeable damage to another, Y sues X for damages to cover the cost to him of his lost production. X denies liability, founding in turn upon the doctrine that damage of a purely economic character occasioned to one party as a consequence of damage to another's property caused by negligence is 'too remote' to be the subject of any obligation of reparation.

In such a case, justification of a decision cannot be achieved simply by subsuming the propositions of proven fact under a governing legal rule and reading off the result. The very point of the dispute is as to what rule or doctrine among rival possibilities governs. Legal theorists such as Kelsen, Bentham, Austin, or Hart, positivists to a man, would say that in such a case the judge's decision is necessarily norm-creating, since it involves answering the question what *is to be* the governing rule for such a case. 'American realists' would broadly agree, subject to reservations on the question whether cases can ever 'turn on' rules and on the question whether all disputes do not leave the judge sufficient of what Karl Llewellyn called 'leeway'[9] to make his own ruling for these parties, guided by the traditions of his craft, or whatever.

For Dworkin all such soi-disant 'realistic' approaches are downright unrealistic. Surely, he insists, the parties have their rights. The law gives or guarantees to citizens certain rights as against each other (Dworkin does not, but we might, call these 'primary rights'). As against political institutions such as courts, citizens must then have secondary rights (what he calls 'institutional rights') that only such decisions will be given as will secure already vested primary rights. Not least among our institutional rights against courts is that they shall not, no more than legislatures may, create retrospective laws to any citizen's disadvantage. However much a projected legal provision might

---

[8] Dworkin's example is *Spartan Steel and Alloys Ltd.* v. *Martin and Co.* [1973] 1 QB 27.
[9] K. N. Llewellyn, *The Common Law Tradition* (Boston, Mass., 1960) pp. 62 f., 219 f.

serve the common interest, it cannot in justice be invented in the course of a litigated dispute and then be applied retroactively to the detriment of one of the parties under a show of upholding a 'right' of the other's which by the hypothesis did not exist when the litigation was started, far less when the matters in dispute actually occurred. To tolerate that would be to tolerate using the unfortunate loser as a means to public ends, which is *the* cardinal sin in the Dworkinian calendar.

Dworkin need not—though he seems to[10]—assert that no such intolerable thing ever occurs, for presumably it is always a possibility that rights, even institutional rights, will be infringed. The fundamental point of his argument is not that judges cannot do injustices, but that there is something fishy about any theory of law which presents the systematic infliction of such injustice as a *necessary*, not a possible but regrettable, incident of adjudication whenever a hard case comes to trial.

This, in his view, is a necessary feature of those theories of law which (whatever their detailed content) represent legal systems as comprising nothing other than bodies of socially operative rules whereby citizens regulate their lives and judges judge cases. The problem which he discerns in such theories is the 'strong' discretion which they necessarily ascribe to judges in any litigated cases which the rules do not 'fit'. If the rules are all there is to the law, then in the cases where (because of 'vagueness', 'open texture', or indeed plain 'gaps') the rules don't determine a clear answer, there is nothing for it but that the judge must make law for the case relying on such standards as he thinks right to justify his decision standards which *ex hypothesi* cannot already belong to the law. Hence the ostensible necessity of the injustice of retrospective legislation, and of the systematic infringement of institutional rights which ought to be taken seriously.

Rather than acquiesce in theories which have such distasteful implications, Dworkin invites us to reconsider how a hard case such as that of *Y* v. *X* might really be decided. No statute governs the matter in hand, and by our hypothesis (which is true in fact) there are precedents and legal doctrines which 'pull both ways'. What then? Dworkin's answer is that we, supposing

[10] *TRS*, ch. 13.

ourselves faced with the task of judging, not merely spectating, must decide which pulls hardest. How can we find that out? By having, he says, a theory of the law; not, be it noted, a descriptive theory *about* law, but a justifying theory *of* the law.

It seems, though the evidence is here a little obscure, that Dworkin accepts that to have laws and courts at all, we must indeed have the man-made rules and humanly established institutions whose anatomy and typology have been so exhaustively explored by positivists. But, he would add, these rules and institutions function intelligibly not because they are there as some kind of brute social fact, but because they are theorized, because social agents operate them through the categories of some normative political and social theory whereby they make sense of them.

At any given point of time, therefore, we can examine a society's established rules and institutions in order to work out by what principles and policies they are animated; that is, if we follow an eccentric stipulation of Dworkin's,[11] we can ask what rights of individuals they are supposed to secure ('principles') and what collective advantages they are supposed to serve ('policies'). By such a procedure, we can work out for any breach of law and, had we but world enough and time, for the whole legal system, a justifying theory. That is, the theory which best makes sense of the law all and whole as an engine for protecting individual rights and beyond that for advancing common public goods. Not every statute and precedent will necessarily be accommodated by such a theory. But the main points of the system as men and women have built it up and tried to live with it will be clarified, and in the light of that we will know which precedents and statutes to reject, or at least to confine within a narrow ambit, as 'anomalies'.

In doing this, we will necessarily be taking account of the theories which have animated agents working before us within the system. We shall not, however, be simply describing their view of it, for we are now no less engaged than were they. As they did, so must we, construct and act upon the best justifying theory of the system that we can contrive, taking account of, but not being enslaved to, their theories. In so far as we may be

---

[11] See *TRS*, p. 90. For the eccentricity of the stipulation see the excursus to ch. 9 of my *Legal Reasoning and Legal Theory*.

called upon to give advice or make decisions within the system we can properly do so only by reference to the 'theorized' system, not just to the inert mass of black-letter rules which in Dworkin's opinion positivists have mistakenly supposed to be the whole body of the law. ·

A particular point of such a theory will be that it goes beyond simply expounding the various principles and policies subserved by the law. It will necessarily rank them in order of priority by assigning 'weights' to them, with a generally heavier weighting for principles concerning rights than for pure policies.[12] (The whole point of 'taking rights seriously' is that in the areas covered by rights individuals are guaranteed against having their interests postponed to some collective interest in which they may or may not share.)

The last refinement is what gives, in Dworkin's view, the possibility of certainty of decision and rightness of decision in our figured case of Y v. X. The assignment of relative 'weights' to the principles and policies which underlie the rules of the law is what enables us to decide who ought to win. For as we saw, X's and Y's sides of the case are each supported by a body of legal 'doctrine', which expounds and explains guiding principles and policies of this branch of the law. But once we have assigned weights to the policies and principles, it must appear either that X's principles and policies outweigh Y's, or vice versa. (There is, Dworkin concedes, a remote possibility of a tie, but the system can and should incorporate some tie-breaking rule.) Accordingly either X or Y has a right to be granted a decision in his favour, and that decision should be handed down which secures the right of X, or, as the case may be, of Y. That is to take rights seriously, and it is the reverse of retroactive legislation.

For the decision to be justified in the full, strong sense which Dworkin demands, it is necessary that the theory which authorizes it is the best possible theory of the legal system in question at the time in question. This seems a tall order. Given the Dworkinian prescription for theorizing the law, it would be hard enough for any mere mortal to construct *a* theory of a legal system all and whole, far less to satisfy himself that he had done

---

[12] See *TRS*, pp. 116–17.

the best possible job. But Dworkin does not claim that we can be sure that we have achieved the best possible theory. He claims only that we can be sure that the best possible theory is what we must try our best to achieve. Real judges, he claims, are engaged in just that attempt when wrestling with hard cases— and that is what a positivistic legal philosopher would find himself trying to do if he were called upon to be a judge and therefore to abandon that external observational position from which alone the task appears an impossibility.

To make this point vivid, a demigod *ex machina*, 'Hercules J.', is postulated,[13] he being endowed with such superhuman mental capacities that he can construct the theory which best justifies and reconciles and conclusively sets the priorities among all the elements of the legal system comprehended together at once. No one can be a Hercules, but the very fact that we can intelligibly postulate such a being justifies the claim that every judge can and should try to get as close to Herculean competence as he can.

This is the very point at which we must cry 'halt', and ask whether the thesis holds. The Greeks' Hercules was a handy man at achieving the physically impossible, but has Dworkin not imposed on his own Hercules the altogether taller order of achieving that which is, by his own premises, logically impossible? If the constructive model is the right model for practical reasoning, can it make sense to claim of one constructed theory that it is the best possible, from all possible points of view? Or can such a claim be sustained only by opting for the natural model with all the problems and difficulties which that faces, the model which in face of such problems Dworkin expressly rejects? Such would be my conclusion, and therfore I find Dworkin unable to sustain his conclusion by his premises.

Let us think some more about the nature of the problem in *Y* v. *X*. The court before whom the case is brought must decide it, and must justify its decision.[14] The decision must be justified according to the law. But plainly 'according to the law' does not for such a case mean 'according to a rule of law uncontroversial in interpretation', for by the hypothesis the case is a hard one.

---

[13] *TRS*, ch. 4.

[14] The following section summarizes some of my main arguments in my *Legal Reasoning and Legal Theory*, chs. 3–9.

The very idea of justifying the decision implies that it is to be decided not on a 'once-off', 'individual merits of the parties' basis. There must be some ruling on the point in issue which is logically universal in the sense that it can cover this and all other like cases which may arise; in this sense the requirement of universalizability applies in legal justification. But that is a necessary, not a sufficient, condition of justifying the decision. In turn the ruling itself must be justified.

But what does that involve? First, there is a requirement of consistency: no ruling can be acceptable which contradicts any previously established rule of law which is binding for that court (what 'rules of law' are 'binding for that court' depends on detailed provisions of the particular legal system concerning formal sources of law). This is a strict test, but relatively easy to satisfy, given the open texture of law and the leeways of interpretation which it leaves open. But there are further tests which must be applied. A ruling upon law which can be entertained by the court must also be shown to be 'coherent' with the rest of the system. That means that it must be shown to be supported by relevant principles of the system, or (what comes to the same thing) to be derivable by analogical extrapolation from the existing body of the law.

From where, then, can we get these 'principles' which authorize such rulings and which secure the coherence of the legal system as a rational and intelligibly purposive scheme for the ordering of a society? The answer is that to some extent we find them, and to some extent we make them. We find them, to the extent that previous judges and doctrinal writers have expounded broad statements of general norms which make sense—in their view—of congeries of interrelated rules and precedents. 'Making sense' implies showing that there is some value or values which is advanced by adherence to the rules in question. We make them precisely by trying to make our own sense of the rules and precedents which confront us, taking fully into account the efforts of our predecessors, giving them the more weight according to their number and authority.

Even at that, we may often find that in just such a case as that of *Y* v. *X both* sides can appeal to settled and sound principles. *Y*, whose factory was plunged in darkness, can adduce the general principle that everyone ought to take reasonable care to avoid

inflicting foreseeable harm on others, and to answer for such
harm as is caused by failure to take such reasonable care. *X*,
who indubitably through his employee caused the harm, can
adduce principles which have been enunciated as restricting
the possible range of liability for negligent acts, in particular the
principle that the duty of care is owed only to those upon whom
one's acts may forseeably inflict physical harm, whether to their
persons or to their property.

What else can come into play at this point of the argument?
My answer would be that a characteristically legal mode of
consequentialist argument does normally, and should in any
event, come into play. A ruling for or against *Y* could be made
consistently with the pre-established rules, and adequately
supported by one or another of the principles mentioned. But
which ruling should be made? Is it not relevant to ask what will
be the outcome if it be ruled that all who engage in activities
which may cause nonphysical damage to other persons owe to
those at risk a duty to take reasonable care, and an obligation of
reparation if they cause such economic loss by failure to take
reasonable care?

The courts in practice certainly do ask such questions, and,
in Britain, in the 'economic loss' cases, they have concluded
that the potential range of liability which such a ruling would
imply in cases such as *X*'s are too extensive and catastrophic to
be acceptable. This is partly what lawyers call a 'common-
sense' point, in the sense that the range of potential plaintiffs is
so large that the defendant could not possibly meet or insure
against all their possible claims; so imposition of liability would
be pointless. It is partly an argument of justice, to the extent
that it is held both that so large a burden of damages cannot
fairly be imposed on defendants, and that those who are
particularly sensitive to loss of electric power can and ought to
insure against it, not come against those who could not know of
their particular sensitivity. So far, that has been the clinching-
point of the argument in economic loss cases.

The evaluation of consequences is not by reference to any
variant of the hedonistic utilitarian principle, but by reference
to such concepts as 'justice', 'common sense', 'public policy'.
But it necessarily follows that any judge or critic in making up
his mind one way or another at this level of argument is doing so

by reference to his conception of 'justice', 'common sense', 'public policy', and whatever else, reflecting on and advancing from what he takes to be the best conception of the justice (or whatever) that the law serves. In so doing he is *ascribing* weight to this or that of the principles in play, deciding which ought to have priority in such a situation as this now before him.

This brings us back to the very argument I made earlier, leading to the point that: 'one position which cannot be sustained is that over and above the various practical theories we may construct, there is some criterion independent of any one of them whereby we can judge of one theory or system as better than another'. Of course we do pass judgment on other theories: but we pass judgment from the perspective of one theory or another, from the perspective of that which to us as judges or critics seems to us the most acceptable. The constructive model cannot take us beyond that, nor should it pretend to, and it is a model which well fits the style of legal argumentation—as also, in my opinion, of moral deliberation. Judges do (and ought to) construct theories of the law, and do (and ought to) use the conceptions of legal justice and so on, which seem to them best constructed, in deciding in the last resort to which of two well-founded arguments to give the greater weight. This is not a matter which can be decided in a theory-independent way, nor can the question which is really best among the theories which people think best be answered in a theory-independent way. If 'constructivism' is correct, Hercules can finish his job only at the far end of an infinite regress.

That knocks out a main point of Dworkinian legal theory, the 'right answer' thesis. Such being knocked out, we are left to conclude that Dworkin has not, in the sense he intended, establised the grounds for his pre-Benthamite programme. He has not succeeded in demolishing the alleged gap between censorial and expository jurisprudence.

Certainly as the foregoing sketch account of adjudication in hard cases implicitly supposes, there must be more to any account of a legal system than simply an account of different sorts of rules and their inter-relations. The making and implementing of such laws presupposes and involves reference to values which can be and sometimes must be rendered explicit in statements of principle or of policy. It would be only a matter of arbitrary fiat answering no good end of understanding if these elements of principle or policy were ruled out in an exposition or description of the law which exists within some jurisdiction.

What that says, however, is only that a good description (or definition) of law must be *expanded* beyond a mere account of 'rules'. It does not say or mean that description as distinct from criticism of law is impossible. No doubt the legal system of the Soviet Union or of the Republic of South Africa is pregnant with principles as well as with rules, and should be seen and grasped as such. The principles, however, may be from my point of view very bad ones; I may rightly wish to proceed from description to criticism and the mere observation that law comprises principles and policies as well as rules in no way impedes that proceeding, or justifies the thesis that expository and censorial jurisprudence are, after all, identical. This pre-Benthamite programme is therefore flawed at the heart.

Moreover, there is a certain sense in which the 'rules' have logical primacy. As Hart[15] and others have shown, 'developed' legal systems develop precisely by establishing more or less clear criteria as to what counts as a rule of the system. This is essential to law as a common and objective standard of conduct in a complex society. It is quite right to say, as Dworkin in effect does, that this law is 'theorized' in action. But the principles which can reasonably be propounded as principles of this or that legal system are limited by the need to fit the more or less objectively established rules. It would be absurd, for example, to suggest that the principle of the equal freedom of all human beings was implicit in the law of the later Roman republic. Among the reasons why it would be absurd would be simple observation of the clear rules concerning slavery then clearly established in Rome.

Whatever his ambition, Dworkin has added to, rather than subverted, the 'ruling theory' which he thinks so inadequate.

III. RIGHTS

It may seem unsatisfactory that Dworkin's key argument about 'rights' has been passed over. In truth, as will appear, it is the

---

[15] H. L. A. Hart, *The Concept of Law* (Oxford, 1961), ch. 5; cf. MacCormick, *H. L. A. Hart* (London, 1981), ch. 9.

argument itself which is unsatisfactory, both in particular and in general.

The problem about rights in hard cases can be dealt with fairly swiftly. Dworkin argues, fairly enough, that if courts in hard cases are not enforcing rights, they are in effect legislating retroactively. He takes this to imply that in every case one party necessarily has a right to the decision in his favour, and that legal theory is committed either to that 'rights thesis' or to the inevitability of retrospection.

This is at best a half-truth. To see *why*, we need only recur to the definition of a hard case as one in which *both* parties have some doctrine or principle or precedent or such-like on which to base their respective cases. Let us suppose that since each party has a principle in his favour, he has a right to something or other as against the other party—for example, *Y* has a right to damages, *X* has a right to be absolved from liability. (Notice: Dworkin *must* suppose this to be the case, since by his definition principles *always* determine rights; the truth is that *some* principles do.)

Then the problem is that *both* parties have rights, but their rights conflict—this is exactly what makes hard cases hard. The rights conflict because the principles conflict. Therefore, just as Sir David Ross[16] conceived as prima-facie obligations those obligations we have under potentially conflicting moral principles, so too we had better adopt 'prima-facie rights'—or some such phrase—to cover the legal rights which potentially conflicting legal principles vest in us.

Thus a hard case is one in which each party has some grounds on which to assert at least a prima-facie right. The problem for the court is not one of inventing a right and applying it retroactively. It is a problem concerning *which right to uphold in preference to the other*. In addition to the merit of being true, this actually follows from Dworkin's own definition of principles, and his definition of hard cases as involving a conflict of principles. If we go on and say, along Dworkinian lines, that judges should decide to which right to give preference by making recourse to a kind of 'constructive' argument, we are left to conclude that the decision can only be justified in a theory-

[16] See W. D. Ross, *Foundations of Ethics* (Oxford, 1939), pp. 84–6; *The Right and the Good* (Oxford, 1930), p. 19. He was confessedly unhappy with the qualifying phrase prima facie.

relative way. Since there may be honest and rationally irresoluble differences of theory between different judges, the decision contains an irreducibly dispositive element. Each judge tries to work out which right ought to prevail. The court's decision determines which *is to* prevail; it establishes a preference, it does not merely record a pre-established preference of one (prima-facie) right over another in the generic circumstances of the case. That conclusion is probably not startling to, and certainly not radically subversive of, the 'ruling theory'.

This preliminary point may well be thought to show that Dworkin is not fully attentive to all the implications of what he variously says about principles and about rights. Nor is he. But what is worse is that he fails to take 'rights' as seriously as he would have us take rights. He variously describes rights as 'political trumps held by individuals', as not being 'spooky things men and women have in much the same way as they have nonspooky things like tonsils', as being an 'individual political aim' which is 'described' (*sic*) by a principle as distinct from a policy; and so forth.[17] He embarks upon an elaborate typology of rights in his essay on hard cases. He distinguishes rights in a 'strong sense' and rights in a 'weak sense'[18] (the distinction turning on that between what it is wrong to do to somebody and what it is not wrong for somebody to do—rather like Hohfeldian 'right' versus Hohfeldian 'privilege'[19]). But the nearest he ever really comes to identifying what he calls a right in the strong sense is when he says: 'A man has a moral right against the state if for some reason that state would do wrong to treat him in a certain way, even though it would be in the general interest to do so.'[20] If that is his main view, it is simply not open to him to argue, as he elsewhere does, that some political theories start from rights and derive duties from the basic set of rights, while others do the reverse, his being of the former kind.

What it is wrong for the state to do is that which the state has a duty not to do. The definition above quoted therefore defines

---

[17] The references are respectively to *TRS*, pp. xi, 139, 91, 90.

[18] *TRS*, pp. 188–92.

[19] W. N. Hohfeld, *Fundamental Legal Conceptions* (New Haven, 1919). Although a former holder of the Hohfeld Chair at Yale, Dworkin takes no time comparing his taxonomy and analysus of rights with that of his distinguished predecessor.

[20] *TRS*, p. 139.

rights effectively in terms of duties. The position can be saved only if he goes on to say that the wrong or duty in question is founded in some right which the individual has. But on that account the definition is viciously circular. A person has the right if he has a right such that the state would wrong him by taking it away. True. But what's a right?

The lesson from this is that anyone who wishes to give rights the kind of primacy Dworkin wishes to give them in political theory must think harder than Dworkin has thought about their nature. In my judgment (more fully explained elsewhere[21]) the direction in which such a person must look is that of the traditional 'interest theory' as against the 'will theory' of rights.

The argument to be made is that rights always and necessarily concern human goods, that is, concern what it is, at least in normal circumstances, good for a person to have. When positive laws establish rights, for example expressly by legislation, what they do is secure individuals (or members of a particular defined set of individuals) in the enjoyment of some good or other. But not by way of a collective good collectively enjoyed, like clean air in a city, but rather an individual good individually enjoyed by each, like the protection of each occupier's particular environment as secured by the law of private nuisance. Such protection is characteristically achieved by imposing duties on people at large, for example, not to bring about certain kinds of adverse changes to the environment of land or premises occupied by somebody else, and further duties, which may be invoked at the instance of any aggrieved occupier, to make good damage arising from adverse environmental change. And there are other ways of securing protection, which I have discussed elsewhere.[22]

One way of conceptualizing 'rights' is to conceive them as goods which are in some way normatively secured to individuals. Another, apparently less profitable way, is to see them simply as the reflex or correlative of the duties for some reason imposed by law, correlativity being determined by the presence or absence in a person of power to waive, or enforce, or demand

[21] See ch. 8 below; also my 'Rights in Legislation', in Hacker and Raz (eds.), *Law, Morality, and Society*, pp. 189–209.

[22] Ibid., p. 205.

remedies for breach of such duties. (The latter is the view held by H. L. A. Hart,[23] among others).

Looking at it from a moral or political rather than strictly or narrowly legal point of view, if we wish to use 'rights' as a ground for arguing that people have certain moral duties to each other, or ought to have certain legal duties imposed on them, it is obvious that the Hartian conception of rights is unuseful, as he himself states.[24] From this point of view, therefore, a theory which asserts the primacy of rights must necessarily postulate that there are goods or values which in their character as goods-which-ought-to-be-secured-to-individuals therefore count as 'rights'. That is an analytical apparatus which will enable us to treat of rights as grounds for identifying duties and justifying various kinds of laws and political institutions. For rights so understood can genuinely be presented as logically prior to duties, or, at least, some duties; and as grounds for determining *what* it is wrong for the state to do to an individual, or indeed for one individual or group to do to another individual or group. 'Or indeed' is important; Dworkin seems far too apt to suppose that rights affect only relations between individuals and the state, which obviously they don't.

I do hold that there are goods which ought to be secured to individuals, goods which it is wrong to withhold from or deny to any individual. To such goods I would say that people have rights, and accordingly I would further say that their having such rights is a good justifying reason for certain duties which I would assert to be incumbent on individuals in their conduct towards others and on the state in its conduct towards individuals. This is perhaps no more than spelling out a more exact meaning for Dworkin's idea of an 'individual political aim'—to reflection upon which I am much indebted. But I do not find in Dworkin any such, or any other, elaborated account of rights.

From this point of view we might say something about the fundamental and about the universal quality (with respect to all human beings) of rights people may have. Goods which are goods for an individual might be ranked by that individual in order from those most valued by him/her to those least valued.

[23] H. L. A. Hart, 'Bentham on Legal Rights', in *Oxford Essays in Jurisprudence, Second Series* (ed. A. W. B. Simpson, Oxford, 1973).
[24] Ibid.

To an individual the goods most valued—those least readily given up in competition with others—are the fundamental ones. If these goods belong within the category of goods which ought to be secured to that individual, they are for that individual rights which he/she holds as fundamental.

That would not necessarily make them universal in the sense of belonging to all human beings. There have been slave-masters who have valued their freedom as a fundamental good, and who have held it as a fundamental right; and there have been slave ideologies since at least Aristotle's time which have justified the existence of freedom as a fundamental right for some but not for all human beings. Even apart from that, some rights which we might think fundamental for all children, we would not necessarily think fundamental, or even rights, for all human beings; for example, the right to care and nurture by parents or parent-substitutes.

In short, the account of rights as goods which ought to be secured to individuals is—as it should be—a formal one which does not settle *what* goods should be secured, nor *to whom*. These are vital questions of moral and political substance, not capable of settlement by mere analysis or definitional *fiat*. To answer them calls for the 'construction' of moral and political theories. Clear analysis is, however, a prerequisite of the construction of a worthwhile theory; with respect, I find no sufficiently clear analysis in Dworkin, though I suspect that what I have said is more or less compatible with what he does say.

IV. LIBERTY AND EQUALITY

These remarks are an essential preliminary to a consideration of Dworkin's political philosophy, which is an anti-utilitarian restatement of liberalism, in which he gives pride of place to every person's right to equal concern and respect with every other. So far indeed is he insistent upon the egalitarian aspect of his theory that he goes to the length of saying that 'In any strong sense of right, which would be competitive with the right to equality, there exists no general right to liberty at all'.[25] His argument for this view is that by his definition of 'right in the

[25] *TRS*, p. 269.

strong sense', there could be a right to liberty in general only if it were wrong for the state to limit any aspect of liberty on simple 'general interest' grounds. Yet laws restricting one's liberty to drive down Lexington Avenue and 'the vast bulk of the laws which diminish my liberty' are in fact justified 'as being in the general interest or welfare'.[26]

The point is dubitable on several counts: first, it turns on the inadequate analysis of 'right' already castigated above; secondly, it makes the somewhat facile assumption that the sole argument for a one-way street system, or other such legal restrictions, is a general interest one, whereas it might well be argued that traffic regulation systems, for example, are an attempt to balance such rights as the right to free and expeditious movement through cities and the right to bodily security (which is plainly put at some hazard by toleration of the motor car); and finally, most seriously, the argument does not treat on the same footing 'liberty' and 'equality'. Let us see how.

The argument concerning liberty is of the form: if there is a right to liberty in general, then no encroachment by government upon liberty can be justified simply on grounds of general interest. Some encroachments on liberty are justified simply on grounds of general interest. Therefore there is no right to liberty in general. To make out the case that 'equality in general' (which would be the relevant comparison) is the subject-matter of a right, Dworkin must therefore be prepared to argue that no departure by government from equality of treatment of citizens can ever be justified on grounds of general interest. I do not find him to make such an argument, and it would be difficult indeed to make and sustain the argument in relation to such matters as military conscription for defence of a nation, or taxation legislation, or legislation regulating different payment of different public-office-holders—and so on and so on.

Of course, Dworkin intends no such argument, for his contention is not that people have a right to equality of treatment in every respect, but only that people have a right to treatment as equally deserving an equal measure of concern and respect from the government. In short, he wishes to say that in this

---

[26] Ibid.

crucial matter, everyone has an equal right: an equal right to concern and respect.[27]

I agree with that, but at the cost of disagreeing with his assertion that the right to liberty cannot compete with the right to equality, for it turns out that they are by his lights on a similar footing: in *some* matters, people have a right to liberty; in *some* matters they have a right to equality.

Unlike Dworkin, I would be content with the traditional definition of liberty as what he tendentiously calls 'liberty as license'[28] rather than his 'liberty as independence',[29] Liberty, in my judgment, is most simply to be understood as freedom from imposed constraint on one's actions, whether such constraints be normative (for example, laws imposing duties not to do this or that) or factual (for example, handcuffs on a prisoner's hands). To have liberty in some matter is to be free from constraint.

To establish that there is some right to liberty by my account of the matter, it is therefore necessary to establish that liberty is a good which individuals ought to have secured to them; and to establish that it is a fundamental right of everyone, it needs to be shown that liberty is a good for everyone, which ought to be secured to everyone.[30]

There is one important reason why we should be inclined to think liberty both a good and a relatively basic good for everyone, namely, that people may have many various and mutually differing values, indeed they do; but whatever different things they value, they can pursue whatever values they have only on condition that they are not normatively or factually constrained against pursuing them. So, for everyone, liberty to pursue what they value is a good precisely because it is a condition of getting anything else they think good.

But to say that everyone ought to be free to pursue whatever he/she thinks good is evidently absurd because the satisfaction of some people's ideals or desires may result in the imposition of constraints by them on other people. Therefore it is necessary to stipulate that everyone's liberty should be constrained at least

[27] *TRS*, pp. 180–3, 227, 272–8.
[28] *TRS*, pp. 262, 267–8.
[29] *TRS*, p. 263.
[30] See ch. 3 above.

within such limits as prevent the imposition of unequal constraints on others.

This stipulation does indeed turn upon recognition that each person does have a right to equal respect with every other, has indeed an equal right to the conditions of self-respect and of the contentment which resides in the ability to pursue his or her own conception of what is a full and rewarding life. But that is a ground for prescribing the *universality* within a population of the right to liberty, not a ground for perceiving liberty as the subject-matter of right. Liberty is not good because people are to be treated as equals. Rather, it is because liberty is a good and because people ought to be treated as equals that there is, with certain qualifications, a right to equal liberty.

What then are the qualifications? First, there are exceptions for children and persons of unsound mind justified by reference to the interests of such persons. Secondly, there is the Rawlsian qualification that within a set of institutions designed for the protection of liberty, it may be legitimate to impose special restrictions on and to give special privileges to those who hold particular institutional offices: e.g. judges are (rightly) subjected to restrictions on their political activity and granted special privileges in relation to their utterances in their capacity as judges.[31] Thirdly, there are rights which compete with the right to liberty, especially those concerning fair shares in economic goods.

The third of these points is worth pursuing. Liberty is one of the conditions of self-respect and the 'pursuit of contentment' as delineated above. But so is life, and so are the means essential to a tolerably commodious existence. A starving peasant may have the fullest possible freedom of speech, but writing letters to the editor of the local paper is not his foremost concern. For him to have an equal opportunity of self-respect with a well-heeled businessman, it is essential to him to have more money, more food, and the chance to sustain himself reasonably commodiously by his own work.

It is at least open to argument that a legal order which maximizes the freedom of property-owners to do what they will with their own and which encourages the fullest possible

---

[31] J. Rawls, *A Theory of Justice* (Oxford, 1971), p. 302; cf. ch. 5 above.

freedom of market transactions will fail to secure for the starving peasant the degree of equality with the businessman which has been postulated. To that extent and within such spheres the right to liberty collides or competes with the right to such a share in general economic resources as is a condition of one's self-respect and pursuit of contentment. Therefore there is good ground for arguing that liberty of property-owners and market liberties ought to be restricted to whatever extent is necessary to secure other no less basic rights to individuals.

This can be argued in a different way: the existence of a liberty to do X being defined solely in terms of the absence of constraints (normative or factual) against doing X, it is evident that one can be free to do X without being capable of doing it. I may be free to swim across the Atlantic without being capable of doing it. But a legal order may secure equality of liberty without in any degree securing an equal capability to exercise the liberties secured.[32] Black children of a given level of native intellectual capability may under a particular system of public education turn out to be incapable of exercising the liberty to enter a professional training which some white children may be capable of exercising, not because of greater native endowments but because of better schooling and greater environmental advantage. And so on.

On the basis of either of the foregoing arguments, or both of them, it is possible to argue for some restrictions either on the general scheme of legal liberty, or on the particular exercise of particular liberties, in the cause of securing economic fairness in general and of making fair allowance for socially induced differences of capability to exercise legal liberties. In constructing a fair legal and social order we inevitably find that there are goods other than the liberties of individuals which compete for recognition. But, so far as economic goods are concerned, the range of possible competition is restricted. Freedom of speech, freedom from arbitrary arrest and seizure, freedom of religion, conscience, and opinion, freedom to come and go in public places as one chooses, political rights of participation, and such like, are in principle neutral as between different systems of

---

[32] This parallels Rawls's point about the distinction between the existence and the 'worth' of a liberty: ibid., pp. 204 f; Cf. Hart, 'Are there any Natural Rights?', 64 *Philos. Rev.* (1955), 175, and MacCormick, *H. L. A. Hart* (London, 1981), pp. 9–10.

distribution and allocation of economic goods. Hence it is always a bogus argument that 'bourgeois liberties' such as these are inimical to a fair distribution of economic goods, or *a fortiori* that liberty in these respects is a mere adjunct of a bourgeois system of private ownership of the means of production, distribution, and exchange. It is an equally bad argument to contend, as some Conservatives appear to do, that liberty in the former respects is logically impossible without the liberties implicit in a private property system.

The rhetoric of the indivisibility of liberty, to which Dworkin objects,[33] makes just that mistake. I wholeheartedly agree with him as to the absurdity of treating all liberties connected with property and the market as being essential to a just and liberal ordering of society, but I venture to think that the conclusion he reaches is preferable to the method of his argument for it. Liberty is a good, and people do have a right to it, but only within an order in which each has in principle an equal liberty, subject to the exception for children and other *incapaces*, subject to the Rawlsian qualification, and subject to other requirements of justice, especially economic fairness; but the last qualification operates only as against those aspects of liberty which can conflict with our favoured conception of economic fairness. Certainly, the idea of *equal* liberty for *everyone* requires as a prior postulate an equal right of everyone to self-respect and to respect from others. But to say, or even to seem to say, that that makes liberty in general subordinate to equality in general would be absurd.

Finally, one aspect of Dworkin's argument for the right to 'liberty as independence' should be challenged. He argues, in effect, that rights of self-expression always predominate over other rights. This he takes to follow from his interesting distinction between 'personal preferences' and 'external preferences'.[34] Preferences of the former kind concern how I want my life to be, preferences of the latter kind concern how I want other people to live, or what kind of relations I prefer to have with other people. If a person wants to be a lawyer, that is a personal preference. If a person wants all lawyers to be white men, that is an external preference.

[33] *TRS*, pp. 277-8.
[34] *TRS*, pp. 234-8; also ch. 11.

One of the quarrels which Dworkin picks with utilitarianism is that in principle it equates personal and external preferences in prescribing principles of governmental action. Thus even if all blacks wanted to be lawyers, a scheme which admitted no blacks to the legal profession would satisfy more preferences if all the whites wanted there to be no black lawyers, and if whites were in the majority. But such a scheme would involve systematically refusing 'equal concern and respect' to the minority, in this case an ethnic minority. And so it would be wrong.

Dworkin argues that it would be wrong because it involves a kind of systematic double counting of majority preferences.[35] They get to be what they want to be (or at least get a chance of being it) in virtue of the weight of their personal preferences. But they also stop the minority, or some members of it, from getting to be what they want to be, in virtue of the weight of their external preferences. Since this is unfair, Dworkin argues that in principle all external preferences ought to be omitted in determining any public course of action. But since in a democratic system this is impossible in practice, the device of entrenched rights must be resorted to in order to secure minorities against the baneful restrictions entailed by majorities' external preferences. And, in turn, this leads to particular interpretations of the rights entrenched in the US Constitution.

Thus, in relation to the right of free speech Dworkin in effect argues that, short of inflicting physical danger on other people, demonstrators must have the right not only to say what they like but to express their position how they like, however that may be.

It may be said that the anti-riot law leaves [a person] free to express [his] principles in a non-provocative way. But that misses the connection between expression and dignity. A man cannot express himself freely when he cannot match his rhetoric to his outrage, or when he must trim his sails to protect values he counts as nothing next to those he is trying to vindicate. It is true that some political dissenters speak in ways that shock the majority, but it is arrogant for the majority to suppose that the orthodox methods of expression are proper ways to speak, for this is a denial of equal concern and respect.[36]

[35] Ibid.
[36] *TRS*, p. 201.

This looks like an attractive argument. But how far does it go? What if the majority of people in a town prefer a beautiful old terrace to stand as it is, whereas a property-developer wants to tear it down to put up a new office block? The developer is also an architect, and claims that carrying out this piece of building here is essential to his self-expression. For my part, I would have no hesitation in saying that the property-developer has no absolute right worthy of entrenchment as against the wishes of the majority. Yet theirs are 'external preferences' and his are 'personal preferences, if I have the distinction aright.

The case seems to be one which casts doubt on the pleasing simplicity of the 'personal' versus 'external' distinction as between preferences. We all live in this town and necessarily share in the physical environment which it offers. Either the environment contains these historically interesting and aesthetically pleasing houses, or it contains the office block, but not both. There is as much risk that the property-developer will fail to show full and proper respect to his fellow citizens as vice versa. And somebody's preferences are going to lose out in the end.

I cannot bring myself to resist the belief that for each of us a physical and social environment which is pleasing to us is a good of the kind which may properly be the subject-matter of rights. So far as concerns public and visible additions to the environment or public actings which necessarily impinge upon all and sundry I cannot see the overwhelming justice of the view which says that everyone must always be free to choose whatever mode of self-expression he or she may choose. Thus for example it appears to me that some forms of obscenity law and of environmental protection law may be justified although they do impose limits on the manner of individuals' self-expression; but they must not limit the substance of what may be said or thought.

This requires an admission that environmental goods may be brought into the balance against the good of freedom of action, which is no doubt a dangerous admission which can readily be abused. But to the extent that constraints are placed only on actings in public and are placed equally on all, such constraints are not inimical to the essential equality of liberty for which I have argued.

With some caution, therefore, I would make that admission. In making it I am driven to conclude that Dworkin's distinction between external and personal preferences, at least as he has so far drawn it, is too crude to be acceptable. Applied to contexts other than those to which he applies it, it appears to yield unacceptable results.

8.
CHILDREN'S RIGHTS: A TEST-CASE FOR THEORIES OF RIGHT

I AM not confident that I could give, far less justify, a comprehensive list of the rights which children have, but I feel no unease in saying that they do have rights. I don't have a theory of children's rights, but I do at least have a theory of rights which can make sense of saying that children have them. Just because the concept of 'children's rights' is difficult to square with some theories of what it is for anyone to have a right, children's rights are a good test-case for theories of rights in general. First things first. Let us be clear that it makes sense to ascribe rights to children at all before we go on to work out substantive theories as to the rights they should be accorded. The former is what will be made clear in this chapter.

In broad and general terms there are two competing theories as to the nature of rights:[1] the theory which says that having a right of some kind is to do with the legal or moral recognition of some individual's choice as being pre-eminent over the will of others as to a given subject-matter in a given relationship, and the other theory which says that having a right is having one's interests protected in certain ways by the imposition of (legal or moral) normative constraints on the acts and activities of other people with respect to the object of one's interests. Between various manifestations of the will theory and the interest theory there has been a long-running, but inconclusive, series of test matches. Here we have a test-case, in the light of which I shall show, to my own entire satisfaction, the untenability of all forms of will theory, in place of which I shall suggest as an alternative a theory more along the lines of traditional interest theories.

Let me start from what seems to me a simple and barely contestable assertion: at least from birth, every child has a right

---

[1] See, e.g., G. W. Paton, *A Text-book of Jurisprudence* (4th edn., Oxford, 1972), ed. G. W. Paton and D. P. Derham), pp. 285–90, for a review of this opposition of theories.

to be nurtured, cared for, and, if possible, loved, until such time as he or she is capable of caring for himself or herself. When I say that, I intend to speak in the first instance of a moral right. I should regard it as a plain case of moral blindness if anyone failed to recognize that every child has that right. Certainly, it has not been a universally recognized legal right—think of the law of republican Rome—but to my way of thinking that only means that some or perhaps many legal systems have been morally deficient, which is scarcely a startling observation. (As it happens, our legal systems do at present grant the right in question, so for us, now, it is a legal as well as a moral right.)

There are, however, morally acute and clear-sighted people who would deny not the substantive moral tenet involved in ascribing that right to all children, but the appropriateness of expressing the moral tenet through the linguistic device of the noun 'a right'. 'Say, if you will, that morality demands, or the law demands, that all children be nurtured, cared for, and, if possible, loved, but do not say they have a right to such treatment, for so to use the term right is to obfuscate.'

That objection is grounded in the will theory of rights. It could be expanded, along lines laid down by H. L. A. Hart,[2] in some such terms as follow: Rights (understand 'claim-rights', 'rights of recipience')[3] presuppose duties as their correlative. Duties exist when there exist legal or social rules of a particular kind, in virtue of which individuals in certain circumstances are required to act or abstain from acting in certain ways. For any individual whose circumstances are those specified in such a rule, it is true to say that he has a duty to act or abstain from acting as specified.

Of the rules which impose duties, some provide that the performance by a duty-bearer of the required act (or absten-

---

[2] See H. L. A. Hart, 'Definition and Theory in Jurisprudence', 70 *LQR* (1954) 37 esp. p. 49; 'Are there Any Natural Rights', repr. in *Political Philosophy* (ed. A. M. Quinton, Oxford, 1968), esp. p. 58, where it is said that to ascribe rights to babies or animals is perhaps to 'make an idle use of the expression "a right"'; 'Bentham on Legal Rights', in *Oxford Essays in Jurisprudence, Second Series* (ed. A. W. B. Simpson, Oxford, 1973). For another recent example of an essentially similar argument, see W. J. Kamba, 'Legal Theory and Hohfeld's Analysis of a Legal Right', *Jur. Rev.* (1974), pp. 249–62.

[3] On terminology, see W. N. Hohfeld, *Fundamental Legal Conceptions* (New Haven, 1919, third reprint 1964), for the expression 'rights of recipience' see D. D. Raphael, *Problems of Political Philosophy* (London, 1970), pp. 68–71.

tion) is to be conditional on some other person's choice, either in the sense that it is to be performed only if and when he so requests, or in the sense that that other person can waive the requirement, and, if he does, the act (or abstention) need not be performed. When A's being required to do his duty is in either sense left in B's discretion, B may properly be said to have a right against A, a right that A act or abstain in the manner contemplated in the rule. On this view, a legal or moral right is equivalent to a legal or moral power of waiver or enforcement of duties, and any rate, rights exist only when people have such normative power over duties of others. (Although this analysis applies to 'claim-rights' in the Hohfeld scheme, the theory suggests that what is common to all types of right is that they make the choice, or the will, of the right-holder paramount in a given relationship.)

If that view is accepted as yielding a satisfactory recommendation as to the usage of the noun 'a right', then it must indeed be inept to ascribe to children the right to care, nurture, and love. A baby cannot in fact, cannot in morals, and cannot in law relieve his or her parents[4] of their duty towards him or her in those matters.

But adherents of the 'will theory' have a standard tactic for avoiding the awkward example of children. They say that it is sufficient if either B or some other person C acting on B's behalf has the relevant powers over A's duty in respect of B.

For the case we are considering, the tactic is unemployable. Standardly, in the case of children, the party who in legal (or indeed in social) matters acts on a child's behalf is his or her parent or guardian. But it is at least possible to imagine a legal system in which a parent's duty to care for and nurture his or her own child is neither subject to the parent's issuing a self-directed request on the child's behalf nor indeed to any possibility of waiver by the parent as the child's representative. That is so whether or not the law accords to the parent powers of waiver or enforcement over duties owed to the child by third

---

[4] Here, and elsewhere, I assume for the sake of simplicity that the duty towards children is a duty primarily owed by the 'natural parents'. But, as is pointed out later, the opinion that children have the right in question does not necessarily entail the opinion that it is the *parents* who bear the correlative duty. Throughout, for the sake of simplicity, I ignore questions of adoption, legitimacy, etc.

parties. What is more, speaking morally, there seems to be no reason whatever to suppose that the child or anyone acting on the child's behalf should be permitted or empowered to waive the parental duty or in any sense to acquiesce in its non-performance.

It might be said that the contemporary British legal systems do give just that power to certain public officials, in that procedures exist whereby in appropriate circumstances children may be removed from their parents' care and transferred to the care of other persons in pursuance of a judical order. Short of that, too, welfare officers acting in the interests of children have power in various ways to 'keep up to the mark' parents whose performance of their parental duties is in some degree deficient.

One who rejects the 'will theory', as I do, can say, as I say, that such legal provisions are desirable because they protect and further the rights of children. To regard such powers as constitutive of rights (as the will theory does), is to foreclose the possibility of justifying them on the ground that they do protect rights which might otherwise be insecure, and thus in my submission to confuse the substantive right with ancillary remedial provisions. It is unduly anglo-centric to erect the brocard *ubi remedium ibi ius* into an analytic truth.

In any event, that example of those legal provisions would not serve to save the theory that powers of waiver or enforcement of duties are essentially constitutive of 'rights', even if it were proferred in its defence. When a child is taken by law out of the tutelage of its parents and put into the care of some other person, the measure is not conceived as being a waiver of the parent's duty—the parent may indeed be penalized for the acts of neglect which justify the order. The point is that in the interests of the child, fulfilment of the functions of care and nurture especially in infancy is so fundamentally important that someone else is appointed to undertake their fulfilment as a duty on the ground that the parent is temporarily or permanently unable or unwilling to do so. It is a case of substituted performance of a duty which is so important in the child's interest that penal or compensatory remedies for its breach are inadequate. Substituted performance is no waiver. The function is not one of 'letting off' the parent; rather it is one of protecting the child. In consequence, the transfer of care is not deemed to release the parent from the duty in the sense of exempting him or her from the possibility of penalties for its breach.

As for enforcement provisions which fall short of transferring care of the child, these lack the discretionary character essential to the 'will theory', it is not the case that the child or someone deemed to be acting on the child's behalf has an option of enforcing the duty of care and nurture, which option may or may not be exercised according to arbitrary choice. If the child needs greater care than is being provided, there is no discretion to be exercised, that greater care must be provided. Of course, there is discretion in judging any question of 'need', but it is discretion of a kind not contemplated by the will theory.

We are put, as lawyers say, to our election. Either we abstain from ascribing to children a right to care and nurture, or we abandon the will theory. For my part, I have no inhibitions about abandoning the latter. It causes me no conceptual shock or mental cramp to say that children have that right. What is more, I will aver that it is *because* children have that right that it is good that legal provisions should be made in the first instance to encourage and assist parents to fulfil their duty to care and nurture, and secondarily to provide for its performance by alternative foster-parents when natural parents are disqualified by death, incapacity, or wilful and persistent neglect. *Ubi ius, ibi remedium.* So far from its being the case that the remedial provision is constitutive of the right, the fact is rather that recognition of the right justifies the imposition of the remedial provision.

Is this merely a trivial issue of linguistic preferences? Only in part, and that a small part. I think that it is morally important that we should recognize the moral importance and the significance of moral rights, and legally useful to have a clear conception of legal right which recognizes the straightforwardly analogical relationship between legal and moral rights. (That they are analogical in form does not, of course, mean that they are identical in content.) In so saying, I do of course court Bentham's posthumous condemnation, if not, in his case, sub-humous rotation. In his view, the locution 'a moral right' was either a devious way of talking about what ought to be done, an obscure way of asserting that the law ought to confer certain rights, or just plain nonsense.[5]

I counter-claim that there is a significant difference between asserting that every child ought to be cared for, nurtured, and, if possible, loved, and asserting that every child has a right to care, nurture, and love. One way of showing the difference is to show that there are statements which could intelligibly be advanced as justifications of the former proposition but which could not be intelligibly be advanced in justification of the latter. For example, along the lines of Swift's *Modest Proposal*, one could suggest as a reason why children ought to be cared for, nurtured, and loved, that that would be the best way of getting them to grow into plump and contented creatures fit to enhance the national diet. Or again, one could argue that a healthy society requires healthy and well-nurtured children who will grow up into contented and well-adjusted adults who will contribute to the GNP and not to be a charge on the welfare facilities or the prison service.

Of course only one of these is a moral, or indeed a serious, argument. But neither is an argument which could be used directly to justify the proposition that children have a right to care, nurture, and love. Why not? Because both advance reasons for giving children care, nurture, and affection solely on the ground that their well-being is a fit means to an ulterior end. I do not say that there can be no moral argument that certain beings ought to be treated in a certain way in order to achieve some end other than their well-being. I do say that such arguments are necessarily inept in justifying the ascription to them of a right to that treatment. Consider the oddity of saying that turkeys have a right to be well fed in order to be fat for the Christmas table, or of saying that children have a right to care and nurture lest they become a charge on the taxpayer. It may not have escaped notice that the same oddity would attach to saying that children have a right to be cared for because that is a . way of maximizing general utility. So it may be no wonder that Bentham was so dismissive of the notion of moral rights. But it would be a wonder if he were believed.

[5] See, e.g., *Bentham's Works*, ed. Bowring (1843), ii. 501 f., iii. 221 f.

To argue, on the other hand, that each and every child is a being whose needs and capacities command our respect, so that denial to any child of the wherewithal to meet his or her needs and to develop his or her capacities would be wrong in itself (at least in so far as it is physically possible to provide the where-withal), and would be wrong regardless of the ulterior dis-advantages or advantages to anyone else—so to argue, would be to put a case which is intelligible as a justification of the opinion that children have such rights. To generalize: the ascription of a right to some class of beings seems to require the following presuppositions: for the class in question (in our case, children) there is some act or omission (in our case, the acts and omissions involved in care, nurture, and love) performance of which in the case of each and every member of the class will satisfy, protect, or advance some need, interest, or desire of each such individual; and secondly: satisfaction of that need, interest, or desire is of such importance that it would be wrong to deny it to any such individual regardless of ulterior advantages in so doing. Of course, the second of these con-ditions is intrinsically contentious, and argument might rage inconclusively over the question whether denial of some form of treatment to every member of a given class would be wrong. But to observe that is to observe only what is obvious, that in relation to their substance, rights belong to the class of essen-tially contested concepts.

Even that generalized formulation is perhaps too specific, just because it unnecessarily begs substantive moral questions in tying an elucidation of the notion of 'having rights' solely to 'want-regarding' categories such as needs, interests, and desires. This is the characteristic failing of the 'interest theory'. It is uncontroversial that satisfaction of needs, interests, and desires is a part of 'the good' for individuals, but it is contro-versial whether it is exhaustive of and constitutive of the good. A formal account of rights can and should be neutral on that substantive moral question. So I shall generalize further and say this: to ascribe to all members of a class C a right to treatment T is to presuppose that T is, in all normal circum-stances, a good for every member of C, and that T is a good of such importance that it would be wrong to deny it to or with-hold it from any member of C. That deals with moral rights: as for legal rights I should say this: when a right to T is conferred by law on all members of C, the law is envisaged as advancing the interests of each and every member of C on the supposition that T is a good for every member of C, and the law has the effect of making it legally wrongful to withhold T from any member of C.

What has been said may suggest that one cannot believe in the category 'moral rights' unless one accepts in some form the principle that sentient beings ought to be respected as ends in themselves. If that is so, I do not regret it. A belief in respect for persons is indeed an essential precondition of a belief in moral rights. And respect for persons is both a fundamental and an ultimate moral principle.[6]

Be that as it may, the above reflections have, I hope, indicated why the proposition that all children ought to be cared for, nurtured, and loved is far from identical with the proposition that every child has a right to be treated so. It is indeed possible, and now possible to see why it is possible, to advance the latter proposition as a specific kind of justification for the former, but not vice versa. It is also trivially true that children's having that moral right can be advanced as a reason why they ought to be accorded the parallel legal right. That the one proposition can genuinely be adduced as a reason for adhering to the other, however, in itself indicates that Bentham was wrong in thinking them identical (or, rather, in thinking that the former was reducible to the latter so far as it made sense at all).

What I have said so far seems to entail at least the possibility that rights are or could be logically prior to duties. That may seem very shocking, but it is true. Austin and Hohfeld might be scandalized, but I can appeal to law to mitigate the scandal, by showing that the law sometimes confers rights which are logically prior to duties. An interesting instance of such a right statutorily conferred upon children is to be found in section $2(1)(a)$ of the Succession (Scotland) Act 1964: 'Subject to the following provisions of this Part of this Act, (a) where an intes-

---

[6] As it stands, this passage is open to the charge of begging at least one question; but I would call in aid David Raphael's very persuasive Presidential Address to the Aristotelian Society (D. D. Raphael, 'The Standard of Morals', XCVI *Proc. Arist. Soc.* (1974–5) 1).

tate is survived by children, they shall have right to the whole of the intestate estate.'

By virtue of that, whenever any person domiciled in Scotland dies having left no valid will, there automatically vests in his children (if any) a right to the whole of that part of his estate statutorily denominated 'the intestate estate'. At the moment of its vesting, the right is not a 'real right' involving ownership of the estate or any part of it. It is a right to receive, in due course, a proportionate share in the assets remaining in the executor's hands after satisfaction of prior claims. But note that at the moment at which the right vests there is as yet no executor to bear the correlative duty. The executor must be judicially confirmed or appointed in due course, and what is more, if the estate is solvent those who have beneficial rights in it are normally preferred to other parties in the appointment of an executor dative. So any child who is of sufficient age may, in virtue of the right conferred by the Act, have a resultant if defeasible right to be appointed as executor. His appointment as such will in turn result in his acquiring the duties of executor, including the duty of distributing the intestate estate to those (including himself) who have the right thereto in virtue of section 2.

The intelligibility of that statutory provision indicates that the vesting of rights may be both temporarily and logically prior to the vesting of duties correlative thereto. Since that is intelligible, it cannot be an objection to the argument herein advanced that it contemplates the possibility of rights being logically prior to duties. On the other hand, it may be noted that the statute could not be intelligible if the will theory were correct.

It certainly does not seem to me in any way objectionable to say that it is *because* children have a right to care and nurture that parents have the duty to care for them. There might be other and different grounds (e.g. saving taxpayers' money) for imposing such a duty on parents or on whomsoever it may be imposed, but recognition of children's rights is one distinctive reason for doing so. I find it a much more peculiar view to suppose that parents' having the duty is a logical prerequisite of children's having the right; *a fortiori* if it is added that someone has to have discretion over its performance.

Surely there is much more sense in the opinion that it is because children have the right, and because their parents stand in a particular natural relationship to their own children, that it is the parents upon whom in the first instance the duty of care and nurture is incumbent. But only in the first instance; in default of parents (death, incapacity, fecklessness), the children's right remains and other means must be sought to fulfil it. That in modern societies the responsibility is deemed a state responsibility indicates only one possible solution to the problem.

There may be other cases in which we are much more certain that children have a right to something than we are certain about what is the right or the best way of giving effect to it. That every child has a right to be educated to the limits of his or her abilities seems to me clear. But whose is the duty and the rightful power to provide it and to rule as to what constitutes a satisfactory education seems to me much less clear. The parents? The local authority? The central government? A church? The child? There can be heated dispute over the rival claims of all these, and more besides, even among those who are in no doubt about every child's right to have a proper education, indeed especially among those.

In the foregoing pages I have suggested that children's rights provide a test-case for rival theories about rights in general, and that the 'will theory' fails the test. What I have offered in the alternative is, in effect, a variant of the 'interest theory' advanced in various forms by such writers as Ihering, Austin and Bentham[7] (whose rejection of the concept 'a moral right' should not blind us to the value or the generalizability of his theory of legal rights). As I have said, to ascribe to all members of a class C a right to treatment T is to presuppose that T is in all normal circumstances a good for every member of C, and that T is a good which it would be wrong to withhold from any member of C. Certainly recognition of a right involves the imposition of duties on other persons than the right-holder, but what duties, and upon whom, is a matter which in any case needs careful

---

[7] R. von Ihering, *Geist des römischen Rechts*, iii. 332; J. Austin, *Lectures on Jurisprudence*, ch. XVII; H. L. A. Hart, 'Bentham on Legal Rights', and references therein. For a contemporary defence of a version of 'interest theory' see also G. Marshall, 'Rights, Options, and Entitlements', in Simpson (ed.), *Oxford Essays in Jurisprudence*, pp. 228–41.

definition in order best to secure the right. When the legislature confers a right *eo nomine*, as in the Succession (Scotland) Act discussed above, it is in effect left to the courts to effect a structure of duties and remedies sufficient to secure the right in question.

Although it appears, for the reasons stated here, that the will theory cannot be accepted as yielding a satisfactory analysis of legal or moral rights, the central point which the theory stresses is one which should not be denied. It is certainly true that apart from such cases as those of children or the mentally incapacitated, the holder of a legal right is normally permitted and empowered in law to choose whether or not on any given occasion he should avail himself of his right by insisting on performance by another party of the relevant duty. What is more, in the case of 'private rights', breach of a correlative duty ordinarily gives rise to a 'remedial' right which in turn the right-holder has an option to exercise or not as he sees fit. The remedial right is enforced by exercising as against the wrongdoer the power of initiating legal proceedings. For quite obvious reasons, out of the whole class of legal rights, it is this subclass of private rights supported by private remedial rights and private powers of initiating proceedings which is of central concern in the practice of the law.

But while conceding the truth, and the practical importance, of these points, I would strongly contend that powers of waiver or enforcement are essentially ancillary to, not constitutive of, rights (whether primary rights or remedial rights). That contention, when coupled with that concession, is acceptable only if good reason can be shown, in terms of the theory here advanced, why it should be normal that rights (as here explained) carry with them the power of waiver or enforcement, and a free option as to its exercise.

To recur to my earlier elucidation of a legal right, and to improve a little on it, let this be said: a law which is conceived as conferring on members of Class C a right to treatment T, is envisaged as advancing the interests of each and every member of C on the supposition that T is (normally) a good for each and every member of C. (Save in the case of legislation expressly conferring 'rights' *eo nomine*, it may be disputable whether a law is so conceived and should be so construed.) On that footing, there would be good reason to leave it to any right- holder to choose whether other parties need or need not on any given occasion respect his primary right, and whether to enforce or not to enforce remedial rights in the case of breach of the primary right, only if there is some good reason to leave it to the choice of individuals whether to have or not have what is, or is from the legislator's point of view believed to be, good for them.

Is there then any good reason why individuals should be permitted to choose whether or not to have what they, or others, think is good for them? From a certain standpoint in political philosophy, that of liberalism as classically expressed, for example, by John Stuart Mill in his *Essay on Liberty*, the answer is 'Yes'. To be a liberal is indeed to believe *inter alia* that nobody should ever be forced to pursue his own good, however that may be defined; but exceptions are allowed for, notably children and the mentally incapacitated.[8] One ground which can be asserted as supporting both the principle and the exception is that people can be presumed to be the best judges of what is for their own good or in their own interest, but that presumption does not hold in certain defined cases, for example young children and mentally incapacitated people. To put it another way: save in such exceptional cases, freedom of action is a good which ought to be accorded to every person except in the case of actions harmful to others. (Notice that on the present theory, that would lead on to saying that people have a right to freedom; a right which would be barely intelligible if we accepted a *definition* of 'right' in terms of the will theory.)

It is now obvious that if anyone accepts the theory advanced in this paper as to the nature of rights, and also accepts (as I do) the liberal principle just adumbrated, he must further accept that in all normal cases rights ought to carry with them powers of waiver or enforcement. That the legal system does in fact normally confer just that power of waiver or enforcement on right-holders should accordingly be taken as implying no more than the unsurprising truth that the liberal principle is deeply embedded in our law, if less so now than in the later nineteenth century. It would be equally unsurprising that questions about private rights should be regarded as being of practical impor-

8 Cf. ch. 2 above.

tance only in legal systems imbued to some extent with liberal principles. I conclude that the theory here advanced can fully accommodate the valid insights of the will theory in the context of a liberal legal system.

On the other hand, the will theory fails as an explanation of rights because it cannot account for such important rights as the children's rights discussed in this essay. The presumption that people are the best judges of what is good for them and of whether to have it or not is not and should not be extended to children, certainly not to young children. Neither in law nor in what I take to be sound morality can children's rights be regarded as carrying the option of waiver or enforcement by themselves or on their behalf. Children are not always or even usually the best judges of what is good for them, so much so that even the rights which are most important to their long-term well-being, such as the right to discipline or to a safe environment, they regularly perceive as being the reverse of rights or advantages. It does not follow that adults act well if they permit their children to waive those rights, or if they enforce them only at their children's insistence.

I am at once glad and regretful to discover that it is possible for me to acknowledge that my children have rights, without being thereby committed to the outrageous permissiveness to which my natural indolence inclines me.

9.
PRIVACY AND OBSCENITY

Is THERE any legally or morally significant connection between the topics of privacy and of obscenity? Does respect for the privacy of individuals tell in favour of banning obscene publications, or in favour of abolishing legal restrictions on the use or dissemination of obscene materials? Is legislative prohibition of obscene publications calculated to protect or to infringe the right of individuals to privacy (so far as they have such a right either in law or in morality)?

These are the questions which will be considered and explored in this chapter. From the outset a paradox, or at least an apparent paradox, must be faced. The paradox is that it appears possible either to argue that respect for privacy requires a regime of freedom in relation to the use and enjoyment of obscene materials, or to argue that respect for privacy requires legal controls upon their use and dissemination. Indeed, it may be possible to advance both arguments at the same time, by contending that up to a certain point the right of privacy entails a right to freedom from restraint in the use of obscene materials, but that beyond that point some legal restraints are required in the interests of privacy.

The best proof that it is possible to advance such arguments is to show that they have been advanced by people whose views are, on the face of it, worth some respect. To do so is of course not to demonstrate that all or any of the arguments are soundly based, but it will pave the way for considering critically and in a fresh light what, if any, are the genuine bearings of privacy on obscenity and vice versa. Such critical consideration is the business of this chapter, so let the way be paved for it forthwith.

My source of arguments for preliminary consideration is a series of recent decisions given by the US Supreme Court in various cases involving review of prosecutions of possessors, users, and publishers of things alleged to be obscene.

The first, the case of *Stanley* v. *Georgia* (1968),[1] concerned a conviction under a statute of the State of Georgia for 'Knowingly hav[ing] possession of . . . obscene matter', namely certain films found in his desk drawer during a search by federal and state agents in his home under a warrant authorizing them to search for materials relating to an illegal wagering business. The Supreme Court, reversing the decision of the court below, held that the First and Fourteenth Amendments prohibit making mere private possession of obscene material a crime, and that the Georgia statute was unconstitutional.[2]

An important element in the justification of the ruling given was concern for the protection of privacy. As Marshall, J., giving the opinion of the Court, said, the First Amendment right to freedom of speech and of the press entails a right to receive information. 'This right to receive information and ideas, regardless of their social worth . . . is fundamental to our free society. Moreover, in the context of this case—a prosecution for mere possession of printed or filmed matter in the privacy of a person's own home—that right takes on an added dimension. For also fundamental is the right to be free, except in very limited circumstances, from unwanted governmental intrusions into one's privacy.'[3] And he went on later to say, 'Whatever may be the justifications for other statutes regulating obscenity, we do not think they reach into the privacy of one's own home.'[4]

Here, then, we have an example of an argument that recognition of a right of personal and domestic privacy, at least as a right associated with that of free speech and free access to ideas and information, is necessarily hostile to an attempted legislative prohibition on the possession or use of obscene materials. It is perhaps worth noticing, too, that the Court was careful to distinguish this area of activity from that of possession of 'other items, such as narcotics, firearms or stolen goods' which in its view could legitimately be made criminal wherever and however privately such items might be kept.[5]

[1] 394 U.S. 557; 22 L.Ed. 2d 542.
[2] 394 U.S. 568; 22 L.Ed. 2d 551.
[3] 394 U.S. 564; 22 L.Ed. 2d 549.
[4] 394 U.S. 565; 22 L.Ed, 2d 549–50.
[5] 394 U.S. 568 fn. 11; 22 L.Ed. 2d 551 fn. 11.

In part, the significance of the ruling in *Stanley's* case is precisely the way in which appeal to a right of individual privacy was used in setting a limit to the extent to which anti-obscenity laws can be held constitutional. This decision departed significantly from the judgment in the case of *Roth* v. *United States* (1957),[6] when it was held that 'obscenity is not within the area of constitutionally protected speech or press'.[7] The point of distinction was that *Roth* and similar precedents all involved some form of publication, or public distribution or dissemination, of materials deemed objectionable. One ground adduced as showing the materiality of the distinction between those activities and mere private possession is of particular interest for the present purpose: 'public distribution . . . is subject to different objections [from private possession]. For example, there is always the danger that obscene material . . . might intrude upon the sensibilities or privacy of the general public.'[8]

In that sentence can be seen a version of the opposite argument about privacy in relation to obscenity: whereas the right to privacy has been advanced as a reason for striking down legislation penalizing the private possession of obscene articles, now the right of privacy is held to entail a right to protection from intrusion by publication of obscene materials. Thus, it appears, privacy may have a Janus-faced relevance to penalties for obscenity, striking them down in relation to a persons's private use and enjoyment of the obscene, backing them up in relation to a person's dissemination of obscenity to others.

It is not obvious and it may appear self-contradictory to argue in this way that the claim of privacy may pull in two conflicting directions in relation to obscenity laws, since plainly there is a difference between my having 'dirty' books or pictures for my own private use and my disseminating them to other people; the idea behind the argument is that it would be an intrusion into my privacy for the state to take action in the former case, whereas in the latter my foisting the materials in

[6] 354 U.S. 476; 1 L.Ed. 2d 1498.
[7] Ibid, 485; 1507.
[8] 394 U.S. 567; 22 L.Ed. 2d 551.

question on to others is itself an intrusion upon theirs. But even if there is no contradicition there is at least a tension between the two arguments, in that one who accepts both faces some problems of balancing. If my right of privacy involves a right to use and peruse materials of my own choosing, it is not (in this respect) worth much if I cannot lay hold of the kind of thing I like to peruse. But on the whole, I cannot get hold of it unless I can acquire it, and I cannot without difficulty acquire it unless someone is disseminating it. Again, if he is passing it to me by my desire and with my consent, the privacy-based objection to trading in obscene articles appears on the face of it to have little force. So if there is (and it remains to be seen whether there is) anything in either the argument for or the argument against anti-obscenity laws so far as they are based on the right of, or the value of, privacy, it appears that at some point a balance has to be struck between the rights of privacy protected by pro-hibitions on obscenity and the competing rights of privacy infringed by such prohibitions. It does not look like an easy task to strike such a balance.

The experience of the US Supreme Court, as evidenced quite recently in a series of decisions handed down in June 1973, confirms that it is not easy. For example, in *U.S.* v. *12 200ft. Reels, U.S.* v. *Orito*[9] the question was raised as to the constitutionality of Federal statutes prohibiting respectively the importation of, and the interstate transportation of, obscene materials. In each case it was argued that since a person has a constitutional right to private possession even of materials judged obscene, he must have an ancillary right to bring such materials into the USA for his own private use, or to transport them from state to state for the like purpose; if he has that right, legislation prohibiting importation or interstate transportation of such material, unless it is limited to the case of importation for commercial purposes, must be unconstitutional. In both cases, the majority of the Court, led by Burger, C. J., rejected the argument.

Here is a sample of the reasoning:

We are not disposed to extend the precise, carefully limited, holding of Stanley to permit importation of admittedly obscene materials

---

[9] 413 U.S. 123; 37 L.Ed. 2d 500 and 413 v.s. 139; 37 L.Ed. 2d 513.

simply because they are imported for private use only . . . We have already indicated that the protected right to possess obscene material in the privacy of one's home does not give rise to a a correlative right to have someone sell or give it to others *(U.S. v. Thirty Seven Photographs)* [10] . . . Nor is there any correlative right to transport obscene material in interstate commerce *(U.S. v. Orito)* [11] It follows that Stanley does not permit one to go abroad and bring such material into the country for private purposes. 'Stanley's emphasis was on the freedom of thought and mind in the privacy of the home. But a port of entry is not a traveller's home' *(U.S. v. Thirty Seven Photographs)*. [12]

In both cases, and indeed in the whole series of recent decisions there were strong dissents from Douglas, J., and Brennan, J., with the latter of whom Stewart and Marshall, J. J., joined. The following passage from the opinion of Douglas, J., in the *12 200 ft. Reels* case, is characteristically pungent: 'Finally, it is ironic to me that in this Nation many pages must be written and many hours spent to explain why a person who can read whatever he desires, *Stanley* v. *Georgia* . . . may not without violating the law carry that literature in his briefcase or bring it from abroad. Unless there is that ancillary right, one's Stanley rights could be realized, as has been suggested, only if one wrote or designed a tract in his attic and printed or processed it in his basement, so as to be able to read it in his study'. [13] The general line of the (conservative) majority of the Court in the recent decision has been to give a very limited ambit to the privacy-based right of possession of or access to obscene material, restricting it indeed to the 'privacy of the home' principle. In the case of *Paris Adult Theatre I* v. *Slaton* [14] the majority gave a ruling that the right of privacy did not extend so far as to confer a protected right on consenting adults to pursue their own choice in the matter of watching obscene and pornographic motion pictures within a theatre which was not open to minors and which gave patrons due notice of the kind of entertainment provided. Accordingly, state statutes of Georgia prohibiting and penalizing such exhibitions were not unconstitutional.

[10] 402 U.S. 363 at 376; 28 L.Ed. 2d 822.
[11] 413 U.S. at 142–4; 37 L.Ed. 2d at 517–19.
[12] 413 U.S. 128–9; 37 L.Ed. 2d 506.
[13] 413 U.S. 137; 37 L.Ed. 2d 511.
[14] 415 U.S. 49; 37 L.Ed. 2d 446.

In justifying his decision, Burger, C. J., quoted with approval from an article by Professor Bickel which again refers to the two-way pull of claims of privacy in relation to permission or prohibition of obscenity.

A man may be entitled to read an obscene book in his room, or expose himself indecently there . . . We should protect his privacy. But if he demands a right to obtain the books and pictures he wants in the market, and to foregather in public places—discreet, if you will, but accessible to all—with others who share his tastes, *then to grant him his right is to affect the world about the rest of us and to impinge on other privacies.* Even supposing that each of us can, if he wishes, effectively avert the eye and stop the ear (which in truth, we cannot), what is commonly read and seen and heard and done intrudes upon us all, want it or not.[15]

Finally, to illustrate that the opinions and concerns expressed in the foregoing are not purely transatlantic in origin or focus, one may point ot the report entitled *Pornography*, published by the 'Longford Committee'. On the one hand, the report notes as a possible 'evil' arising from anti-obscenity laws 'the invasion of privacy or an unjustifiable restriction of an individual's liberty of moral choice' and asserts that 'there would . . . seem to be weighty objections to any attempt to restrict by law what books an individual reads or pores over in privacy'. On the other hand, in the section on 'Conclusions and Recommendations', the committee avers that 'an important aspect of what we have called the "problems" of pornography [is] the overruling of choice or invasion of privacy where sexual display cannot be avoided'.[16]

The foregoing section confronts us with instances of two potentially conflicting, but not self-evidently contradictory arguments: that respect for the privacy of individuals is inconsistent with the existence of laws against obscenity, at least in certain respects; and that respect for the privacy of individuals is a justifying reason for the existence of laws against obscenity, at least in certain respects. Can either or both of these arguments withstand critical examination? That is the question for discussion in the rest of this chapter.

[15] 22 The Public Interest 25–6 (Winter 1971) (emphasis added by Burger, C. J., in citing quoted passage at 413 U.S. 59; 37 L.Ed. 2d 458).
[16] *Pornography: The Longford Report* (London, 1972).

I propose to begin by considering the second-mentioned argument, that laws against obscenity are protective of privacy. As to that, the view for which I shall argue is that there is at best a very loose and indirect connection between restricting obscene displays, publications, etc., and protecting privacy. (Whether there are other, and better arguments for maintaining, or for that matter strengthening, the law on obscene publications is a question which I shall not pursue in depth).

In the fairly recent past, a British philosopher might have been expected to deal with the question simply by demonstrating that the terms 'privacy' and 'obscenity' as they are used in common English speech (at least, in the speech of philosophers) are, in fact, used in different ways. From that demonstration, it would follow that the words have different meanings. If the words have different meanings, it follows that the right to privacy and the right to protection from obscene displays are different rights. As a matter of observation, I am inclined to think that the premise is true; but I doubt if it will bear the weight of the conclusion which depends upon it.

Even if it is true that ordinary English-speakers do not make any very close connection between privacy and obscenity, that cannot supply a sufficient argument to show that the moral or legal reformer is unjustified in seeking to exhibit important analogies and similarities between the areas covered by the two terms, and in the light of those to argue that the good reasons supporting a right of privacy are equally good as supporting a right to protection from obscenity. That established, he may if he chooses go on to argue that the concept of a 'right of privacy' should be recognized as including within it a subsidiary right to protection from obscene displays, literature, etc. If there were important analogies and similarities between the two areas, then there could surely be nothing objectionable in this extension or development of linguistic conventions. There is an obvious danger of moral as well as linguistic conservatism in excessive worship of common usage. It will not do, therefore, to rest one's whole argument in such a field as this merely on an attempt to elucidate common usage.

What is clear is that any attempt to justify protection from obscenity as an instance of protection of privacy depends essentially upon the thesis that the same values, the same reasons of principle, are the underlying justifications of each form of protection. If that thesis is unacceptable it would merely be a form of mischievous obfuscation to treat protection from obscenity as an element in the protection of privacy. The attempted redefinition of terms would result solely in the introduction of a gratuitous equivocation into any argument about either privacy or obscenity. I believe the thesis to be false and shall forthwith set out my reasons for believing it so.

Let me start by asking what we protect when we protect privacy. What kind of legal right would a legal right to privacy be? I have asked and answered the same question before, and so may be tolerably brief here.[17] Our right to privacy, in so far as it is what is sometimes called a 'claim-right', is essentially a right to non-intrusion. As such, it must be a right to non-intrusion in some respect which can be specified. My right to domestic privacy, for example, is a right that no one else shall intrude into my home or home life save by my invitation or permission. Such a right presupposes as correlative a duty incumbent on some other person or persons (indeed, in this case, all other persons) not to intrude upon me in the specified (or understood) way. To be rather exact about it, the right of privacy is a right which sustains a series of claims against a large, perhaps indefinite, group of other people all of whom owe me the duty not to intrude upon some aspect or aspects of my life and affairs.

To confer upon people legal protection of their privacy is, in effect, to invest in them certain rights against other people, and to impose upon other people correlative duties of non-intrusion in the affairs of the people protected. Either in a strict, or at least in a metaphorical, sense, privacy is always in some degree 'territorial'. That is to say, there is some sphere within which the individual is in the relevant sense protected from intrusion. The sphere in question may be some geographical area, such as his home or his office at work; or again, it may be the 'sphere' of his personal activities and interests which are protected from snooping or interference wherever he is. (It can be as much an invasion of privacy if a stranger in a train seeks to prise from one

[17] D. N. MacCormick 'A Note Upon Privacy', 89 LQR (1973) 23–7; 'Privacy: a Problem of Definition?' 1 *British Journal of Legal Studies* (1974) 75–8. But note also N. S. Marsh's rejoinder to the former, at 89 LQR 183.

detailed personal information, as if somebody tries to do so on one's own front doorstep).

'Intrusion' however is a wide concept. The burglar who ransacks my house, or the hoodlum who mugs me in the street, intrudes upon the security of my home, or, as the case may be, my person. In neither case, however, is the gist of his offence adequately captured by saying simply that he has invaded my privacy. To take something which belongs to me, or to injure me physically, albeit kinds of 'intrusion', are, I think, objectionable on other grounds than invading my privacy. To give an example, a burglar may break into my house and steal what he hopes is a valuable document; on leaving the house he discovers that it is nothing more than a personal diary which he has stolen, and in disgust he burns it without having scrutinized its contents at all. He is clearly guilty of theft, though I think not guilty of intruding upon my privacy as such. By contrast, a visitor to my house might perhaps take the opportunity of surreptitiously reading the contents of my private diary. Here there is neither theft, nor, at any rate in Scots law, any form of trespass. But there is, as most of us would say, a serious breach of personal privacy.

How then shall we account for these differences, and how shall we capture the notion of intrusion which is special to the case of privacy? The answer, as it appears to me, is that we must postulate the existence of a general human interest in being able for some purposes some of the time to 'keep oneself to oneself'. The basis of privacy is some kind of desire for seclusion. Taking our earlier concept of a 'sphere', we can say that within certain spheres at least some and probably all human beings desire to be able to seclude themselves. This desire for seclusion should not be construed in all cases as a desire to exclude all other human beings from one's life or some aspect of it; rather it is a desire to have the last say on which other human beings will be brought within the circle of one's seclusion for certain purposes. It has indeed been argued by some that the basis of a desire for privacy or a desire for seclusion is precisely that intimacy presupposes the possibility of seclusion.[18] I can make myself

---

[18] See C. Fried, *An Anatomy of Values* (1970), p. 139; also 77 L. J. Yale (1968) 475; and P. Stein and J. Shand, *Legal Values in Western Society* (Edinburgh, 1974) ch. 8, esp. pp. 192–3.

intimate with my friends or my wife or whomsoever, only given that I am granting to them some special privilege which is not shared by other people in general. Real relationships of love, friendship, and trust are created by the sharing of intimacy within areas of life which we do in fact ordinarily keep secluded from other people.

To the extent that any individual in respect of some area or aspect of his life takes steps to exclude all or most other people and/or demands that others concede him seclusion, to that extent we may say that he asserts *de facto* privacy. Plainly not all claims to *de facto* privacy are such as would be generally regarded as legitimate. A private meeting of the heads of Mafia families might be one which the 'public interest' would be best served by busting. But in the light of legal or moral norms it may be that some claims to *de facto* privacy are recognized as being legitimate claims. It is hard to imagine any viable system of positive morality within which no claims to privacy are recognized as legitimate, although it is easy to point to legal systems which do not grant a parallel legal right.

These reflections suggest that rights to privacy (in addition to entailing a series of claims against all other human beings), being claims against intrusion, also entail a 'normative power'[19] possessed by each individual, to waive his claims in respect to individuals chosen by him. These are to the extent of his permission admitted within his circle of intimacy in some particular matter or 'sphere'. That helps us to specify the particular forms of intrusion against which the right avails. It is that intrusion which consists in seeking to know about or to observe or to find out about an individual in those contexts in which he desires that knowledge about himself or observation of himself and his activities should be restricted either absolutely or to those alone to whom he himself reveals such knowledge, or whom he admits to watching him lounging in his armchair, or whatever.[20]

It seems to me likely that the matter of privacy is, in many ways, culturally relative. The spheres within which people

[19] For dicussion of the concept, see D. N. MacCormick and J. Raz, 'Voluntary Obligations and Normative Powers', in *Arist. Soc. Sup. Vol.* XLVI (1972) 59–102; also MacCormick, *H. L. A. Hart* (London, 1981), ch. 6.

[20] For the notion of privacy as involving control, see A. F. Westin, *Privacy and Freedom* (1967), e.g., p. 7.

actively desire self-seclusion, and the spheres within which a common social morality concedes the legitimacy of self-seclusion, may indeed vary greatly from time to time. What is more, there may be from time to time and from place to place wider or narrower ranges of desire for privacy or of the concession of the legitimacy of some aspect of privacy.

There seems indeed to be abundant evidence for some degree of cultural relativity in these matters. There is probably even very considerable difference between different social subgroups within a larger society. It may well be for example that desire for and respect of privacy are more keenly felt among certain segments of middle-class society in contemporary Britain than in other strata of society.[21] All that this would amount to saying, however, is that there are some crucial cultural variables within what is a quite general concept of privacy.

It seems on the face of it by no means unlikely that for any individual and for any society there will be some areas within which there is both a general desire for seclusion and a general concession of the reasonableness of such desire. There is so much which seems to depend on the possibility of seclusion that one is almost inevitably driven to this conclusion. I have mentioned earlier the notion that intimacy with some people presupposes a possibility of excluding all others. To that one may add the perhaps general desire in most people to 'be themselves' some of the time, as distinct from playing some public role, as they do, and desire to do, at other times. We all, it seems, have a need for some degree of autonomy, some degree of self-regulation, unimpeded and uninfluenced by the demands or judgments or even detached observation of other human beings.

I have suggested, and I can see reason to believe, that such desires are very generally felt by human beings. But the thesis that all people ought to have and to be recognized as having a right to privacy in at least some of the spheres in which privacy can be exercised is not dependent on empirical evidence as to how many people (if any) actively desire it at a given time in a given society. It is sufficient for the justification of that thesis that we should judge autonomy of this kind, together with the

[21] Cf. *Report of the Committee on Privacy* (1972), Cmnd. 5012, paras. 98–113.

possibility of 'power over intimacy' as being values important in themselves. There' is nothing wrong with conferring or recognizing human rights to things which not everyone (even not many people) wants; for, of course, to have a right is, normally, to have the option whether one exercises it or not. Those who don't want privacy are in no way inconvenienced by being given a right to it. If they don't want others to have privacy, the question is whether their wish in that matter is legitimate; at which point we come back to the value question, not to an empirical question. All this is true whether we have in mind the recognition of a moral right or the conferment of a legal right.

To that extent I think that there are grounds for arguing that (even if the desire for privacy were not entirely general) there would be good reason for conceding some degree of seclusion to every human being whatsoever, and for recognizing a right to such seclusion. There are doubtless many ways of making and arguing such points as these, and there is indeed a most voluminous literature exploring such arguments. I shall not take the argument any further here. To sum it all up: when a right of privacy in some respect or respects is granted or conceded to all individuals within the range of some normative system (legal or moral), the recognition or grant of that right creates a sphere of individual (or it may be of small group) autonomy. Within the sphere acknowledged, the individual (or the small group) has the right of choice, the right of admission or exclusion of observation or knowledge or 'joining in' by others. Some may value such autonomy more, others may value it less; but the value upon which privacy rests is, surely, the value of autonomy in shaping a personal, as distinct from a public, dimension of one's life. The wrong of intrusion is the wrong of infringing that aspect of an individual's autonomy contrary to his wish and without his permission.

If the argument presented above is acceptable, it follows that the right (if any) to be protected from obscenity can be subsumed under the right to protection from intrusion upon privacy only if there is some substantial and important sense in which the former protection can be seen as furthering the claim of autonomy in the way in which protection of privacy furthers it. To say the least, it would be hard to sustain that argument.

At any rate if one starts by considering the somewhat

tendentious legal definition of obscenity which characterizes it in terms of its tendency to produce effects (depraving and corrupting) which no clear evidence has shown that it does produce, the wrong done to an individual who is exposed to some obscene production does not seem in any way more analogous to the wrong of breach of privacy than is the already mentioned case of wronging a person either by stealing his property or assaulting his person. It may be said that to deprave and corrupt somebody is to deprive him of the possibility of making a good use of his autonomy; but to kill somebody or to assult him so seriously that he is hospitalized, is equally, or more, to deprive him of the capacity of using his autonomy, for ever or for some time. Equally if you steal my car, you deprive me of one place in which to have private conversations with my associates, but you do not *eo ipso* invade my privacy.

What is more, if one departs from the rather tendentious legal definition of obscenity, and if one considers the cognate notions of obscenity and indecency without regard to their alleged effects, one finds that their gist concerns the doing in public what ought not to be done in public if at all. There is probably a line to be drawn between sexual and sadistic obscenity and indecency. The former consists in making public display of things the public display of which is held to be objectionable though the private existence or practice of them is unobjectionable. Sadistic obscenity and indecency depict or display acts of violence and cruelty which ought not to be practised at all.

If the essence of obscenity and indecency is the public revelation, display, depiction, or description of such matters, there is on the face of it some oddity in subsuming such conduct within the rubric of intruding upon other people's privacy. It appears that those who indulge themselves in obscene displays or whatever are rather waiving their own privacy than impeding or intruding upon that of others. Indeed it seems as if that which is willingly done in public falls outside the sphere of any individual's privacy. We have noted earlier how the concept of privacy involves drawing a literal or metaphorical sphere around each individual person; within that sphere he has a choice whom, if anyone, to admit to intimacy with him. As with all concepts of seclusion or exclusion, the drawing of such lines of seclusion presupposes that there is something, as it were, on the other side of the line. What is not within the special power of any particular individual lies within the general domain in which all are free to take as much or as little interest as they choose without regard to the desires of others. I may be shocked, horrified, or titillated against my wishes by matters which other people choose to bring into the public arena. I may experience such shock, horror, or titillation as offences; but the offence is not the offence of intrusion into my sphere of privacy. What is more, so long as I have the right and the freedom to avert my gaze or go elsewhere, the offence is one which I can escape precisely by availing myself of my own privacy.

There is an objection to this line of argument which, if well founded, would be fatal to it. If people, as they go about their daily business in public places, are confronted on cinema hoardings or news-stands or wherever with materials which they find offensively obscene, is that not, from their point of view, a kind of 'intrusion' into their private consciousness, a thrusting-in of undesired images and thoughts? And if so, is this not then one form of invasion of privacy as contended by Professor Bickel in the passage cited above?[22]

The last thing which I would wish to deny is that people may well feel such a sense of offence as is here mentioned, perhaps even to the extent of finding their freedom to go about the public streets constrained and restricted, in that one has to choose whether to sustain serious offence or to keep away from certain parts of the town. But for my part, I cannot see this as a question of privacy, if only because at that rate almost every aspect of one's concern for one's environment would involve an element of concern for privacy. If a beautiful old Georgian terrace is torn down and a brutal concrete tower-block substituted for it, some people may be deeply offended by that, and may even feel obliged to stay away from the place rather than sustain the offence. Or if the garbage collection services were removed from part of the town, so that it became smelly and unhealthy, or if raw sewage were wantonly pumped into a beautiful river, such conditions would be very offensive to most of us.

But what all that shows is that we have a legitimate interest in a tasteful, salubrious, and healthy environment, not that our interest in it is the same as our interest in privacy, or an element

---

[22] This is indeed an objection to the present argument which has been most forcefully put to me by my colleague Professor Robert S. Summers.

in it. Even given the degree of figurativeness which I am willing to admit in the notion of 'intrusion' into a 'sphere' of privacy, I do think it would be stretching things to the point where the concept loses all its distinctive utility if we were to extend our conception of privacy to include all aspects of environmental offence. And if we don't include them all, I cannot see the rationale of including one, that of the offence provided by publicly displayed obscene articles. So I remain unconvinced by the objection.

It is sometimes said that obscene matter in television broadcasts and the like may amount to an invasion of privacy, in the case of a viewer who dislikes such matter, and does not wish it to be thrust into his home. The argument is a bad one, since one has a simple method of 'averting one's gaze', namely switching off. All the same points can be made as will shortly be made in relation to mail, but in a stronger form, since one has the option of not owning or possessing a TV receiver.

There is a different and interesting argument, that public-service broadcasting, supported from public funds (i.e. the BBC particularly) should not use the public's money to produce what the public doesn't want. 'I pay my licence fee in order to get programmes I like in my own house, not this rubbish.' Interesting and important arguments about democracy and accountability of public bodies arise here, and there are (at least) two sides to the argument. But it would be a blatant case of 'persuasive definition' for either side to claim support on the ground of the 'right to privacy'.

Indeed, in general terms, it appears to me that whatever offence there is in the areas of obscenity and indecency, it can only be characterized as offence against everyone in general and no one in particular (though this is subject to exceptions which will be considered). The analogies of obscenity and indecency are most clearly and closely to be found in such areas as breach of the peace, public nuisance, environmental pollution, and the like. Somebody who pollutes an estuary does not harm anybody in particular; he harms 'the public in general'. That may be a harm amply sufficient to justify prohibitions and penalties. But it would surely be a mistake to view the offence as an invasion of the right of any individual in particular. Public nuisance and private nuisance are plainly distinguishable.

In this respect one finds an entire distinction from the case of invasion of privacy. Although there may be good general utilitarian reasons why the privacy of each and every person should be respected, every manifestation of breach of privacy is breach of some specific individual's privacy. In so far as there are laws protecting privacy, and in so far as those laws are to the general good, the general good is secured by protecting individuals severally. By contrast, in the case of, say, environmental pollution, the general good is directly secured by prohibiting certain activities which are considered harmful to the community at large even though there may be no identifiable and specific harm to any specific person. At any rate identifiable and specific injury to a particular person is not essential to the offence. Students of jurisprudence will readily recognize here a tacit reference to John Austin's famous distinction between absolute and relative duties.[23] It is submitted that Austin made a perfectly valid point in drawing that distinction, whether or not each and every instance which he mentions as a case of the distinction is well conceived.

As has been conceded in advance, there are exceptions to the general point just made. The exceptions, however, on scrutiny rather support than weaken the case put. Let us suppose that a magazine publishes a photograph of a man and a woman in the act of sexual intercourse. Let us further suppose that the photograph has been obtained illicitly by the unknown and unpermitted use of a surveillance device in a private bedroom. The individuals whose photograph is displayed are plainly the victims of a breach of their privacy. There is nothing wrong with their activity; there is everything wrong with uninvited surveillance of it, and the wrong is compounded by the publication of the visual image. A similar case may be made out in relation to what may be called exploitative obscenity. If it is the case that severe economic or other pressures can be put upon actors and actresses or photographic models to secure that they unwillingly participate in public displays of an indecent or an obscene character, then, to the extent that their consent was not really free consent, they have suffered an infringement of their privacy. They have been forced into a position of making public that which they would not otherwise have wished to make public.

[23] See. J. Austin, *Lectures on Jurisprudence* (5th edn., ed. R. H. Campbell, London, 1885). lecture 17.

But in each case the element of intrusion is entirely separate from the element of obscenity or indecency. If we consider the case of persons who of their own free consent, without either duress or illicit observation, permit precisely such displays of themselves as those already considered, the resultant photographs may be indistinguishable from a visual point of view. If either set of pictures is obscene or offensive, both are, considered simply in themseles. In the former case there has been an offence against specific individuals as well as the postulated offence to people in general resulting from publication. In the latter case the element of offence to specific individuals is missing, but the public offensiveness of the display is neither greater nor less.

Another, at least arguable, exception is presented in rather different vein by the instance of delivery by mail of unsolicited obscene materials of an advertising or indeed of any other kind. To the extent that such materials are deposited in people's houses without their desire, consent, or invitation, that constitutes an intrusion on privacy. But non-obscene materials cascading through one's letter-box can be just as intrusive. The fact is that the existence of a postal service facilitates a minor form of intrusion into people's homes, to the extent that outsiders can pester them with materials which they do not wish to receive or see. Perhaps many people strongly dislike obscene materials. But it is specifically the undesired rather than the obscene quality of the mail which makes it intrusive. (Consider the converse case of the person who likes and hopes to get unsolicited obscene material but who can't stand political pamphlets).

It seems to follow from what has been said that offensive obscenity and offensive intrusions on privacy are entirely different categories and types of wrong, except for the areas of overlap in which the production of obscene materials may involve intrusion in other people's private affairs either without their consent or at least without their free and willing consent. It seems therefore that it must be wrong to treat any case of obscenity as such (apart from the issue of the means of obtaining obscene material) as being a wrong (if wrong at all) of a similar kind to breach of privacy.

There is perhaps one line of argument which might be advanced as supporting some degree of connection between respect for privacy and repression of obscenity, at any rate by way of obscene publications or public displays. It might be said that the essence of obscenity lies in some gross breach of those standards of decency or modesty which are held in a given society or social group. No doubt such standards are variable, and do vary, from place to place and from time to time, and no doubt legal moralists are much too prone to considering that for even large and complex societies it is possible to find or to prescribe some single set of common standards of modesty and decency. But having expressed all due reservations, it seems true as a matter of common observation that some standards of decency and modesty in sexual and other matters are observed in almost all groups, and that their being observed is thought important. Whatever may be the justification of such standards and conventions, there too is to be found whatever justification there may be for prohibitions on obscene displays and publications (therein, too, if anywhere, is to be found a workable definition of obscenity, if definition be desired). But has all that anything to do with privacy?

Very tentatively, I should suggest that there may be some connection between respect for such standards and respect for privacy. Given that standards of modesty are indeed change-able and changing, and that they may be more or less extensive, rather as clothing may be longer or shorter according to fashions of different times, it might be argued that recognition of and respect for duties of modesty can lend support to individuals' claims for privacy. If there is some range of emotions, activities, etc., which one is expected not to disclose or display in public, those who do wish to keep themselves to themselves in such matters may have an easier task in asserting their right to do so than they would in a society in which more or less 'anything goes'. There may at least be some concomitance in attitudes as between an attitude of respect for people's privacy and an attitude of respect for norms of decency and modesty in sexual and other matters. And it may be that respect for modesty and decency requires the support of some kind of legal regulation of the obscene. But, as is obvious, the connection here with privacy is at best tenuous, and is in any event only tentatively suggested. It seems that a sound justification of anti-obscenity laws will need to be based on stronger and more directly apposite grounds than this somewhat tenuous link between attitudes of respect for privacy and attitudes of hostility to obscenity, indecency, and immodesty.

Among the reasons for adopting a cautious and tentative view of this last-mentioned argument is the rather obvious consideration that the preceding discussion led to the conclusion that it is a form of individual autonomy which is the basic underlying value essentially involved in recognition of a right of privacy. The freedom to be oneself, to choose one's intimates, and to choose how far, if at all, certain aspects of one's thoughts and activities and way of life in general should be opened to others, is the core of liberty which the right of privacy protects at the perimeter. But if that is so, any legal or moral restrictions upon one's choice to keep things to oneself or impart them to others is a restriction which conflicts with the underlying principles on which recognition of a right to privacy is founded. There may be independent and forceful reasons for requiring people to keep private matters—or indeed private parts—private, but I cannot believe that such requirements can be founded on the same principles as those which may move us to recognize or to assert a right of privacy. The protection of privacy is essentially an aspect of the protection of individual freedom of choice, of choice what kind of person to be. The discouragement or restriction or prohibition of obscenity is a limitation on freedom of choice, limiting in some areas one's choice as to the kinds of things one does, whether or not one sees them as expressing the kind of person one wants to be. Such restrictions cannot therefore be credibly justified on grounds of protecting privacy, whatever other grounds may be advanced in support of them.

And so we are back to the considerations which moved the Supreme Court in *Stanley* v. *Georgia*. For by contrast with the attempt to use the value of privacy as a support for anti-obscenity laws, an attempt which must fail, the assertion that protection of privacy involved protection from such laws is vindicated by the considerations most recently advanced. The kind of respect for individual autonomy which is manifested in recognition of individual rights of privacy, demands as a minimum the degree of freedom from supervision or restriction upon one's private reading, viewing and acting which the Supreme Court held to be constitutionally entrenched in *Stanley's* case, Whatever else one may doubt, one can surely entertain no doubt that state or other public regulation of the contents of an individual's personal library or his collection of pictures, films, or records and the like would be fundamentally inconsistent with recognition of any worthwhile right of individual privacy. Here, surely, we find an uncomplicated instance of John Stuart Mill's conception of self-regarding acts and activities in relation to which public regulation of individual taste would be wholly contrary to quite fundamental rights of freedom and autonomy.

It is not clear that any ground of principle worth serious consideration can be advanced against extension of such a claim based on privacy to cover the case of one's personal and private possessions wherever one may for the moment have them, whether in one's brief-case on a train, in a car on a journey, or packed in a removal lorry or a freight-carrying plane. The limits recently set by the US Supreme Court restricting the *Stanley* ruling to the narrow ambit of the 'privacy of the home' cannot, it is submitted, be upheld on any substantial grounds of principle (unless, perhaps, by reference to what Professor Gordon has elegantly styled the principle of disfacilitation:[24] to accept the argument, 'I was shipping these films solely for my own use', even when it is true, is to establish too easy a loophole for the commercial distributor of things which it is held undesirable and unlawful to distribute commercially).

How much further can the argument from privacy be pressed as an objection to anti-obscenity laws? That I should be free to peruse what I choose in the privacy of my own room may not avail me much if the choice available in published form is restricted, say, to uplifting works on Marxism or religion, and on science and mathematics. At this point, the argument should perhaps be viewed in Rawlsian terms as concerning rather the worth of liberty than the existence of liberty; or, rather, to re-express his point in directly relevant terms, the worth rather than the recognition of the right of privacy. If we look at the matter first from the point of view of the consumer (so to speak)

---

[24] G. H. Gordon, *The Criminal Law of Scotland* (Edinburgh, 1967), pp. 218–20.

of literature, painting, photography, drama, and all the rest of it, we can with reason say that whatever is a good reason for recognizing such a right is *a fortiori* a good reason for maximizing its worth. If there are good reasons, as has been contended, for recognizing a right of privacy in such matters as those under consideration, there are equally good reasons for extending to the maximum possible range the modes and manners in which, and the subject-matters on which, the right may be exercised; for that is to maximize its worth.

One of the practical ways in which the worth of such a right of privacy can be diminished is by restricting the publication of works of whatever kind people may wish to acquire. So from the consumer's point of view the right of privacy, and its underlying value of autonomy, are at least diminished in worth to the extent that the law imposes restrictions on the production and distribution or exhibition of whatever kind on grounds of their objectionable content. But what of the producer or distributor? The act of producing or creating any literary or artistic production, however limited in aesthetic merit it may be, is always (or, at the very least, and in dubious cases, may always be claimed to be) an act expressive of the personality of the individual creator. A concern for individual autonomy can be extended to the protection of the rights of the creator here too, as part of or analogous to his basic right of privacy. Private communication or display of such productions among the circle of one's intimates can be no less included within the realm of privacy.

But do these rights extend to cover distribution in an open market? Here, I think, the answer must be negative. The mere fact that an act is an act of a private citizen does not make it a private act. The right to draw or write or take photographs howsoever one wishes to do in private, and the right to communication of one's creation to chosen individuals of one's own acquaintance are both rights which belong within the wider ambit of a right of individual privacy. They are different in substance from an asserted right to address oneself openly and generally to the public at large, or to vend one's productions in an open market to people in general.

To say that freedom of public debate, discussion, and display is different from, and raises different issues from, the freedoms

entailed by rights to privacy, is not to accord them less importance. The right to public speech is indeed no less vital than the
right to private thought. But it is different, and it rests upon
different considerations, and may be opposed by different
countervailing considerations. The problem of public order and
disorder is posed here as it is not directly posed by private
activities. And here, by parity of reasoning, the question of the
legitimacy of the laying down of norms and standards of public
decency must be confronted, and (apart from the question of
the worth of the consumer's right of privacy) it does not seem
possible to set up the right of individual privacy as a directly
relevant counter to the claim of public decency, whatever it is
worth.

This is not the place to pursue that point much further. The
arguments in favour of the greatest possible freedom of public
speech, discussion, and debate are too well known to require
further rehearsal here. Whether one looks at the matter from
the point of view of a general interest in the furtherance by free
discussion of truth in all its manifestations, or from the point of
view of the individual's freedom and dignity as a participant in
the processes of a free society, the setting of limits on freedom of
speech and expression must always be subject to the most
stringent scrutiny, and there is a formidable onus to be borne in
justifying such limits. However, there may still be a greater
range of legitimate limitations on public than on private conduct.

For myself, I am far from convinced that prohibitions on
publication of material based solely on the ground of their
breach or flagration of canons of decency do constitute legitimate limitations (save in so far as particular publications are
directly invasive of the rights of determinate individuals,
including rights of privacy in the exceptional cases discussed
above where they are so invaded). But I would suggest at least
this: that such restrictions on public conduct would be at least
in some degree less difficult to justify if they were drawn in such
a way as to secure a clear protection for genuinely private
activities in the sense of activities private to voluntary partici-
pants and not obtrusive to the view of those having no wish to
join in. If a majority favours the legal maintenance of given
canons of public decency, it does not follow automatically that

the majority is justified in so doing. But at least one of the obvious objections is met if the majority concedes clear rights of privacy to minorities who do not share or respect the same canons of decency. I strongly doubt whether either the Scots or the English laws on obscenity or obscene publications do achieve any such balance, in the way of a full recognition of rights of privacy in such matters. It seems clear that the current majority of the US Supreme Court does not do so either.

But that is not the issue which this paper set out to consider, and on the issue proposed the argument may now be drawn to a conclusion. Privacy and obscenity are indeed mutually relevant topics, but in a more restricted sense than is sometimes supposed. It is certainly true that recognition of a right of individual privacy is inconsistent with certain forms of restriction on the possession, use or private enjoyment or circulation of materials deemed obscene. Considerations of the worth of such a right tell against the legitimacy of restraints on publication or distribution of such materials, as do other arguments concerning the importance of securing the freedom of public speech and expression by private individuals. But the right of privacy cannot itself be set up in direct opposition to prohibitions on obscene publications or public displays or performances. The drawing of a clear and justified distinction between public and private activity, in so far as it genuinely secures a generously defined right of privacy may indeed remove one common and strong objection to legislation on obscene publications and cognate subjects. Whether there are, and what might be, the positive justifications of such legislation, has not been here considered; but it has been demonstrated that, contrary to a widely and influentially held opinion, obscene publications cannot, save in special and exceptional cases, be attacked on the ground that they themselves are intrusive upon privacy or rights thereto.

10.
VOLUNTARY OBLIGATIONS

I. INTRODUCTION

CIVIL lawyers at least since the time of Gaius have been in the habit of taking 'the law of obligations' as a separate branch of study; within obligations, the practice of distinguishing 'voluntary obligations' from what Lord Stair called 'obediental obligations'[1] is also fairly venerable. Voluntary obligations are of course those which arise from contracts and promises, obediental include, e.g., those whose incidence is determined by the law of delict. The point of the distinction is clear enough; I can choose whether or not to buy your house, and only if I choose to do so will I incur an obligation to pay you the price. If on the other hand I wilfully burn your house down, I am in breach of a duty which applies to me whether I like it or not; and the existence of my consequential obligation to compensate you is equally independent of my choice. In the seventeenth century, at least, legal theorists such as Grotius, Pufendorf, and Stair treated it as a very significant question to inquire into the nature and basis of voluntary obligation—how can the will obligate itself? Sometimes such disputes had significant practical results. For example, according to Grotius, it is of the essence of promises that they cannot bind without acceptance, whereas Stair took the opposite view. Grotius's view prevailed in most continental systems, but in relation for example to the rights of third parties under contracts, Stair's view is the basis of the modern Scots law.

It might be thought, however, that speculation as to the nature of voluntary obligation is essentially a misconceived activity, especially when it is supposed to yield solutions to practical legal problems. To common lawyers, there must appear to be a certain futility in the efforts of French doctrinal

---

[1] *Institutions of the Law of Scotland* (ed. D. M. Walker, Edinburgh, 1981) I. i. 19. Cf. ch. 4 above.

writers to settle the question of when a contract made by postal correspondence is to be deemed complete—whether on declaration of acceptance, posting of it, delivery to the offeror's address, or actual scrutiny of it by him. Such problems are not to be solved by theorizing as to the true nature of *accord de volonté*, but by laying down more or less arbitrary rules.

The point of the objection could be put thus: in law, contractual and other 'voluntary' obligations presuppose the existence of power-conferring rules.[2] Because, and only because, certain rules exist in virtue of which persons may by performing certain actions place themselves under obligations to perform further acts specified by themselves, it therefore follows that performance of the rule-defined actions 'generates' valid legal obligations. Thus English law contains a rule by virtue of which persons who sign, seal, and deliver a certain sort of document called 'a deed' thereby incur a duty to perform the acts specified in the document. There would be no point in dedicating ourselves to a study of 'deeds' as such, or of the acts of will or other mental states of parties who execute deeds, with a view to discovering what it is in their intrinsic nature which explains why they generate obligations. The only answer to that question 'why?' is to point to the power-conferring rule. A serious question which *might* then be raised would be to ask for the justification of that power-conferring rule; but the answer to that should be in terms of the general expediency of providing 'facilities' (Professor Hart's term) of this sort.

It need scarcely be added that this legal–philosophical thesis is neatly paralleled currently both in moral philosophy and in the philosophy of language. Promising, it is said, can be analysed as a speech act in an intelligible way only if it is observed that particular promissory utterances essentially 'count as' promises only because they are intended to be and are recognized as instances of a social 'practice', or 'institution'. The act presupposes the practice; the practice is rule-defined in that widely recognized social rules exist under which if any person S says to another A 'I promise that I shall ϕ' it becomes obligatory upon S to ϕ, unless he can point to some defeasing or excusing circumstance which either exceptionally negates the

---

[2] Cf. H. L. A. Hart, *The Concept of Law* (Oxford, 1961), pp. 42–3, and see MacCormick, *J. L. A. Hart* (London, 1981), ch. 6.

existence of the promise or excuses him from his obligation under it. The conditions of defeasance or excuse are themselves defined by existing social rules, which are no doubt constantly evolving and being further refined and developed by the usages of persons in society.

Thus if anyone were so misguided as to ask *why* promises generate obligations, the answer must be, 'because the rules of the practice are such that the serious utterance of certain sentences has a specified illocutionary force and therefore counts as incurring an obligation'. Then it becomes clear that what has to be morally justified is the existence of the practice, not the judgment that performance of this or that promise is prima facie obligatory. Utilitarian arguments may well be advanced at this stage, and John Rawls once indeed suggested that this might rescue utilitarianism from certain of the traditional objections to it.[3] The practice as a whole can be justified on grounds of utility, but the rightness and wrongness of particular acts of promise-keeping and promise-breaking are to be judged by reference to the rules of the practice, not by immediate considerations of utility. The utility of the practice in this view presupposes the existence of the rules which constitute it.

So the overall picture appears to very neat and tidy. The law of voluntary obligations confers upon people a power to create legally enforceable obligations by making promises which satisfy certain formal and/or substantial conditions laid down in the law. The concept of 'promising', which the law rather takes for granted than defines, is itself to be explained in terms of a logically prior social practice whose constitutive rules confer on people a normative power to perform certain speech acts which 'count as' promises and which give rise to obligations upon the people who perform such speech acts.

Neat though the picture is, I find it quite unconvincing. My object in this paper is to show that it is indeed unconvincing because it is wrong. It is quite unnecessary in the explanation of promising and of the obligation to keep promises to invoke the concept of a power-conferring rule enshrined in a social practice as a necessary condition of the possibility of promising. If, on the other hand, it is necessary in analysing the law of voluntary

---

[3] See J. Rawls, 'Two Concepts of Rules', 64 *Philos. Rev.* (1955) 3–32.

obligations to make reference to normative powers (i.e. powers conferred by rules), that is a consequence not of the nature of promising but of the legal enforceability of those promises which constitute legal contracts.

II. PROMISES AND RELIANCE

To take the first of these assertions first, promising as a speech act will here be explained in its simplest form as an utterance of the speaker's about his own future conduct which is characterized by the speaker's intending his addressee to take it as being intended to induce the addressee to rely upon the speaker's taking the action in question. The relevant concept of 'reliance; does not itself presuppose the existence of rules under which the addressee is entitled to rely on the promisor's keeping his word. And the fact of the addressee's reliance on the promisor is sufficient ground for asserting that the promisor has an obligation to keep his word.

If these propositions are well founded, then promises *need not* be represented as instances of the exercise of normative powers conferred by rules. But of course it will still be *possible* to represent them in terms of a power-conferring rule, thus: 'A person having the following characteristics [age, soundness of mind] may by the following acts . . . "make a promise"; anyone who so makes a promise has an obligation to perform the acts mentioned in his promise.' But, so far from being the only terms in which 'promise-making' and 'promissory obligation' are explicable, that rule is itself explicable in terms of the existence of good reasons why promise-breaking should be regarded as wrongful, given the essential nature of the activity of promising.

It will be helpful to make clear the point of this suggestion by drawing a contrast with two other speech acts which are also 'acts-in-the-law'. In some legal systems, a man can divorce his wife simply by the act of saying 'I divorce thee, I divorce thee'.[4] In the laws of the UK an auctioneer who declares the subjects of the auction 'sold to Mr So-and-So', thereby effects the sale. But the concept 'divorce' can only have meaning, and an act can only count as 'divorcing', if there exists a legally defined status

---

[4] Cf. *Qureshi* v. *Qureshi* [1971] 2 All ER 325, [1972] Fam. 173.

of marriage whose commencement is effected by certain legally defined acts, whose continuance entails the applicability of numerous laws granting privileges, imposing duties, creating powers, and so forth, and whose termination is likewise regulated by the law. So, too, the concept 'sale', implying as it does the passing of ownership from one person to another, presupposes a concept of 'ownership' which can be accounted for only in terms of laws, that is, investitive, constitutive, and divestitive laws, as Dr Raz has pointed out,[5] following Bentham. Thus the utterances 'I divorce thee' and 'Sold to Mr So-and-So' are incomprehensible save in the context of such laws of status and of property. And they can take effect as they are intended to only if the particular legal system in question does actually confer the appropriate power. Does the system recognize *talaq* divorce? Does it recognize ownership, and does it recognize a principle of agency such that an auctioneer can validly sell goods on behalf of this owner? If so, these speech acts can be felicitously performed as meaningful acts-in-the-law, and if not, not.

A full analysis of the *talaq* divorce or the auction sale as speech acts would therefore necessarily include an intention on the speaker's part to be taken as invoking such laws. The clear-headed husband or auctioneer addressing a comprehending audience intends it to be recognized that his utterance is intended to take effect as 'a divorce' or 'a sale'; the addressee of the act is clearly aware that the act is done with that intention, and that he is intended to recognize that intention, and so on. Necessarily, the act is performed and understood in the light of 'secondary' social and legal rules.

From such acts promising can be radically differentiated. It is not necessary to suppose that promisors either intend to invoke, or to be taken as invoking, any particular moral, social, or legal rules in making promises. Contrary to John Searle's view,[6] promises can be shown to be speech acts explicable in terms of an intention to bring about a specific perlocutionary effect, and an intention that that intention be recognized. Searle's summary dismissal of the possibility of such an explanation is unconvincing: 'There is no perlocutionary effect of . . .

[5] J. Raz, *The Concept of a Legal System* (2nd edn., Oxford, 1980), pp. 175–83
[6] J. Searle, *Speech Acts* (Cambridge, 1979), esp. pp. 33–72, 175–88.

promising which will distinguish promises from firm statements of intention and emphatic predictions. All three tend to create expectations in the hearer about the future, but "I promise" does not mean "I predict" or "I intend."[7] The tacit supposition that 'creating expectation' is the only conceivable such effect which might be adduced in explanation of promises is a false supposition; so that argument doesn't amount to much. There is an alternative which will both satisfactorily serve to explain promising and clearly distinguish it from predicting, etc., namely that promises do, and are calculated to, induce their addresses to rely upon future performance by the promisor. This involves more than merely creating expectation. If A believes that B intends to take some course of action, or to refrain from taking some action, and if A then himself acts (or refrains from acting) in a manner which is, or is likely to be, detrimental or at least unprofitable to himself unless B acts as A believes he will, then A may justly be said to have acted 'in reliance' on B. So reliance involves not merely having expectations about others' conduct, but basing one's own conduct on such expectations, as when a host takes trouble and expense in preparing dinner for an expected guest, or when a man deliberately refrains from catching a train because his neighbour will give him a lift to work. 'Inducing reliance' means intentionally or knowingly inducing a person to base his conduct on expectations about one's own.

This concept of reliance can be well illustrated by references to the law, for example, to the English case of *Inwards* v. *Baker*.[8] In 1931 young Mr Baker was contemplating buying land to build a house, but the site he had in mind proved too expensive. His father ('old Baker') said to him, 'Why not put the bungalow on my land and make the bungalow a little bigger?' So young Baker set about doing this, with his father's help and encouragement; in 1933 he completed his bungalow, and there he resided until his father's death in 1951. After his death, the plaintiffs who were trustees of his will (old Baker's mistress and her two daughters) permitted him to continue in residence until

---

[7] Ibid., p. 46.

[8] [1965] 2 QB 29. Since the decision in this case, whose facts well fit my present purpose, the courts have further developed the equitable doctrine of proprietary estoppel. See *Crabb* v. *Arun District Council* [1976] 179. I am indebted to Mr R. Austin of Sydney University for advice on this and related points.

1963 when they instituted proceedings for possession of the house. They lost their action. The grounds for the Court of Appeal's decision in young Baker's favour were:

(1) young Baker had put himself to trouble and expense in building the house because he believed that his father would let him stay there as long as he wished

(2) that belief was actively encouraged by his father, who knowing that such was his belief stood by and let him go ahead with the building

(3) generally, if any person has encouraged, or knowingly acquiesced in, another's acting irrevocably to his detriment in reliance upon expectations as to the former's future conduct which the former has knowingly or intentionally induced in him, then the court must restrain the former from going back upon the understanding (or provide some other sufficient remedy)

(4) the principle applied equally to the trustees of the will as successors in title to the land.

To non-lawyers, this no doubt seems a rather roundabout way of doing obvious justice; but the reason why the round-about route was chosen is most instructive. The arrangement made between old and young Baker was not such as to imply any agreement to transfer any legal estate recognized by the English law of property which the court could enforce by directing that the appropriate estate be vested in young Baker. Precisely because the powers of transferring ownership created by property law had not been invoked by the parties, they could not be invoked by the court. It followed that the son's position could be protected only under the principle of 'proprietary estoppel'—you may not go back on an arrangement to let someone occupy your land if you have stood by and let him spend money on it in the belief, encouraged by you, that you will let him stay there.[9]

Another type of case relates to action in reliance upon representations of present fact rather than of future conduct. The old case of *Neville* v. *Wilkinson*[10] arose out of negotiations for the marriage of the young and aristocratic but profligate Mr Neville

---

[9] Under the doctrine of *Crabb's* case (see n. 8) the court may provide an appropriate remedy to do substantial justice in an individual case.

[10] (1788) 1 Bro. CC 543.

to the daughter of a rich merchant. Before he would consent to the marriage, the merchant insisted upon seeing a statement of all Mr Neville's debts. The latter's agent, Mr Wilkinson, prepared a statement showing that Mr Neville owed the sum of £18,000, but deliberately excluded from the total the further sum of £8,000 owing to himself. The merchant paid all those debts, and the marriage went ahead, whereupon Mr Wilkinson, confident that he had secured his debtor's means, proceeded to sue him for the sum owing to him. It was held that he was 'estopped', that is precluded, from giving the lie to his earlier statement, since the parties had acted in reliance upon its truth, as he had intended and foreseen that they would.

Be it noted that these legal doctrines do not depend upon any concept of intent to incur a legal obligation. Whether or not the parties intended to act with reference to legal rules under which they might incur obligations towards other parties who acted in reliance upon their words is a perfectly indifferent question at law. What matters is whether one side did in fact rely upon the other's representations about future conduct or present fact; and whether that other intended that they should or knew that they would. Sometimes it is even the case that persons make statements hoping to evade rather than incur obligations, as when a contract requires in law to be reduced into writing, and *A* falsely assures *B* that it has been so written; *B* performs his part, then *A* tries to plead as against *B* that the contract cannot be enforced for want of writing; but *A* is estopped from giving the lie to his earlier assurance, upon which *B* has acted. Here *A* neither intended to incur an obligation nor to be taken as incurring an obligation; he intended to evade an obligation, and he intended *B* to take it that he already fulfilled an obligation. But at all events he intended that *B* should act irrevocably in reliance on his assurance, and that will suffice to debar him from now taking advantage of *B* by pleading the lack of writing as a defence.[11]

In all these situations there are two elements: (1) the fact that one person has taken detrimental action in the belief either that

---

[11] A partially relevant example is that of *Wakeham* v. *Mackenzie* [1968] 2 All ER 783, though the actual decision in that case turned on the doctrine of 'part performance'. The fundamental principles of that doctrine and of 'proprietary estoppel' seem to me the same.

another will take certain action in the future or that present assurances of the other are true, that is the fact of reliance; and (2), the fact that the speaker *intended* the other to rely upon him, or, we may add with equal force, *knew* or *thought it likely* that he would so rely. I hope we can quickly agree that the first of these, the bare fact of reliance, is ordinarily quite indifferent morally, as it is and should be legally. A student applies for admission to a university because he wishes to do research with Dr Jekyll. Dr Jekyll does not know that this is the reason for the student's application, and after recommending its acceptance he himself takes up a post at a different university before the student comes into residence. The student did in fact act in reliance on Dr Jekyll's staying put, but Dr Jekyll neither encouraged him to do so nor knew he had done so. He has therefore no obligation to avoid disappointing him. It would have made all the difference if Dr Jekyll had intentionally or knowingly induced the student to act in reliance on him. A further illustration will show why that makes so great a difference.

Suppose that Jones has been swimming from a beach at the foot of a cliff on a stormy day. He has failed to notice the speed with which the tide is rising, and is now in such a position that a desperate dash along the beach will perhaps enable him to reach the path up to safety before he is cut off by the tide. Macdonald happens just then to be strolling along the cliff-top carrying a few hundred feet of stout climbing-rope. He spots Jones's predicament and lowers the rope down the cliff-face to him. Jones sees what he is doing and waits for the rope to reach himself, thus losing time so that he can no longer conceivably reach the path before the tide comes in. He then starts to climb the rope.

These facts entitle us to infer in relation to Macdonald's state of mind:

either (1) He intended Jones to climb up the rope, and intended Jones to recognize that he intended him to climb up the rope in reliance upon Macdonald's holding it till he reached the top.

or (2) He knew or thought it likely that Jones would suppose that Macdonald intended him to climb up the rope in the belief that Macdonald would hold on till he reached the top.

Even if Macdonald could, in very exceptional circumstances, satisfy us that he acted without adverting to the possibility of Jones's making such suppositions, we should be justified in saying:

(3) Macdonald ought to have realized that Jones would make the supposition mentioned in (2) above.

From the moment at which it ceased to be possible for Jones to reach safety by running, because he had waited for Macdonald's rope to reach him, as Macdonald intended he should or knew he would, we can surely say that it would be wrong for Macdonald to abandon the enterprise, drop the rope, and go away—it would be wrong even if he could do equal good, save another person, even two other persons, by going and rescuing them from some other predicament. Jones has acted in a way which is now irrevocable, and which will be greatly detrimental to him unless Macdonald holds on to the rope till Jones has climbed up. Jones so acted because Macdonald intended him to take it that Macdonald intended him so to act (or knew that he would). Macdonald therefore has an obligation to hold on to the rope till Jones reaches the top.

Why do we say that Macdonald has this obligation? Need we suppose that he belongs to a society which recognizes some practice or institution according to which persons have a power, by throwing ropes over cliffs, and suchlike acts, to incur obligations? What if in that society it is accepted that nobody is ever deemed to have made a promise unless he uses the explicit performative formula 'I promise to ϕ ', rather as in republican Rome stipulations could (according to one widely held view) only be made by the promisor's replying '*spondeo*' to the stipulator's question '*spondesne* . . .?' I venture to think not. Is it not sufficient that we should assert and accept the following principle: if one person acts in a potentially detrimental way in reliance upon beliefs about another's future conduct, and if the latter person has by some act of his intentionally or knowingly induced the former to rely upon him, then the latter has an obligation not to act in a manner which will disappoint the other's reliance.

The use of the word 'obligation' in that principle signifies the force and function which the principle is conceived to have.

That is to say (following but perhaps modifying Professor Hart[12]), it is a principle breach of which will justify serious criticism, as wrongdoing not mere solecism, and which involves the existence of morally significant relationships between persons.

Since it has often been suggested that promissory obligations are inexplicable in utilitarian terms, it is worth while to point out, briefly, that the principle mentioned is certainly justifiable in utilitarian terms, at least in terms of negative utilitarianism. If there is a general obligation not to cause preventable harm to others, it must presumably be taken to imply an obligation not to cause harm by two successive and mutually related acts. Contemplate the Jones and Macdonald case in that light: Jones could perhaps have got to safety if Macdonald had not thrown down the rope, and if Jones had not delayed himself in waiting to catch it. If Jones is now killed, by drowning because Macdonald lets go before he starts to climb, or by falling if Macdonald lets go later, his death will be a direct consequence of his having taken Macdonald's first act of lowering the rope down the cliff as Macdonald either intended him to take it or knew he would take it. By the two acts: first, of inducing reliance intentionally or knowingly; second, of letting go the rope; Macdonald can do Jones harm which he would not have done by any one act. Jones's death by Macdonald's second act will only become possible if the first act has the consequences in relation to Jones's action which it was intended to have or thought likely to produce. *Mutatis mutandis* the act of breaking a promise causes one's earlier act of promising to have harmful consequences which were foreseeable at the moment the promise was made, given that the promise was intended to be taken by the promisee as giving him grounds to act in reliance upon the promisor's promised performance.

Even if it so happened that when Jones was half-way up the rope, Macdonald spotted someone else whose life was in danger, and whom he could also rescue, the general negative utilitarian principle which I mentioned shows that it would be wrong for him to let go the rope and rush off to save the other life. Though the good he can do Jones and the other is at this

12 Hart, *Concept of Law*, pp. 84–8; MacCormick, *Hart*, ch. 5.

moment equal, Jones will suffer harm as a direct and readily foreseeable result of Macdonald's series of acts; but the harm which the other will suffer is not a morally significant consequence of Macdonald's actions. It is not morally significant, because he did not, when he started to rescue Jones, know of the other's plight; so he could not forsee that his so doing would prevent him going to the rescue of another in equal or greater danger.

So, too, in a situation of promising. You invite me to dinner with you on Tuesday night, explaining that your nephew, who wishes to meet me, will be asked also. I accept, and you then make arrangements with your nephew for him to come too. If I subsequently decide to go somewhere else on Tuesday night, the inconvenience and disappointment which you and your nephew suffer is directly caused by my two acts, of accepting the invitation in the first place and of subsequently failing or refusing to come. If, conversely, you make an arrangement with your nephew for dinner on Tuesday in the hope that I can come, then telephone inviting me, whereupon I refuse the invitation, both of you may be disappointed and inconvenienced. But I cannot here be blamed for disappointing an expectation which was brought about by no act of mine.

It is thus reasonable to claim that a negative utilitarian principle can justify the principle that we must not so act as to disappoint the reliance of others when we have intentionally or knowingly induced them to rely upon us. What has been assumed rather than demonstrated so far is that the case of promising itself falls under that second principle of not disappointing reliance. But that is easy enough to show. I propose the following partial definition:

The utterance 'I shall ϕ '[13] addressed by S to A is a promise to ϕ at least if:

either (1) S intended A to take it as signifying that S intended to ϕ and intended A to rely upon S ϕ *-ing*, by making plans or taking actions in the expectation that S will ϕ

or (2) S knew or thought it likely that A would take it as

[13] Or any other utterance expressly or implicitly referring to the future conduct of the speaker.

signifying that S intended A to rely upon S ϕ -*ing*, in the sense mentioned in (1).

In order that the promise should be successfully made, it is essential that A should realize that S intends him so to take his utterance 'I shall ϕ '. It is not essential to the constitution of the promise that A should subsequently take any irrevocable action in reliance upon it. So soon as an utterance is made by a speaker intending knowing or thinking it likely that his addressee will understand it in the manner mentioned, and provided the latter does so understand it, a promise has been made. The extent to which the addressee then acts, by making plans or proceeding to overt acts or omissions, relates not to the existence of the promise but to the seriousness of breaches of it. (It is, for example, obviously worse to cancel a dinner engagement when the meal is already half-cooked, than half an hour after accepting the invitation and three weeks in advance of the date fixed.) So the definition given looks only to the speech act and the intention with which it is uttered; if the definition is correct, any such speech act clearly falls within the ambit of the principle against disappointing reliance wilfully or knowingly induced. Hence the obligation to keep promises is derivable from that more general principle.

The definition seems to me to be preferable to Searle's suggestion that that promising always answers and necessarily requires an intention to incur an obligation, and an intention to be taken as undertaking an obligation. The trouble with Searle's approach is that it is either incomplete or wrong. Let me show why. How could we make sense of the doctrine that a promisor essentially intends to incur an obligation? Only by supposing a logically prior rule or principle under which some obligation arises, which rule the promisor intends to invoke. What is the rule? Presumably, it is the rule or principle that it is obligatory to keep promises. Thus far, the definition is incomplete, because the concept 'promise' in this rule has yet to be explained. One possible way of going on to explain it is wrong: suppose the rule to be, 'Whoever says "I promise to ϕ " with the intention to be taken as invoking this rule, has an obligation to ϕ .' This would keep us out of the vicious circle, but at the expense of leading us straight into nonsense. For it would follow that there might be numerous occasions on which

S says to A, 'I promise to ϕ', afterwards claiming that he had no intention to be taken as invoking that or any other rule, whereupon it would follow that he had neither made a promise nor incurred an obligation. And that will not do. We must not 'provide Hippolytus with a let-out, the bigamist with an excuse for his "I do" and the welsher for his "I bet"'.[14] Moreover, it would make it very hard to understand how any utterance not using the explicit performative could possibly count as a promise.

The thesis which I have been advancing does indeed enable us to give a particularly clear account of the function of explicit performatives such as 'I promise . . .'. If I do intend you to take it that I intend you to rely on me, or know, etc., that you will take it so, then I promise when I say 'I shall ϕ'. Usually the context makes it clear enough whether I have such intention or knowledge. But sometimes doubt may arise. Because the word 'promise' has the meaning it has, someone who says 'I promise to ϕ' necessarily settles all doubt, if he knows the language. We need not trouble about his intentions; *knowing* the language, he must *know* that his addressee will suppose that he intends him to rely upon the act being done. He is therefore 'estopped' from denying that he promised, and whether or not *he* has the least intention actually to ϕ, and whether or not *he* regards it as obligatory to ϕ, *we* need have no doubt that he has in fact promised to ϕ, and that now he has indeed a duty to ϕ, whatever morally eccentric views he may hold.

It would be silly to deny, and I do not deny, that consciousness of the obligatoriness of promise-keeping, in a society in which the obligation is clearly recognized, in itself reinforces the practice of promising in a variety of ways. A promisor who makes a promise in the knowledge that his associates will take a very serious view of his misconduct if he does not keep it, is thereby the more likely to weigh seriously whether or not to make such and such a promise at all in the first place, and whether or not subsequently to break it. The promisee is more likely to take the promise seriously, and go ahead to lay plans and so on in the unquestioning assumption

[14] J. L. Austin, *How to do Things with Words* (Oxford, 1962), p. 10.

that the promise will be kept. The more likely it is that the promisee will seriously rely on the promise being kept, the more important it is that the promisor should keep it. Thus observance of the rule reinforces the practice which in turn reinforces the rule, in an entirely virtuous circle. In such circumstances it is indeed likely to be the case that people who assure others that they will ϕ , with the intention that those others take it they are to rely upon that performance, do in standard cases have a conscious intention to incur an obligation. In stable societies, people who promise probably do consciously intend to incur obligations by promising. (The difference between Searle's position and mine is that the last sentence is necessarily tautologous on his view; on mine it is synthetic, which I take to be a merit.) It does not follow that we need stipulate 'intention to incur obligation' as a necessary condition of promising; 'intention to induce reliance' is an alternative possibility, and one which provides us with intelligible reasons why promises *should* generate obligations, and therefore why it may indeed be the case that promisors do in fact sometimes consciously intend to create them. Further, it explains why we can quite justifiably impute to a person who says 'I promise to ϕ ' an intention to create an obligation, given the kind of social setting mentioned above; for whatever he intends, he knows or ought reasonably to realize that such words are (save in exceptional cases) calculated to convey such an intention to an addressee.

When this essay was first written,[15] I falsely supposed that 'intention to create reliance' was a *necessary* condition of promising. But that view shares a defect with other attempts to produce *necessary* conditions for promise-making. The defect rests in the supposition that everyone has the same understanding of what is required for making a promise. Yet the voluminous philosophical literature on this topic is itself evidence for the opposite view. What a person has to do in order to be deemed to have made a promise (e.g., is an *explicit* 'I promise' necessary or not?) may indeed vary in accordance with varying social usages. There is probably a family of varied understandings,

---

[15] In 1972, for publication in XLVI *Arist. Soc. Sup. Vol.* (1972), as part of a pair of essays (with J. Raz) on 'Voluntary Obligations and Normative Powers'.

usages, or even conventions about the making (and keeping) of promises, varied as between different social groups and for different occasions of varying solemnity, in much the same way as comparative law reveals a variegated family of legal provisions about voluntary obligation and contract among differing legal systems, all of which allow in some form of such obligations.

Provided there is some non-conventional reason why promises of some sorts should be held to generate obligations, then it is possible that some persons or groups evolve or stipulate conventions whereby intention to undertake such an obligation is either sufficient or necessary (or both) for the constitution of a promise. What the theory of 'intention to create reliance' shows is that such a non-conventional reason can and does exist precisely in cases covered by that theory. Hence that theory should be accepted as elucidating a logically primary or fundamental kind of promising, by reference to which other kinds and conventions can be rendered intelligible.

As I have pointed out, in the case of promises (any kind of promises) which do induce reliance, it is obviously wrong for the promisor to go back on his word once the promisee has acted in reliance on the promised performance. It is wrong in that the promisor thereby harms the promisee in a way for which he is responsible. Hence, as I said, a negative utilitarian morality (which gives priority to not harming people, as against failing to benefit them) can account for the bindingness of such promises.

But this merely shows that utilitarianism in its 'negative' form is not defeated by the example of promissory obligation. It does not itself establish the case for negative utilitarianism. And one need not be any sort of utilitarian to believe that harming people is wrong. In any moral theory in which respect for persons is deemed of fundamental value, it may be said that deliberately letting down somebody whom you have induced to rely upon you is a plain instance of disrespect for that other.

Nor need this be a simple, unanalysed, case of disrespect. For making promises shares a certain feature with giving serious factual information or advice, namely that a promisee's acceptance of the promise or the information or the advice depends upon the existence of some relationship of trust between the two parties (as I have pointed out elsewhere in a discussion of deceit[16]). Hence I can only let down by breaking promises those who think they can trust me and who believe that some relationship of friendly trust and confidence obtains between us, just as I can only deceive by telling lies those who think they can trust me as an informant or adviser on the ground of some supposed relationship of friendly trust and confidence obtaining between us. Quite apart from particular detriments arising from particular acts of reliance, any breach of such a relationship of trust is in some degree injurious to the trusting party. It is injurious to the exent to which people set value on such relationships; and I for one am attracted by John Finnis's argument that such relationships are of fundamental and non-derivative value to human beings.[17] Such an injury is a case of more or less serious disrespect to a person who values the mutually trusting relationship in which he believes himself to stand with the promisor (or, in the other case, deceiver). A non-utilitarian may hold that any such injury is wrong *even if* worse harms follow from keeping than from breaking the promise, and that reparation of some kind is due to a promisee who has been let down even if, all things considered, the right thing to do in a given case was for a promisor to break his promise. Hence, although some versions of utilitarianism can account for the binding force of promises, there still seems reason for supposing that non-utilitarians may yet give a better account.

All this is founded on the supposition that breaking promises does involve 'letting people down'. But that is not obviously true of purely executory promises—where a promise refers to a date some time in the future, and the promisor notifies the promisee that he will not perform as promised, the latter having as yet taken no steps at all in reliance on the promise. This can be thought an injury only if we involve the idea that the promisee is *already* trusting the promisor. But that will be so only if there is some reason why purely executory promises should not be broken or cancelled, and thus some reason why the promisee's attitude of trust includes trusting the promisor not to cancel. What such reason can there be?

---

[16] MacCormick, 'What is wrong with Deceit' (1982), *Sydney Law Rev.* (forthcoming).
[17] See J. Finnis, *Natural Law and Natural Rights* (Oxford, 1980), chs. 4.2.A and 6. 2–4, esp. pp. 141–4.

Here, surely, the answer must rest in convention and usage as justified by utilitarian considerations. There are advantages which flow from treating the obligation of a promise as perfect and uncancellable save in exceptional cases or with the promisee's consent from the very time at which a promise is made. It is advantagous for a promisor to exhibit a character of rigorous trustworthiness and reliability. It is generally advantageous to members of a community to be able to regard promises as firm commitments from the moment they are made, without regard to nice questions about the degree to which the promisee has perfected the promisor's commitment by acting in reliance on the promise. Rule-utilitarianism may not be a sufficient moral theory, but to account for such matters as this it is a necessary part of any sound moral theory. Consequentialism cannot be the whole of morality, but no adequate morality can ignore either the consequences for which particular agents are responsible or the consequences in general terms of the adoption or rejection of principles of conduct.

In any event, in its simplest and logically fundamental form, promising is plainly distinguishable from such concepts as 'marriage' or 'divorce' or 'conveyance' or 'sale' which are not explicable save by reference to rules which define the status of marriage and providé as to its commencement and termination or to rules which define the institution of property and provide for its investment and divestment or transfer. Therefore a parallel distinction exists between the speech acts involved in that simplest case of promising and the speech acts (or other acts-in-law) essential to marrying, divorcing, selling, and conveying.

III. VOLUNTARY OBLIGATIONS AND LEGAL INSTITUTIONS

Turning now to the law of voluntary obligations, we should recall a point made earlier, that questions of intention are frequently difficult to settle, so that it may be a difficult question to answer whether a man who said that he would do x meant to be taken as promising to do x, or merely as predicting that he would or stating an intention to do it, or whatever. Such uncertainty is an unavoidable inconvenience of social life, and perhaps not much can be or need be done about it—after all, someone to whom such an equivocal utterance is made, can there and then ask 'Is that a promise?', and the speaker's prompt reply one way or the other is necessarily conclusive. In the law, however, certainty one way or another is highly desirable if the machinery of state coercion is to be used in enforcing voluntary obligations. It is in this light interesting to recall how in the earlier Roman law, no promise as such was enforceable unless couched in a formal answer to a formal question: '*Spondesne . . . ?*' '*Spondeo.*' This requirement only died out when it had become universal practice to reduce stipulations to writing. The fondness for writing has descended to modern civilian systems; Scots law requires proof by writ or oath of all gratuitous promises, and of most private non-commerical transactions, and French law likewise requires all private contracts of a non-commercial type to be proven by an appropriate written instrument, or at least to be proven in part by writing, in all save a few exceptional cases where it is thought unconscionable for the promisor to plead the want of writing as a defence. In English law, the only way in which a gratuitous promise may be made enforceable at law is by couching it in a solemn written instrument known as a 'deed' which takes effect when signed, sealed, and delivered. In cases of contracts properly so called in which consideration 'moves from' all the parties, it is interesting to observe that the questions whether a promise was made, and what promise was made, are settled by what lawyers call an 'objective test'. After proof of what the parties actually said and did, the court concerns itself only with asking what 'a reasonable man' would in that light have assumed to be the intention of the parties; not what it actually was.

Another difficulty which we noticed earlier was the difficulty in which a promisor may find himself if he does not know that the promisee has properly understood him, nor whether or not he wishes to 'take him up' on the promise. Again, one way in which we can tackle that problem in ordinary life is by *asking* the promisee, and again in the nature of the case his answer is conclusive. To be on the safe side, one can even expressly make it a condition of one's promise that it must be expressly accepted. The law can clarify such problems, either by ruling that the matter is, so to say, at the promisor's risk unless he expressly makes acceptance a condition of his being bound;

Lord Stair favoured this rule, and it found its way into Scots law. In French law on the other hand, acceptance is, as a requirement of law, essential to the completion of *any* contract, even a gratutious one. In all systems, of course, bilateral contracts, which essentially consist in an exchange of promises, necessarily require some form of acceptance. In such cases, further problems can arise as to the *time* of completion of the contract, or to the *place*—for example when dealings are by post. In this, it may be convenient that the law should lay down a rebuttable rule that acceptance takes place, for example, at the moment of posting of a letter of acceptance. It is then up to the parties to prove that a different condition was stipulated by the offeror, or the presumption contained in the rebuttable rule stands.

One way to represent legal requirements of the kind which I have discussed is as follows: they are designed to provide safeguards relating to the legal enforcement of promissory obligations. Certain possible areas of doubt and difficulty relating to whether or not a promise was genuinely made, or genuinely 'taken up' by the promisee, and to when it was 'taken up', can be clarified by stipulating certain procedural and evidentiary rules as conditions, not of the existence of a promise as a matter of social fact, but of the enforceability of promises at law. This implies that the *concepts* of 'promises'; or 'agreements' are pre-legal and extra-legal. The law adopts them and enforces the obligations arising from them, but only if certain clearly established conditions are fulfilled with regard to the mode of making promises. Whether or not such conditions are said by lawyers to go to the 'constitution' or only to the 'proof' of voluntary obligations is comparatively unimportant. The function which they essentially fulfil is to secure, as far as may be, that promises are not enforced unless it is clear that the 'promisor' really intended to be taken seriously, and had grounds to suppose that the promisee really took him seriously. They are rules laying down procedural prerequisites for the enforceability of voluntary obligations. Unless these prerequisites are satisfied, undertakings and promises are not to be enforced at law.

Such prerequisites can indeed be characterized as parts of legal power-conferring rules. Whoever observes them succeeds in establishing a legally enforceable obligation, provided other legal requirements are also met. A 'contract', or whatever, now exists, and it is the duty of courts to enforce by civil remedies the rights and obligations which flow from valid contracts, in cases where one party will not do so voluntarily and the other raises an action at law.

This exhibits the 'sanction' which attaches to procedural and other prerequisites for the validity of contracts and voluntary obligations generally. The facility which the law offers is not the bare ability to undertake obligations, but the ability to undertake enforceable obligations. The price of this facility is the observance of the legal prerequisites in question. The case is a classic case of one of Bentham's 'praemiary' sanctions— reward as a sanction. If I follow the law's requirements I achieve the reward of legal enforceability of the arrangements I make. Even when the law's requirements are burdensome, the reward may justify the trouble and expense of fulfilling them. Those who purchase houses often grudge their conveyancing costs, yet find the security and enforceability of title achieved thereby a reward sufficient to justify the cost.[18]

The very fact that certain steps are required to secure the particular end of establishing a legally binding and enforceable obligation is what makes it reasonable to treat the rules for creating obligations as distinct from the rules about fulfilling them or procuring their enforcement. As much as anything else, this is a matter of intellectual tidiness and convenience. Those concerned with the law's operations as doctrinal writers, as practitioners, or as judges evidently find it convenient to split off the question of the making of a contract from logically secondary questions as to the consequences of its validity and as to the mode of its termination. All these specialities, however, arise from the institutionalization of legal contracts and legal voluntary obligations of all sorts as generating enforceable rights and duties. We delude ourselves if we suppose that the same elaborate analysis is required in the case of those ordinary promises which we make and fulfil daily in our ordinary lives.[19]

The conclusion is that there are important differences and important parallels between voluntary obligations in morality

---

[18] Cf. MacCormick, *Hart*, pp. 83–7.

[19] For a fuller statement of this line of argument, see MacCormick, 'Law as Institutional Fact' (1974) 90 LQR 102.

and in law. The law, in adopting for its purposes, and in giving protection and security to, ordinary moral obligations, nevertheless transforms them. Such transformation occurs in consequence first of the legal enforceability of certain such obligations, and secondly of the elaboration of special prerequisites for securing such enforceability.[20]

---

[20] The adjustments to this essay since its first publication represent my response to views put by P. S. Atiyah in *Promises, Morals, and Law* (Oxford, 1981), pp. 38–42, 64–6, by P. S. Árdal in 'Promises and Reliance', *Dialogue* 15 (1976) 54–61, and by H. Beran in an unpublished paper 'On Psycho-Behavioural Analyses of Promising and Consent' (1981).

THE OBLIGATION OF REPARATION

SOMETIMES, when harm has befallen one individual another person may be held bound in some way to make good that harm, wholly or in part, on the ground of his having been in some sense responsible for the harm. Having borrowed from Scots legal usage the term 'obligation of reparation', I intend (by a slight extension of that usage) to apply it to any such case of a person's being bound to make good another's harm on the ground of his responsibility for it. I envisage that such an obligation may be either a moral or a legal obligation, or indeed both together.

In the most extensive possible sense, such an obligation may arise both in the context of a breach of promise and entirely independently of any promissory obligation. To consider briefly the former: suppose for example that a university teacher has promised to take his children to the beach one afternoon, but before setting off he is visited by a student in a condition of apparently suicidal depression; that he gives himself over to helping the student for the rest of the day by talking over his problems, and thus fails to keep his promise to his children.

In such a case, there are two judgments which I would make: that he acted rightly in responding to his student's urgent need, even at the cost of breaking his promise; but he now owes it to his children as soon as possible to make good their disappointment by taking them to the seaside. He has an 'obligation of reparation' even though he did not do the wrong thing in failing to keep the promise—just as much as if he had simply forgotten to turn up or had knowingly neglected to do so in pursuit of some diversion or other. For that reason, the example raises two points of interest.

First, in relation to conflict of duties: my impression is that many discussions of conflicts of duties proceed on the assumption that the less compelling duty is simply overridden by the more compelling, and there's an end of it. But surely it is not so.

The morally justified decision not to fulfil the overriden duty may nevertheless result in an obligation of reparation—the promisee's rights are not abrogated by the circumstances which genuinely overrode the promisor's specific promissory duty. This indeed ought to be a material consideration to be borne in mind when duties conflict—can either, and, if so, which, of the conflicting duties be more or less made good by some substitute performance offered later? (The relevance of that to the deliberation involved in our figured case is obvious: the beach will still be there tomorrow, but the depressed student may not be.)

Secondly, in relation to the question of fault: the existence of an obligation of reparation is not necessarily conditional upon fault or blameworthiness of the bearer of the obligation. So far from incurring just blame for letting his children down, the teacher did the right thing in all the circumstances. Had he done so deliberately and without good cause, or forgetting, he would have incurred blame as well as the obligation to make good the disappointment. But our example shows that fault or blame in the *moral* sense are not conditions of the obligation of reparation.

But, of course, to say that there is an obligation of reparation is to imply that it *would* be blameworthy if subsequently he refused or neglected to make up for the lost trip by going another day, or giving some similar or better treat. As suggested a moment ago, this seems to depend on respecting the rights of the disappointed promisees rather than on a consideration purely of the duties in the given circumstances of the promisor.

These reflections, albeit brief, may indicate that there would be much interest in examining obligations of reparation in the widest sense. But space will not permit that in the present chapter; instead, I wish to let my initial example stand only for the purpose of introducing two ideas: that obligations of reparation may be independent of anterior moral fault, and that their primary moral foundation is perhaps found in respect for the rights of the person hurt or harmed in a given case.

These two ideas are of great importance to the topic to which I mean to restrict my attention in the rest of the chapter, that of reparation in a narrower and more specific sense akin to that in which lawyers have traditionally used it: I mean those cases in which there is held to be an obligation of reparation for some harm inflicted by one person on another independently of any promissory or contractual relationship between the parties; the cases covered by what English lawyers call 'the Law of Torts' and (in a modern usage paralleling the English) Scots lawyers call 'the Law of Delict'.

Subject to a number of important exceptions, the broad principle of the contemporary law in both jurisdictions is that liability to make compensation for harm done is based on 'fault'. That means: I am liable to you to pay damages for harm you have suffered, if it was caused either by some wilful act of mine aimed at causing such harm, or by my negligence, that is be some failure on my part to take what could be 'objectively' regarded as reasonable care in the circumstances of the case. Regardless of the kind or degree of 'fault' involved, the measure of damages to be awarded is the extent of your injuries, which you must mitigate as far as you reasonably can. The rationale of this, as expressed again and again by judges and doctrinal writers, is that the object of the award of damages is not to punish me, but to secure compensation for you, so far as money can achieve that.

In the three main sections of this chapter I shall do three things. In the first, I shall discuss what, if any, is the moral foundation of obligations of reparation in such cases. In the second, I shall use the principle worked out in the first as a critical principle in relation to the law concerning reparation of injuries. In the third, I shall consider the significance of the obligation of reparation in the analysis of legal systems, having particular regard to the notions of legal sanction and coercion.

I. THE MORAL FOUNDATIONS OF REPARATION

The argument of this section is that the justifying ground of obligations of reparation, from a moral point of view, is that individuals have as a matter of principle a right to reasonable security in their persons and possessions, and accordingly a right to be compensated when that reasonable security is infringed. No argument from retribution or deterrence can satisfactorily justify the obligation of reparation.

The argument may again start with an example: Mrs A being

in hospital having just given birth to a child, Mr A sets out by car to visit her, being in the state of agitated excitement appropriate to the occasion. Unhappily, in reversing his car out of his drive, he fails to notice, and collides with, his neighbour B's new car parked on the roadside opposite. There is a collision, and the side panelling of B's car is severely crumpled and dented.

Without regard to any question of insurance or of legal liability, what now is the moral position? It seems to me clear that A ought to at once tell B of the accident, explain the circumstances, apologize, and offer to meet the cost of making good so far as possible the damage to the car. That is for me a clear matter of 'intuition'. But can I articulate any principle which would justify my judgment in this case, and cover like cases?

It might seem that the relevant principle is that of retribution: when a person does wrong, he must pay for it. Applying that in this case: A has done wrong to B, and so must pay to make good the consequences.

This is not, however, good enough. It is not as if A had maliciously and wilfully smashed his old banger into B's new car just for the sake of hurting him. In that case, A's act would be plainly wrongful. But in the case envisaged, A has at worst been guilty of an understandable lapse from care. If what we were concerned with were matching a deserved adverse reaction to A's misdeed or mishap, we would differentiate considerably between the two hypotheses. But by my judgment, on either hypothesis A would bear the same obligation to B: to make good the damage, no more and no less. Since that is the judgment which is to be justified, the principle of retribution (even if acceptable for some purposes) is simply irrelevant.

Moreover, in the case principally envisaged, it is far from clear that in moral terms A has done a wrongful act to B. 'Ought implies can' is a well-entrenched meta-ethical principle; but it is not obvious that in his circumstances A was actually capable of having taken better care, or of having paused and reflected on the question whether to drive at all that evening. Let us indeed strengthen the example by stipulating that such was A's agitation over the onset of paternity and concerning the well-being of his wife and child that the necessary self-command was, in the given case, entirely beyond him. Then since he could not have taken better care, it cannot be true that he ought to have taken it; and it cannot therefore be true that in failing to take it, he committed a moral wrong towards B.

Yet even these suppositions would not lead me to withdraw my judgment that now, after the accident, it would be wrong for A to repudiate any responsibility for it. Evidently, retribution is out of court, and we are still left seeking a justifying principle for that judgment.

What about a principle which would in some way replicate the point of deterrent or disincentive theories of punishment? Perhaps an obligation of reparation ought to be accepted in such circumstances, since its acceptance will secure greater care among drivers. Again, this seems defective since in no way is the disincentive proportioned to the gravity or otherwise of the carelessness involved in any particular case. A further element of 'overkill' can be detected in just such a case as the strengthened version of A's case, when, by the hypothesis, it could not have been the case that the disincentive could have been a factor in A's deliberations. A more rational principle to enunciate from this point of view would be that a harm-causer ought to make compensation in all cases in which he would have avoided the harm by taking better care, and that the quantum of compensation ought to be limited by the degree of culpability. And such a principle would exclude A, on the strengthened version of the case, from any obligation of reparation. On a weaker version of the case, he would be morally obligated under this principle only to make a contribution to the cost of the repairs to B's car.

And here we hit upon the defect in both of the previously reviewed ways of considering the case. Retributive and deterrent principles alike concentrate on the matter exclusively with reference to the harm-causer. But what about the sufferer of the harm? Hard luck as it is on A to have had a shadow cast over an event traditionally deemed happy, it is yet harder luck on B that he has had his car dented in this way. Would we not say that people who park their cars on well-lit roadsides are entitled to expect that others will avoid banging into them? Does that not point towards a rather different sort of justifying principle, concerning the right of individuals to be secured from certain kinds of harm which others may inflict on them?

Of course, to accept such a principle is not to suppose that harm will not be inflicted ever—obviously, rights can be infringed. But precisely what such a principle does entail is that when a right has been infringed reparation ought to be made. This is not then seen as some measure of punishment of a 'wrongdoer' but rather as a matter of restitution to the sufferer—hence the irrelevancy of notions of retribution or deterrence. We may well regret that A has incurred this obligation; we may sympathize with him in his predicament; we shall be glad if he is able to recover from an insurer the cost to himself, for that will not be a way of dodging a just punishment, but a way of meeting an unfortunate liability.

A principle along these lines would then fit our case. But what would be its content, and how would it be justified? Following a point which I have made elsewhere,[1] I would suggest that a justificatory argument for such a principle must be in terms of identifying 'goods' for individuals, in whose enjoyment they ought to be secured. Freedom from physical injury to oneself and to one's possessions is fairly uncontroversially a good for any individual. Ought it to be secured to individuals? Security of the person from harm may I think be treated as uncontroversial; security of possessions is more controversial, in that the extent to which we hold it ought to be protected is properly conditional on our view as to the justice or otherwise of the distribution of assets within a society. But at least we may say that those who assert their own rights over their possessions (as A may be presumed to do in our case) are estopped from raising that point in particular instances as distinct from general proposals for reform and redistribution. At any rate, in conditions of relative distributive justice, which I presuppose for the sake of the present argument, I do believe that each ought to be secured from harm to his/her possessions. My reason is the Humean one that otherwise there must be a breakdown in any kind of ordered existence; my belief in that does not preclude me (as Hume thought it did) from thinking reform in the direction of a more nearly equal distribution both possible and desirable in the interests of justice.

But what of the content? To what precisely are we to assert a right? Not, I think, to total and absolute security from harm

[1] Ch. 8 above; see also 'Rights in Legislation' in *Law, Morality, and Society* (ed. P. M. S. Hacker and J. Raz, Oxford, 1977).

howsoever arising—not that, because we who are at risk of harm to our persons and possessions are the self-same people as are at risk of being unduly inhibited in our actings by the restraints of the very principles which we wish for our passive protection. On that ground I would settle rather for the principle that each person has a right to be secure from harm to person or possessions caused by any lapse from a reasonable standard of care and attentiveness on the part of any other person.

The lawyer's notion of 'reasonable' in that context is of course somewhat question-begging, in that in itself it makes appeal to further, unstated, standards. Suffice it here to say that in my view legal experience shows that such an objection is not insuperable. For want of space, I shall leave it at that, and not argue out the detailed implications of the term 'reasonable'. But the point to be emphasized is that what the term envisages is a certain 'objective' standard of care, not calculated in terms of what this or that individual was subjectively capable of achieving in given circumstances, but calculated in terms of what a 'reasonable person' could and would achieve given the degree of risk of a certain kind of harm occurring in given circumstances.

There is a reason of justice for setting an objective standard: every person is to have the *same* right against every other person—not a standard of protection varying according to the degree of forgetfulness or absentmindedness or clumsiness or excitability of this or that other in his vicinity.

But it is for that reason that an attempt to frame the basic moral principle in terms of a duty to take care must necessarily fail. It is by no means a new point to make, that moral rights may be objectively founded but that moral duties have an essential subjective element related to the particular capabilities of any individual.[2] In a case like our strengthened version of *A*'s case, the point is not that he has acted wrongfully, in a morally blameworthy way, in violation of moral duty; it is simply that he has infringed *B*'s right to reasonable security, and that he is accordingly obligated to make reparation.

That obligation is no doubt itself restricted by his ability to pay, and it may also be restricted by a possible duty on *B*,

[2] See W. D. Ross, *Foundations of Ethics* (Oxford, 1939), ch. 7.

having regard to his own and *A*'s relative means, not to demand or even accept payment by *A* beyond what he can reasonably afford. But to that, surrounding social circumstances are relevant. If there is a possibility for those engaging in risky activities to insure against the risk of their harming others, there are good moral—as well as compelling legal—reasons why people ought to take out such insurance. If I as a car owner wish to assert my rights as against others, I ought to put myself in a position to cover their possible justified assertions as against me. *Qui sentit commodum sentire debet et onus.*

It may be thought objectionable that I should have postulated a right to which there is, morally speaking, no perfectly correlative duty. That objection rests, in my view, on an unfounded dogmatism about 'correlativity' in such cases, which I have tried already to refute. The right which my principle asserts is not one which has any perfectly correlative duty, although it would indeed be pointless to assert any such right without having in view some derivative or consequential duties. Such indeed there are: primarily, there is indeed under the rights principle a duty upon all persons to do their utmost to achieve the proper standard of care; breach of that duty would in itself attract just censure. But secondarily, and regardless of any such 'subjectively' measured breach, there is the resultant obligation of reparation which arises whenever the '*objectively*' measured right is infringed.

The reason for this is the simple analytical connection which obtains between any 'right *in rem*' such as we are here considering, being a right which holds good as against everyone in general, and the personal right to remedial action which arises as against any specific individual who infringes the primary right. The remedial right is indeed an exact correlative of the obligation of reparation. If we did not insist upon fulfilment of that in relevant cases, we would show that our original assertion of the primary right was insincere. If rights concern goods which ought to be secured to individuals, we must secure individuals in those goods or in their equivalent as nearly as possible. That is why there would be moral blameworthiness in failing to make compensation for an injury in relation to one which was not morally blameworthy but for which one was responsible.

The conception of 'responsibility' here involved is plainly different from that involved in cases of moral censure or legal punishment. The elements of intention or wilfulness or gross carelessness essential to real wrongdoing are not necessary ingredients of responsibility in the present sense. It is based simply on the common-sense notion of causation expounded by H. L. A. Hart and A. M. Honoré in *Causation in the Law*[3] and taken up in A. Harari's *The Place of Negligence in the Law of Torts*.[4] When from among the necessary and sufficient conditions of an untoward event's occurrence, we single out one or another as 'the cause' of the event, the justifying ground for doing so is that 'the cause' so chosen is itself an event which falls outwith the ordinary and reasonable run of expectations. (Observe, for example, that in *A*'s case, *B*'s car being parked at a particular point in the road is as much a necessary condition of the collision as *A*'s backing his car out of the drive without keeping that degree of watchfulness which is ordinarily and properly expected of drivers. That suffices to justify ascribing to *A*'s act the status of 'the cause' of the accident. But of course it is necessary for 'responsibility' that there was a relevant act of *A*'s, as distinct from something which just happened to him. If his car had run out of control because he had been stricken by an unpredictable coronary thrombosis, the case would be different. Then the heart attack, not the act of driving, would be the cause of the collision, for which *A* would not be held responsible.)

It is interesting to observe that the conception of what is within the 'reasonable' run of expectations figures here in the notions of causation and responsibility in much the same way as an objective conception of reasonableness figures in the rights principle itself. This exhibits the interlocking quality of the principles at stake, without in any way involving a vicious circularity.

In the introductory part of this chapter, it was suggested (with respect to reparation for breaches of promise) 'that obligations of reparation may be independent of anterior moral fault, and that their primary moral foundation may be respect for the rights of the person hurt or harmed in a given case'. The

---

[3] Oxford, 1959.
[4] Sydney, 1962.

case which I have argued in the present section further reinforces that view in the different context of injuries suffered
outside of any promissory or contractual relationship. Although
no such argument can be conclusive, it has been shown that
there are good grounds for asserting as a principle that every
person has a right to be secure from harm to person or
possessions caused by any lapse from a reasonable standard of
care and attentiveness on the part of any other person. To
respect such a right entails acceptance that an obligation of
reparation is incumbent on a person responsible for an infringement of another's right, regardless of his being morally at
fault or blameworthy in the matter.

For those who share my pre-analytical intuition in relation to
a case like *A*'s, that principle will I hope seem acceptable as
justifying and making sense of such an intuitive judgment. To
those who do not, I hope at least that it has been shown capable
of being accommodated within a coherent moral position. My
next task is to consider the law of reparation in the light of that
principle.

II. REPARATION IN THE LAW

As was said in the introduction, as a matter of general principle
legal liability for harm caused by one person to another is based
upon 'fault', upon 'duty owed and [duty] neglected'.[5] To this,
the principle which I have expounded above may seem irrelevant; but it is not.

The conception of 'fault' or *'culpa'* which is operative within
English and Scots law is that of 'objective', not 'subjective'
fault. Whatever care 'a reasonable man' would take to avoid the
causing of some harm which is reasonably foreseeable in a given
situation, that care is demanded of any person in that situation,
and failure to achieve that degree of care is deemed a breach of
legal duty. Given breach of the duty, one is liable for foreseeable
harm arising therefrom. No account is taken of the 'personal
equation' of the defendant/defender; the law does not ask
whether given his particular character or circumstances he
could have done anything other than he did, whether his conduct was in any sense morally blameworthy. The sole question

[5] Per Lord Macmillan in *Donoghue* v. *Stevenson* [1932] AC 562 at 610.

is whether he was in breach of the legal duty to take 'objectively' reasonable care.

For that very reason, it has indeed been suggested that *culpa* is 'amoral'.[6] Legal fault is not coextensive with moral fault, and so lacks any moral point or moral justification. The arguments put in section 1 enable us to resist that conclusion. Although the law's conception of 'fault' in this context is indeed different from and wider than any acceptable conception of moral fault, the legal application of the doctrine of fault liability does not necessarily lack moral justification. what it achieves, by and large, is that protection of individuals to which our expounded principle declares their moral right. That principle can therefore, if accepted, serve as a critical principle to which reference may be made in justifying or criticizing the operation of the law.

In fact, the legal 'duty of care' just because it is a so-called objective duty is nothing other than an exact correlative of the right for which I have argued. That legal discourse has tended to expound the relevant branch of law solely in terms of duty has indeed tended to obscure the moral justification of the law, because of the evident absurdity from a moral point of view of such objective duties. Similarly, it may have led us to conceive of awards of damages in negligence cases as some kind of 'sanction' for wrongful conduct—in which light the law cannot but seem arbitrary and unjust, because the 'sanction' is in no way proportioned to the degree of fault involved, and is sometimes applied in the total absence of any kind of moral blameworthiness whatsoever.

Let me stress how inapposite is this notion of 'sanction' in the present context. Criminal punishment is the central instance of a legal sanction. There we are properly concerned with conduct which is wrongful from a moral point of view in the sense that by the intention or will or recklessness of an individual, a pro-hibited act has been committed. Suppposing the prohibition to be itself justified, it follows that moral censure is appropriate to the case. As Sir Walter Moberly has convincingly argued,[7] one essential element in punishment properly conceived is that it is a public and symbolic expression of such justified censure. That

---

[6] J. J. Gow, 'Is *Culpa* Amoral?' 65 *Jur. Rev.* (1953) 17.
[7] Sir W. Moberley, *The Ethics of Punishment* (London, 1968), discussed in ch. 2 above.

requires, among other things, a proper proportionality between punishment and seriousness of offence or degree of guilt. That is of course not a sufficient justification of particular penal practices; but it is a necessary element in the justification of any.

To represent awards of civil damages in negligence cases as being in any degree analogous to penal sanctions would thus be to dismiss them as wholly arbitrary and unjustified. But the civil 'duty of care' is not simply a bad replica of the duties which criminal law imposes. It is the correlative of a right to reasonable care which every citizen does or ought to have as against every other. The justifying aim of the law is not the repression of misconduct but the protection of a right. When that protection fails at the first level, in that some harm has been inflicted, it is then secured at a secondary level, so far as possible, by the award of compensatory damages to the person harmed from the resources of the person whose act caused the harm—on condition that there was a failure on his part to take reasonable care. The genuine element of coercive legal sanction here is to be found not in the judgment awarding the damages, but rather in the coercive steps which may be taken to enforce performance of the duty to pay these damages in cases of recalcitrance.

In any justification of this branch of the law, it is evident that we must start from the right, not from the duty which lawyers put at the centre of the map but which is by itself unintelligible.

All this is by no means irrelevant to current legal controversy, nor indeed to the various projects for law reform set forth by the Pearson Commission.[8] Perhaps the most powerful contemporary critique of the fault principle is that set forth by P. S. Atiyah in his *Accidents Compensation and the Law*.[9] His specific indictment of that principle has seven counts, of which I shall here consider two: the first, that the burden of compensation under the principle is unjust to defendants since the extent of liability bears no relation to the degree of their culpability; and the third, that 'the fault principle is not a moral principle

---

[8] See 1978 Cmnd. 7504, I–III.

[9] London, 1970; see esp. pp. 445–77. I should stress that this chapter does not deal with the argument from efficiency against the 'tort system', which seems a stronger argument for Atiyah's position than the moral argument.

because the defendant may be [legally] negligent without being morally culpable'.

These and other related criticisms are readily rebuttable as moral criticisms by reference to the principle for which I have argued in this paper. The conception of justice upon which Atiyah relies is that apposite to criminal penalites. If we are concerned not with the imposition of just penalties on defendants but with securing justice as between plaintiff and defendant on the ground of an infringement of the former's right, that conception of justice is wholly inapposite. Just as in *A*'s case discussed earlier, it is no doubt the case that we sympathize with a defendant who is subjected to a heavy liability for a momentary lapse from attentiveness; but that cannot justify leaving the victim of the lapse to bear the cost thereof.

One aspect of the contrast between civil liability and criminal liability is indeed that the law permits us always and sometimes requires us to insure against the former, whereas in the latter case any attempt to insure against paying the law's penalties is struck down as illegal and contrary to public policy. The law is concerned to secure that plaintiff's rights are met, not that defendants are beggared in meeting them. When we indulge in activities which may be hazardous for others we can, and we ought to, ensure that we can meet such obligations of reparation as we may, however forgivably, incur.

These moral criticisms which Atiyah and others have made of fault liability are therefore in my opinion not well founded. It is, however, the case that they have other arguments, by no means negligible, against continuance of 'the tort system'. There are, for example, arguments of fairness as between the victims of different types of accident. In an industrialized society, a large number of accidents predictably happen every year involving death, injury, pain, and suffering to many individuals, and much damage to property. Only a proportion of these accidents do in fact result from someone's legal fault, and only a smaller proportion can be proven so to have resulted, proof being the essential prerequisite of a successful claim for damages. So some victims of these accidents obtain compensation, while others do not, though they are no less deserving.

This occurs within a context in which large sums of money

are annually paid to insure against risks of such injury. These very sums are disproportionately distributed among the actual victims of injuries—but only after a large cut has been absorbed by insurance companies and lawyers and others involved in operating the 'tort system' with all its complexities and difficulties surrounding the proof of fault.

Since the system is on this account both wastefully expensive and distributively unjust as between victims of essentially similar accidents, it is suggested that a preferable solution would be to institute schemes of comprehensive insurance to cover the victims of all accidents, or of all accidents involving personal injury or death, or of all accidents of a certain type (e.g. road accidents, accidents at work) involving personal injury or death. The British industrial injuries legislation goes already some distance along that line; other states have special road-accident schemes, and New Zealand has recently enacted legislation securing compensation for all victims of accidents, however caused, which result in personal injury or death. So far as the present law provides any disincentive to carelessness, it could more rationally be replaced by an extension of the categories of negligence punishable criminally.

It would be well beyond the scope of this paper, and my own competence, to enter into the debate at the level of cost–benefit analysis, with a view to establishing the possibility or otherwise of eliminating wasteful expense by instituting such schemes of comprehensive insurance. But quite apart from such questions, the moral point at issue is a disputable one.

True it is that under the present law, some victims of, e.g., road accidents have no right to compensation because no one was or can be proved to have been legally at fault, whereas other victims of such accidents can establish and enforce a legal right to compensation. But should the fact that there are some accidents for which no one is responsible lead us to deny the existence of obligations of reparation as against those who are responsible, in cases in which responsibility in the relevant sense can be established?

Social justice, in my submission, indubitably requires the provision of care and assistance for the victims of uninflicted misfortunes of all kinds, including illness, congenital defects, unemployment, and indeed 'sheer accidents' for which no one, or no one other than the victim, is responsible. Distributive justice in such cases is founded upon the principle that certain needs of individuals ought in all circumstances to be satisfied, and there is then no room to discriminate between victims of accidents and victims of such misfortunes as disease.

The justice of the obligation of reparation is, by contrast, corrective justice, and its ground is that one person's right has been infringed by another. Therein is to be found, indeed, a materially differentiating factor as between the victims of negligent accidents and the victims of sheer accidents—and all other types of uninflicted misfortune.

We have recently been reminded that we ought to take rights seriously,[10] and so we ought. The rights protected by the law of reparation are in my judgment worthy of being taken with real seriousness, as also is cultivation of a sense of our responsibility towards those whose rights we have, even unintentionally, infringed. To that extent, this branch of the law, even as it stands at the moment, replete with blemishes and imperfections, has some positive moral worth. So far from thinking it a blot on the moral landscape which ought to be abolished if a cost-effective substitute could be found, I think that one of the costs of its abolition would be a moral cost—whether or not so great as to price an alternative scheme out of serious consideration.

Finally, the idea of extending the criminal law to deal with negligent acts seems to me utterly unacceptable on all the grounds which have already been impliedly covered in dismissing the idea that damages are or should be thought to be analogous to penalties. A further ground is this: as W. G. Carson has pointed out,[11] offences of 'strict liability'—which ought to include at least 'objective' negligence—when admitted in criminal law deprive the criminal sanction of its crucial symbolic force, and thus of its principal potency as a disincentive. The more we admit of such offences, the more we blur the function of the criminal law, to the detriment of its efficacy as an instrument of expressing genuine social disapprobation of those acts which genuinely merit that reaction.

[10] See R. Dworkin's theory discussed in ch. 7 above.
[11] W. G. Carson, 'The Sociology of Crime and the Emergence of Criminal Laws' in *Deviance and Social Control* (ed. P. Rock and M. McIntosh, London 1974), pp. 80, 87.

No more has been done here than to show the eligibility of the principle of each person's rights to reasonable security in body and possessions as a critical principle for justifying the law of reparation. While it does lend broad support to the main outlines of the existing law, there would be many points upon which it would ground adverse criticism of the existing law, and related practice, such as the practice whereby insurance companies oblige their policy-holders never to acknowledge fault or liability in any accident. The scope of such an essay as this, however, leaves no room for consideration of such points.

III. COERCION AND SANCTION: A PRELIMINARY ANALYSIS

Finally, we must turn from moralizing to analysis. The substantive points made in the first two sections have an obvious relevance for theories of legal system, especially for those who insist that every legal duty is necessarily supported directly by some legal sanction. If there is so strong a disanalogy as that which has been asserted between civil damages and criminal penalties, such an insistence must be false; and, on the other hand, an adequate analytical framework must be found which will fully accommodate both of these very different institutions.

The best instance of a carefully worked out version of the wrong theory is that provided by Bentham's *Of Laws in General*.[12] Bentham's conception of an offence includes both civil offences and criminal offences, and his conception of duty is analytically connected with his conception of offence. It is of the nature of all offences that their commission justifies the imposition of a punitive (as distinct from praemiary) sanction. In this light the essential difference between civil and criminal offences is or ought to be located in the quality of punishment therefor; hence his distinction between ordinary and extraordinary punishments. The former are essentially pecuniary and are calculated so as to charge the offender with a fraction more than the exact cost of his offence; the latter require some excess over that, and normally include the infliction of some non-pecuniary loss on the offender. What would justify this differentiation, in Bentham's view, is the degrees of mis-

[12] Ed. H. L. A. Hart (London, 1970); on this topic, see esp. his ch. 17, pp. 209–19.

chievousness of different offences, the crucial difference of degree being discovered in the intention of the offender. An offence ought properly to be treated as criminal, and as attracting therefore extraordinary punishment, if it was committed in full awareness of the law's prohibition and with intent both to violate the law and to escape detection in so doing.

The weakness of this account is that it systematically assimilates legal institutions which those who operate the system assert to be distinct. If judges and others continually tell us that they make orders for civil damages, and justify them, not as 'punishments' upon 'offenders' but as awards of compensation to those whose rights have been infringed, ought not our legal analysis to admit that distinction? Of course it is possible that the judges misunderstand and misdescribe what they are doing, but acceptance that it is so ought to be a last resort, adopted if no other convincing analysis can be found.

What is wrong with Bentham's account is not his insistence on the coercive quality of law, but that he misconceives the way in which it is coercive. In relation to our subject-matter, Kelsen gets nearer the truth in his statement that 'There exists . . . according to the civil law of all the legal orders, a legal duty to repair an illegally caused damage . . . A general legal norm attaches a civil sanction directly to the fact that an individual does not repair an injury caused by his behaviour, even without any previous legal transaction . . .' Unfortunately he proceeds to add the words: '. . . just as a criminal sanction is attached to certain behaviour of an individual. Then there is in this regard no difference between the technique of the civil and that of the criminal law.'[13] The first part of the quotation grasps at the truth that the civil duty which the law can plausibly be said to enforce by coercion is not any postulated duty to avoid causing harm, but the duty to make reparation if one does cause it. That is not a way of coercing us not to cause harm, since *ex hypothesi* the harm has already been caused. In case of the obligation of reparation, either the party who owes it pays up voluntarily, or the other takes him to court and (if he proves his case) obtains an order of the court that appropriate damages be paid. If the 'judgment debtor' continues recalcitrant, the creditor may then

---

[13] H. Kelsen, *General Theory of Law and the State* (tr. A. Wedberg, Cambridge, Mass., 1945), p. 139.

take further steps to enable himself or some official to seize property of the debtor's in satisfaction, or to intercept payments due to him from third parties, or to impose direct physical constraint on him to make him pay up, if he has resources and refuses to disgorge them.

What is the point of all this? It is to make the defaulter fulfil a legal obligation which it is still open to him to fulfil, the obligation of reparation. Successful or not, the attempt is to make him do what he legally ought to do, on the assumption that he actually can do it but is contumaciously refusing to do it.

So far from replicating what the criminal law does, as the second part of the quotation erroneously suggests, this is actually quite different from the 'technique' of the criminal law. That 'technique' is one which authorizes the imposition of penalties on those who commit offences. *Ex hypothesi* criminal sanctions do not coerce people into not committing offences, since they become operative only after an offence has been committed. The crucial element of civil law technique, the forcing someone to fulfil a duty which it is still open to him to fulfil, is quite lacking. What is actually and directly coercive about the criminal law is that once sentence is passed upon somebody the sentence is carried out whether he 'goes willingly' or not, except in the case of fines, in case of which a sentence of inmprisonment is normally passed to take effect in the event of non-payment. In this respect, the penalties imposed by law are coercively enforced in a manner which contrasts with those of, e.g., football associations, universities, churches, etc.

No doubt a part of the point or purpose of a regime of penalties for offences is to provide disincentives, discouragements, or deterrents to the commission of undesirable or at least undesired acts. The threat of a penalty may therefore be considered as a coercive measure. But it remains more or less conjectural whether apprehension of a threat ever coerces anyone or any large number of people into doing that which they would not otherwise have done. It is at least as likely that any influence which the criminal law exerts upon people's conduct it exerts by being perceived as an authoritative mode of expression of social disapprobation of the prohibited acts. That the law's sanctions are coercively enforced does not entail that the threat of legal sanctions is itself coercive in remotely the same sense. What is certain about the law is that it is coercive in the former sense; the latter is a matter of conjecture.

That civil remedies are ultimately coercively enforceable at the instance of pertinacious judgment creditors is the point which they have in common with criminal penalties. *Non sequitur* that on that or any other ground they should be deemed to belong to the same genus of 'sanctions'. The remedy of civil damages has the function of securing pecuniary reparation for the infringement of a right, and the coercion offered is aimed to make sure that he who ought to and who can make such reparation, does. So far from clarifying the coercive character of legal systems, the crude and undifferentiated notion of 'sanction' which so many legal theorists have adopted is better calculated to obscure it.

It is indeed possible, even likely, that citizens' knowledge that infringements of others' rights may lead to enforceable obligations of reparation provides them with an incentive to carefulness in respect of others. Especially in the conduct of large industrial and commercial enterprises, where costs of operations have to be calculated and met, the risk of large-scale civil liability may provide a motive for care to which unaided moral sensitivity would be insufficient. To the extent that this is the case, it is a highly desirable aspect of the law of reparation. But such incentive effect as the law in this case has, it has not by being quasi-penal but by being genuinely reparative.

We see therefore how untenable must be the view that 'sanctions' enable us to identify 'legal duties' which in turn enable us, if we wish to, identify 'rights'. The truth is utterly the opposite. The law institutes various rights (and modes of acquisition and transference of rights, like contracts, trusts, wills, and so forth); the special character of a legal right is not that its infringement gives rise to an obligation of reparation, but that the obligation of reparation to which it gives rise is judically cognizable and, in case of satisfactory proof, coercively enforceable under the authority of legal officials. In this context we may indeed postulate a duty such as the legal 'duty of care' perfectly correlative with the primary right protected. But we will be led into the grossest error if we suppose that there is or must be some 'sanction' for breach of that duty.

We must consider the obligation of reparation, which arises

when damage is occasioned by breach of such a duty, for what it is, not as an imperfect simulacrum of something else. That it is sanctioned by coercion does not make it a sanction itself. To me it seems that the obligation of reparation is interesting enough in its own character to need no disguise as something else.

12.
COERCION AND LAW

FOLLOWING on from chapter 11, this chapter will examine the widely held view that law—positive law—is essentially coercive. That view seems to me wrong. To show why it is wrong, I shall here offer an analysis of the concept of coercion, and shall then discuss the questions of whether law does actually, and whether law must tautologically, involve coercion in any of the senses analysed. In the bygoing, I shall cast doubt on the currently received views about 'legal sanctions'; indeed, I shall suggest abandonment of that concept as it is currently understood. My argument runs parallel to some of the points made by Joseph Raz in the concluding sections of his *Practical Reason and Norms*.[1]

I. COERCION

My first step is to tackle the concept of coercion, and I shall start by reflecting on physical force, particularly on the ideas of enforced action and suffering. As Aristotle points out in Book III of *Nicomachean Ethics*,[2] being forced to do something does not altogether exclude the idea of 'doing', but only that of 'voluntary doing'—a sea-captain forced off course by a storm does indeed change course, but not voluntarily.

Analogously, human beings can force other humans to do things, albeit what is done is not done voluntarily. Mounted policemen may charge upon a mob rioting in a city square and force them despite all resistance to leave the square. People may be forced to undergo, submit to, or suffer various processes, despite resistance; as, for example, in some cases of rape, or in the case of a prisoner who does not go quietly to gaol, but is dragged there despite resistance, or who is forced to undergo corporal or capital punishment, rather than submitting to it without resistance.

Such cases of being forced to do or suffer something against

[1] J. Raz, *Practical Reason and Norms* (London, 1975), pp. 154–62.
[2] Aristotle, *Nicomachean Ethics*, III.i.

one's will and despite one's resistance seem to me plain enough instances of coercion. But others (e.g., Robert Nozick[3]) have doubted the point, holding that, properly speaking, coercion always involves threats and submission to threats rather than the simple application of overwhelming force on an unwilling victim. Their view seems to me false, for reasons which will be sketched in a moment.

What is indubitable is that the clearest cases of coercion by threat involve reliance on an ability to use force in just the way considered. The policeman may address the rioters with a loud hailer and tell them unless they leave the square within ten minutes they will be driven out forcibly; a man may make it clear to a woman that if she does not forthwith submit to intercourse he will force her to do so anyway; a prisoner may be made well aware that even if he does not submit quietly to his punishment, he will be made to suffer it anyway. In all such cases, the victim has no choice about the outcome, though he or she has a choice as to the way it comes about. He or she may choose to struggle and resist or not; but as to what is in the end done or suffered there is no free choice—no choice at all. And this doing or submitting without any real choice is, I submit, the central element in coercion. To give the present particular type of coercion a label, I shall call it 'coercion by direct threat'.

A victim of coercion by direct threat may of course decide to risk calling the other party's bluff—'You say you are going to make me do or suffer x if I don't submit quietly; all right, go ahead and do that if you can.' The risk is that there was no bluff, that the other party has and uses sufficient brute force to bring about x despite any resistance offered. Since I see no point in saying that making a direct threat is 'coercion', but carrying out is something other than coercion, I shall call every case of using force to make somebody do or submit to x against his will and without real choice a case of 'direct physical coercion'.[4]

---

[3] R. Nozick, 'Coercion' in *Philosophy Science and Method* (ed. S. Morgenbesser, P. Suppes, and M. White, New York, 1969), p. 444.

[4] Nozick's argument is to the effect that coercion always involves at least an implicit threat; merely beating someone up is not coercion of itself, but would be in a case where it was clear that the beating would stop if the victim did something or other desired by the assailant. To some extent, I agree. The coercer has some purpose in view, and what he does he does with a view to obtaining that purpose. Hence, if the victim is ready to comply without (further) use of force, so much the better from the coercer's point of view.

Aside from that and from 'coercion by direct threat' we find that there are other cases of coercion which involve somewhat more indirect means. A blackmailer credibly threatens to publish compromising photographs of the ambassador unless he gives some secret information. A kidnapper credibly threatens to kill the millionaire's child unless a ransom is paid.

Here the threat is not to bring about x by force in case the victim fails to do so. It is to bring about y in case the victim fails to bring about x. So I call this case 'coercion by indirect threat'. The hope and intention of the coercer here is to deploy a threat whose seriousness for the victim is such that he will treat it as leaving him no real choice about doing x however unwilling he is to do it.

We must notice that both logically and physically it is actually open to such a victim to refuse. The ambassador *can* refuse to give away the secrets at whatever cost to his reputation and career; the millionaire *can* withhold the ransom at the cost of his child's life. Subjectively, of course, each may experience the threat as excluding real choice. The ambassador may so value his reputation and career that their preservation constitutes for him what Joseph Raz calls an 'exclusionary reason' for action requiring him to exclude from deliberation the ordinary weight of the reasons against disclosing state secrets, and to act as required in order to save reputation and career. The millionaire may treat preserving his child's life as excluding serious consideration of the normally compelling reasons for holding on to his own money.

Notice, however, that there may be 'objective' (not necessarily moral) reasons which do not automatically correspond with the victim's subjective evaluation and ordering of reasons for action in the case.

To take seriously the legal point of view under which the ambassador has an obligation to protect state secrets at all costs, is to hold that objectively the ranking of exclusionary reasons is the reverse of the one which the ambassador subjectively applied to his dilemma. We understand that the ambassador *felt* obliged to do as he did (and perhaps we sympathize with his plight); we hold that he was *actually* obliged to do the reverse of what he did; to keep the state secrets safe even at the cost of his reputation and career.

As Alan White points out,[5] the key test for the question of whether somebody had no real choice about doing something is to determine whether he was (from some point of view) obliged to do it. Those who judge from some point of view that the ambassador was not obliged to do as he did, especially if they hold him to have been obliged to do the reverse, in effect judge that objectively he was not coerced even though subjectively the threat was for him a compelling one.

The millionaire's case is easier in a way, because most of us would indeed hold that parental obligations do objectively count in just the way the millionaire subjectively accounted them in deciding to pay the ransom and save his child's life. He both felt and was obliged to do so given the threat credibly put to him. Subjective and objective coercion here happen to coincide.

Obviously, coercion by indirect threats is a more problematic category than our other two, because of the way in which a gap opens up between possible 'subjective' and 'objective' evaluations of a case, and because of the necessary relativity even of objective judgments about what a person is or was obliged in a given case to do; such judgments are relative to a point of view or schema of judgment. For example, what I am obliged to do for self-preservation may conflict with what I am morally or legally obliged to do. (That is the very point of conflict which is at the heart of the perennial controversy whether 'duress *per minas*', coercion by indirect threats, should be admissible as a defence to criminal charges.[6])

So be it. My analysis of coercion is a far from complete one. But it justifies us in supposing that, subjectively or objectively, by physical force or otherwise, coercion entails deprivation of any real choice on the victim's part as to what he is to do or suffer. To be one who coerces is to act purposively; it is to act with a view to bringing about certain actings or submissions by another person, the method adopted being a serious attempt at the exclusion of real choice on the other person's part, whether through the application of direct physical force, the application of direct threats of physical force, or the application of indirect threats. Accordingly, we have classified three types: direct

[5] Alan R. White, *Modal Thinking* (London, 1976), chapter on 'Obligation'.
[6] See, e.g., *Director of Public Prosecutions for Northern Ireland* v. *Lynch* [1975] AC 653.

physical coercion, coercion by direct threats, and coercion by indirect threats. We have seen that the third is, by contrast with the first two, both relativistic and thus problematic, in application, if not in conception.

II. CIVIL REMEDIES AS COERCION?

Let me now start to show the jurisprudential relevance of such an analysis. It is a widely held view that positive legal orders are not merely systems of operative social norms, but are also uniquely and distinctively coercive systems. Positivistic jurists such as Jeremy Bentham, John Austin, Hans Kelsen, Alf Ross, Karl Olivecrona, and, in his earlier work, Joseph Raz have held that view;[7] sociologists such as Max Weber and anthropolgists such as E. A. Hoebel have held it;[8] so have most natural lawyers from Aquinas to the present day, the question for them being what forms of coercive order properly participate in the rational character of law.[9]

The key step in the construction of this view is through introduction of the notion of 'legal sanctions'; laws are norms to some or all of which 'sanctions' are directly or indirectly annexed; legal sanctions are themselves coercive or at least they are means of coercion.

Let me mention as exemplars of this thesis the work of Jeremy Bentham and Hans Kelsen. In *Of Laws in General*, Bentham, in characteristic pursuit of analytical clarity, seeks to portray all complete laws[10] as establishing offences and as providing for punitive sanctions to be imposed on whoever commits an offence. Kelsen, though with vital differences of framework and

---

[7] Reference may be made to the standard juristic works of Bentham, Austin, Kelsen, Ross, Olivecrona, and Hart. Joseph Raz's position on this question in *Concept of a Legal System* (Oxford, 1970) has been amended in his later *Practical Reason and Norms*.

[8] See *Max Weber on Law in Economy and Society* (ed. M. Rheinstein, tr. E. A. Shils and M. Rheinstein, Cambridge, Mass., 1954); E. A. Hoebel, *The Law of Primitive Man* (Cambridge, Mass., 1954).

[9] See. e.g., Aquinas, *Summa Theologica*, Prima Secundae Partis, Quaestio XC, Art. 3. As translated in A. P. d'Entrèves (ed.) *Aquinas: Selected Political Writings* (Oxford, 1959), at pp. 109–11, the passage reads: 'A private person has no authority to compel right living. He may only advise . . . But law, to be effective, must have such compelling force . . . But the power of compulsion belongs either to the community as a whole, or to its official representative whose duty it is to inflict penalties.'

[10] The qualification as to 'complete laws' is important; cf. Raz, *Concept of a Legal System*. See J., Bentham, *Of Laws in General* (ed. H. L. A. Hart, London, 1970), ch. 14.

of detail, likewise insists that the 'technique' of civil law and of criminal law is a single one:[11] namely, to authorize the imposition of coercive sanctions on persons who commit certain acts (these acts therefore counting as 'delicts' or 'offences'). Thus, for both authors, the class of legal sanctions includes both an order by a court requiring payment of civil damages and an order by a court imposing a criminal penalty. And Kelsen makes explicit what Bentham leaves implicit—that such sanctions are essentially coercive in character.[12]

Quite apart from the philosophical authority and influence of Bentham and Kelsen, the opinion they advance on such matters belongs I believe to the received wisdom of our times— it is just a matter of what every person of common sense knows about the law. Nevertheless, it is false. We ought at least to hesitate before assigning civil remedies and criminal penalties to the same class of 'sanctions'. We ought to review whether and how they involve coercion, our minds uncluttered by any prejudice in favour of treating the two 'techniques' as identical.

I propose here to consider further civil remedies and criminal penalties as separate legal institutions, taking as my exemplar a model based on current Scots law, which in this regard seems a tolerably representative case of a developed legal system. I start with civil remedies.

Suppose that Donald (D) unlawfully injures Patrick (P), that is, infringes by some act or omission a right invested in P by law (whether a right arising from contract, or a right of a proprietary kind, or a right to bodily security, or however characterized among the 'institutional facts; of law[13]). In that case P has automatically remedial rights against D, namely, (i) the right that D forthwith desist from committing the injury; (ii) the right that D make reparation for the injury already suffered by P. These rights are themselves independent of any decision by P to litigate. D can and should fulfil them, if the facts are clear.

But such facts are not always clear. D may refuse to acknowledge or satisfy P's rights. Then P can, if he chooses, start

---

[11] See, e.g., Hans Kelsen, *The Pure Theory of Law* (Berkeley and Los Angeles, 1967), pp. 24–35; id., *General Theory of Law and State* (New York, 1961), pp. 50–1.
[12] Ibid.
[13] See MacCormick, 'Law as Institutional Fact' (Edinburgh, 1973); also in 90 LQR (1974) 102.

litigation. He must first aver and then prove a wrongful infringement by *D* of his rights, and show the court that there are particular legal remedies to which he is therefore entitled.

Suppose that *P* succeeds—for example, the court issues an order requiring *D* (i) to desist from further infringement of a copyright of *P*'s; (ii) to pay *D* £1,000 as damages for loss occasioned to *P* by the original infringement of the copyright. At this stage it is again open to *D* to satisfy quite voluntarily the now judically determined rights of *P*. In a case in which liability has been genuinely disputed by *D*, there is now an authoritative determination of the disputed points, and he may well be entirely willing to change his line of conduct and to pay up now that the dispute is thus resolved.

If he does not do so, yet further processes have to be set in motion by *P* in order to secure satisfaction. If *D* defies the order to desist from infringing the copyright, he can eventually be imprisoned for contempt of court, and kept in prison till he has purged his contempt and given satisfactory assurances as to amendment of his conduct. As to payment of damages, assets of his may be seized by various processes of diligence, and if *D* resists these processes by force he may again find himself committed to prison for deforcement of officers of the law. As in most legal systems, these processes are fairly long-drawn-out, and can at most stages be simply terminated if *P* decides to abandon his rights.

Now let us ask: what forms of coercion are involved in all this long story? Certainly, acts of direct physical coercion are clearly involved in the final stages, for example if *D* is ordered to be imprisoned for contempt or on conviction for deforcement: he will be taken to gaol by the use of such force as is necessary, in case he does not go quietly. The same may hold for forcible seizure of his goods under a judicial warrant. Secondly, the very issuance of orders for imprisonment or seizure of goods in such circumstances obviously and necessarily amount to what I called 'coercion by direct threats'.

Thirdly, at least from the time of the initial judicial determination of the original dispute, there are implicitly present various indirect threats, since it is common knowledge that at *P*'s instance *D* may be subjected to the series of processes mentioned unless he satisfies *P*'s judicially established remedial rights. Subjectively, D may experience these implicit threats as coercive, in that they constitute for him the only and a sufficient reason for unwilling compliance with the court's orders. Objectively, there are perhaps adequate grounds for supposing that these implicit threats fully constitute a form of coercion by indirect threat; this element of coercion lies behind, but is not constituted by, the orders awarding P his remedies.

As to the remedies themselves, there is an abundance of legal principle and legal rhetoric to the effect that their primary function and justification is to compensate the victim and secure him in his rights, not to deter or punish wrongdoers.[14] Especially as to civil damages, these assertions have the ring of truth. The measure of damages is the extent of P's loss, not the gravity of any guilt of D's. The possibility of reasonable mitigation by P of his loss is taken into account. If D has prudently insured himself for such liability, the contract of insurance is not struck down as being illegal or contrary to public policy, for this is no matter of seeking to nullify a just punishment. And so on.

Of course, knowledge of the civil remedies available at law may be fairly widely disseminated in the community. Both in general terms and in particular cases, such knowledge may constitute an inducement to respect for the legal rights of groups and individuals—all the more so to the extent that there is some sort of vague and diffuse awareness that there are available processes of coercion for enforcing judicially awarded civil remedies.

But the existence of such general awareness and its effect as an inducement is by no stretch of imagination any form of coercion. In the present state of sociological knowledge, its existence and effect is a matter of mere conjecture, well worthy indeed of empirical investigation.[15] Even, however, if it were shown to be no sort of operative inducement, or a weak one, that would in no way rob the institution of civil remedies of its point and utility. To recognize remedial rights and to provide for

[14] Cf. Chapter 11 above; Kelsen, of course, concedes here a 'relative' difference between civil and criminal sanctions—see *General Theory of Law and State*, p. 50.

[15] Some work on the attitudes of businessmen to contracts and breaches thereof is highly suggestive on this point. See S. MacAulay, *Law and the Balance of Power* (New York, 1966).

judicial processes aimed at satisfying them is of itself an essential part of taking legal rights seriously—whether or not it has the side-effect of providing a general inducement to respect for those rights.

The general theoretical approach on which I am relying here represents civil law as instituting various forms of rights invested in persons and groups of persons, consequential to which is an obligation on anyone who infringes any such right to make reparation of the injury. That is intelligible (though certainly needing further analysis and elucidation) quite apart even from formally institutionalized litigation and adjudication. But it is an old truism that even among people of good will, rights and infringements of rights are disputable points—a fact which justifies the adoption of some form of authoritative and institutional judicial process for settling disputes.

To all that, processes of the coercive enforcement of judicially awarded remedies are an addendum, an additional security. They are not constitutive of nor definitive of nor conceptually essential to laws and legal rights. They may be a practical necessity in a world in which some people (whether justly or unjustly) will not voluntarily respect the rights instituted by positive law (whether justly or unjustly) in favour of others. If we must here use the terminology of 'sanction' at all, we had better revert to the eighteenth-century usage, and conclude that the remedies of the civil law are not themselves 'sanctions' but are 'sanctioned', that is *confirmed*, by measures of coercive enforcement. As John Erskine put it, the 'sanction' in this sense 'gives [an] enactment its full force and effect, and chiefly preserves if from being violated by perverse men, who would disregard the true ground of obedience'.[16]

---

[16] John Erskine, *An Institute of the Laws of Scotland* (Edinburgh, 1773), I. i. 5: 'When laws have a tendency to promote the real happiness of the subjects, that alone creates an obligation to obedience, called by Heineccius and other writers, the internal obligation of law. This, however, would be insufficient of itself for enforcing obedience, if these laws were not also guarded by a commination of some punishment or evil which is not the natural consequence of the transgression. That part of the law which inflicts the punishment upon disobedience is called its sanction, from *sancire*, "to confirm" because it is that which gives the enactment full force and authority, and chiefly preserves it fom being violated by perverse men . . .'

III . COERCION AND CRIMINAL LAW

A. M. Honoré in his recent essay 'Real Laws'[17] has pointed out that most criminal statutes do not in fact command, prescribe, or prohibit conduct directly. They stipulate what acts and omissions shall constitute offences, and they prescribe penalties for the offences they define. Unlike civil laws, criminal laws do not directly establish rights, though (as in the case of theft) they may allude to rights otherwise instituted. No doubt, indeed, a satisfactory system of criminal law would be justifiable at least in part by reference to the desirabilty of protecting rights of persons and groups, and of registering adequate public disapprobation of conduct manifesting an agent's wilful disregard for the rights of others. But not all criminal laws are satisfactory, and the specific gist of criminal law is only offences and penalties.

It is certainly the case, in all those societies which have developed a specialized criminal law, that coercion is involved in many of the processes of the criminal law. Every day human beings are forcibly arrested and detained and committed to prison pending trial. Public order is regularly secured by coercive action like that of the mounted police in one of my earlier examples. People who have been tried and convicted are sentenced to various forms of punishment, pecuniary and physical (including imprisonment, beating, even death); these punishments are carried out when necessary by direct physical coercion, and even when the convict goes quietly to his fate, he does so in the shadow of coercion by the direct threat that whether he resists or not the punishment will be carried out by main force.

Now you may say that just such measures of coercion are what the very idea of punishment or penalty conceptually requires. I beg to differ. There is no self-contradiction in the idea of unenforced penalties or even of voluntarily undertaken penalties. To see that, one need only reflect on the closely analogous concept of penance. What is absurd about the idea that persons in some organization—not necessarily a church— make regular confession of offences they have committed, and

[17] In *Law, Morality, and Society* (ed. P. M. S. Hacker and J. Raz, Oxford, 1977), pp. 99–118.

accept and act upon the ruling of some institutionally authorized person that they accordingly subject themselves to some
more or less burdensome penance appropriate to the gravity of
the offence?

Apart from such penances, what about penalties in the context of sports and voluntary associations of individuals? I don't
have to play football; I don't have to continue a member of my
social club or my trade union. But so long as I choose to play, or
to be a member, I am subject to a body of law and to processes of
judgment when I break it, and authorized officials (referees,
committees, etc.) can exact penalties from me if I am shown to
have committed some offence. These are truly penalties, not
penances—but they are voluntary, because I need pay them
only if I choose to go on playing the game, or to remain a
member of the association.

It is merely stating the obvious to remark that states as at
present constituted are not in fact voluntary associations and
that criminal penalties in our present states are, by contrast
with penances and with other types of penalty, always or as
often as possible coercively enforced. But it is a *logical* absurdity
to suppose that the penalties of the criminal law could be
non-coercive? What if all the processes of prosecution, trial,
conviction, and sentence took place as with us, only with this
difference: the judge sentences the convicted person to subject
himself to some punitive process—for example, go to a penitentiary ('penitentiary' would then be a well chosen name) and
stay there under a spartan regime for a certain period?

Is this logically absurd as a form of punishment, or is it
merely practically unthinkable given human nature as we
understand it? Is it only ruled out by contingent human and
social facts? (I am tempted to ask if we have any known grounds
to suppose that *even* contingent facts rule it out. Such a scheme
wouldn't work perfectly, but it seems to me a discussable
question whether its imperfections would be any more
damaging to the social fabric than the glaring imperfections of
existing coercive penal systems.)

Here is a final question for those who doubt my analysis: do
you remember whether classical Athenian ostracism was
coercively enforced or not? Could you doubt whether it was,
and still be certain it was a punishment?

Possibly I am still missing the point of the theory that criminal law is essentially coercive. Whether or not penalties have to be coercively enforced, it may be said that the very existence of a standing body of law defining offences and appointing penalties to offenders marks in itself an intrinsic coercive feature of state societies. To have penalties of any kind is to subject ourselves all and sundry to standing threats aimed at securing our compliance with law for fear of the consequences of non-compliance. That is what legal penalties intrinsically are—a mechanism of coercion by indirect threat: 'Refrain from x or suffer y', to adopt the formula I used earlier.

I would be quite glad if it were true that the criminal law did indeed form a standing inducement or *a fortiori* an effective mode of coercion for making people respect the law. I would sleep all the easier in my bed at night the more it were true. But whether or not it is true is a contingent question of fact, one which my criminological friends assure me still remains to be satisfactorily answered.

Still, the theory I am disputing does not depend on the facts of the matter. It makes a conceptual point about what penalties essentially are—threats aimed, however effectually or ineffectually, at coercing or inducing people to respect the law. My fundamental objection to that theory is that it illegitimately works into the definition of penalties one particular theory of the justification of punishments, the theory of general deterrence. But the justification of punishments is a controversial question for normative legal and moral philosophy. Retributivism, or the kind of symbolic expressive theory of punishment advanced by Moberley and implicit in Durkheim, may both be wrong.[18] But they are not wrong by definition; they are not self-contradictory. So we must reject the theory that the institution of penalties is essentially and intrinsically a variety of coercion by indirect threat. We must reject it even if in some societies people seek to make the criminal law coercive in that way, and even if in some societies a regime of sufficiently barbarous and brutal penalties could effectively coerce the subject population into compliant behaviour.

---

[18] Cf. ch. 2 above, and MacCormick, *H. L. A. Hart* (London, 1981), ch. 11; and Sir W. Moberley, *The Ethics of Punishment* (London, 1968), chs. 8, 9; Emile Durkheim, *De la division du travail social* (3rd edn., Paris, 1907), ch. 2, § 4.

So the conclusion I reach about criminal law parallels the conclusion I reached about civil law. In modern state societies, the exaction of criminal penalties proceeds by way of coercion; both direct physical coercion and coercion by direct threat. In this sense these penalties are indeed sanctioned (or 'secured' or 'confirmed') by measures of coercion. This may well be a practical necessity for social peace; H. L. A. Hart may well be right when he says that 'voluntary co-operation in a coercive system' is the best that can be hoped for in human societies.[19] But the necessity, if it exists, is only practical; it is not logical; it is not inherent in the very concepts of 'penalty', 'offence', and 'law'.

That which sanctions and secures existing legal orders is or includes coercion to some significant extent. Our analysis shows that this is a contingent feature of the societies we live in now, whether or not it is a practically changeable feature of them or of any human society; it is not a logically necessary feature of a legal order which determines rights and defines offences for the members of a society.

Certainly it is one possible and useful point of a regime which defines offences and penalties that it establishes a standing inducement to refrain from what is authoritatively deemed to be undesirable behaviour. But we only have to reread Kant and Hegel[20] to be reminded that it is not the *only* possible point of such a regime, or to be reminded that such regimes may perhaps be the more morally questionable the more they are or function as pure systems of coercion by indirect threats.

My argument at present concerns what is logically possible, not what is morally desirable. Once it is accepted that law is not *essentially*, though it may often be *actually* coercive, interesting moral and practical questions are opened. (And it is one aspect of the value of analytical enquiry that it can and does open such questions; though it only opens them.)

It would be a different question again to consider whether in any event law is as much 'sanctioned' by pains and penalties as

---

[19] H. L. A. Hart, *The Concept of Law* (Oxford, 1961), p. 193.
[20] I. Kant, *The Metaphysical Elements of Justice* (tr. John Ladd, Indianapolis, 1965), p. 140; *Hegel's Philosophy of Right* (tr. T. M. Knox, Oxford, 1952), pp. 70–3.

by rewards.[21] My thought on this is that, at least in commercial or capitalist and post-capitalist social democratic societies, the rewards and advantages open to law-abiding citizens far outstrip those open to persons who deviate seriously from the path of the law.[22] My thought is that here may be found the predominantly effective inducement to respect for law in such societies. Here certainly is a fascinating area for investigation and exploration by empirical rather than analytical techniques. Common-sense observation already suggests an answer.

It has been put to me by a colleague[23] that the prospect of such rewards (and of losing them) is at least as coercive as any of the penalties formally regulated by laws. My answer is that not every inducement of this kind is happily labelled 'coercion'. Some people may perhaps experience the prospect of such rewards (or their loss) as 'subjectively coercive'. But the claim by anyone that he has no real choice about doing x, since he can only obtain some advantages by doing x, seems to me likely in most circumstances to be a highly doubtful one, viewed objectively.[24] More often than not, such a claim involves a mixture of the crude animism which ascribes to 'society' in itself purposive activity like coercing people into doing things, and the moral flabbiness whereby people who have made real choices are after the event allowed to claim that they had no choice about doing what they did. In general, that it is less comfortable to be a nonconformist does not mean that people have no choice about conforming. Nor does it mean that those who have opted for the comforts of conformity have done something other than opt for them.

---

[21] Bentham (*Of Laws*) and Erskine (*Institute of the Laws of Scotland*) both thought that rewards could be sanctions. Whether they can be 'coercive' or not is another story; though as to this, in general there is a flourishing literature on coercive offers or proposals as distinct from coercive threats. See, e.g., Nozick, 'Coercion', p. 444; V. Haksar, 'Coercive Proposals', 4 *Political Theory* (1976), 65–79; H. Frankfurt, 'Coercion and Moral Responsibility', in *Essays on Freedom of Action* (ed. T. Honderich, London, 1973).

[22] These rewards are not all or mainly specifically determined by the law itself; is that an important difference between them and penalties?

[23] Mr Z. K. Bankowski; I must add that I do not at all impute to him the vices mentioned in the succeeding sentences.

[24] But the difference drawn earlier between 'subjective' and 'objective' coercion may be helpful in relation to the general question about the possibility of coercion by offers of rewards, discussed by the authors cited above, n. 21.

In short: not every inducement is coercive: there appear to be many strong inducements to law-abiding behaviour which are non-coercive; once we have ditched the misleading notion of 'sanction' which we have inherited, we can usefully speculate upon the extent to which positive law is actually sanctioned by rewards and other inducements built into the social structure of state societies, rather than by pains and penalties alone. We might reflect also on the question whether, conceptually, positive law has to be so sanctioned. All I have shown here is that 'law' as such does not have to be coercively sanctioned.

A final thought may be added, by way of reflection on the horrifying wave of rioting which struck a number of British cities in July 1981. It appears from reports on this that the rioters belong mainly to the disadvantaged youth (of all races) from the inner city areas and other socially disadvantaged parts of great conurbations. Without seeking to generalize too much from thin evidence and mere speculation, it does appear as though attacks on 'the system' stem mainly from those who least share in the benefits it provides and who have had most experience of the coercive force of the law, as expressed in police powers of stopping and searching, of pursuing enquiries, and of making arrests on broad and ill-defined legal charges.

One possible response to such events might be a resort to the more extensive use of 'direct physical coercion'. Certainly, the Home Secretary did, in July 1981, authorize the use of water-cannons, plastic bullets, and other such weapons for restoring or preserving public order. Fortunately, however, police forces found it unnecessary to use such extreme measures of control. Obviously, the long-term utility or effectiveness of extreme forms of coercion is more than doubtful, to say nothing of their moral desirability. Law is not necessarily most effective where it is most coercive.

What ought to be of the greatest concern is a sense of alienation among so many from the legal order of the country. If they think that 'there is nothing in it for them', the rest of us ought to consider most anxiously what justification their view has. As often happens, we may find strong reasons of mere self-interest for seeking a greater measure of social justice in others' favour. That is not a particularly admirable motive for doing the right thing; but let the right be done regardless of motive. Let the law be founded on mere coercion, and we shall all be the losers.

13.
NATION AND NATIONALISM

I F T H E previous chapters of this book appear to espouse an unreflective form of individualism, this chapter may go some way to administering a necessary corrective. Only a partial corrective, however. I mean neither to deny nor to qualify the proposition that individual human beings are the primary bearers of moral value and of moral and legal rights. I continue to affirm that the good society is one in which individuals—*each* individual—are taken seriously; in which each human person has that fair opportunity of material well-being and that just extent of civil liberty which are essential to the flourishing of each one's individuality as a person.

There is a problem about this, though. It is the problem as to the concept of 'an individual' which is presupposed in the affirmation of such a principle. Does it not presuppose the untenable ideas that 'individuals' are logically prior to 'society', and hence that 'society' results from the coming together of preconstructed individuals? Such ideas are as untenable as the idea that anyone could literally be a 'self-made man'; for they are the same idea. The truth about human beings is that they can only become individuals—acquire a sense of their own individuality—as a result of their social experiences within human communities. Thus 'the individual' is as much a product of 'society' as vice versa. Even political individualism is a programme for *social* organization.

Among the concepts through which we can explore the connection between the individual and the social are those of 'nation' and 'nationalism'. On the one hand, appeals to the nation and to nationalism have often served to legitimate the ruthless suppression of individuals and minority groups. On the other hand, it seems an arguable proposition that nations (and hence a certain kind of nationalism) are among the pre-conditions of human individuality and therefore of that version of political individualism intrinsic to my view of 'legal right and social democracy'. Whether 'nation' and 'nationalism' are antithetical to or compatible with 'individual' and 'individual-ism' is therefore a question of some moment.

It is also a question of acute personal concern to me. I have been for a good many years a member of the Scottish National Party, and yet remain in some perplexity about the justifiability of any nationalist case within the terms set for me by the other principles to which I adhere and which I have expounded in this book. With a view to resolving both the general question and the particular perplexity, I present here an exploration of the concepts of 'nation' and 'nationalism'. I do so with par-ticular reference to the Scottish case.

Nations are manifestly groupings or communities of people. Manifestly they are not necessarily identical with states, for while there are some nation-states, there are some states which are not nations (e.g. the USSR) and some nations which are not states (e.g. the Basque nation, whose members inhabit areas within two adjacent states). States are political entities which have a legal definition.[1] Wherever there exists a relatively independent and self-sufficient legal order having defined organs of government of a relatively centralized kind exercising effective jurisdiction over a certain territory, there is a state. The members, or citizens, of a state are defined by laws belong-ing to that legal order, which normally make some natural or specifically chosen connection with the given territory a con-dition of citizenship.

On this view, the United Kingdom is certainly a state; equally certainly, none of England, Scotland, Wales, or Northern ireland is a state. Yet most people would consider that 'England', 'Scotland', and 'Wales' are the names of nations; and at least some would say the same of 'Northern Ireland', though that is manifestly a more than disputable point.

Many people would say that there is also a 'British nation' which in some sense includes all the internal nations or parts of the UK. What is more, those who act on behalf of the UK as a state (members of governments and governmental officials) manifestly use and deploy the concept of 'nation' in their actings on behalf of the British state. For example, the 'National

---

[1] Broadly speaking, I follow Hans Kelsen's account of the state. See Kelsen, *General Theory of Law and State* (tr. A. Wedberg, Cambridge, Mass., 1945) and cf. ch. 2, § iii above, at note-cue 21.

Industrial Relations Court' bore that name because it had, unusually, jurisdiction throughout the UK; likewise the 'National Enterprise Board'; in legal terminology 'nationality' is the name for citizenship, as in the 'British Nationality Acts'; and by those who favour it, 'nationalization' is a preferred term to 'state control'. 'Nation', it seems, is a term with favourable connotations or resonances, 'state' not so. States are legalistic impersonal entities, nations are communities with culture and personality. It should not be surprising if those having charge of the cold legal persona, the state, seek to infuse it with the warm moral personality of 'a nation'.

But still that term rests unexplained. That a nation is a grouping or community of people not identical with a state is an essentially negative observation which fails in any event to distinguish nations from, e.g. churches, universities, or, for that matter, private clubs.

The basic point to be made in a positive elucidation of nationhood is that nations are constituted by a form of popular consciousness, not by a mode of legal organization. In this consciousness, as Ernest Renan suggested in his lecture 'Qu'est-ce qu'une nation?' of 1882, there is included a sense of a common past, and of a present will to live together. A nation is constituted by a relatively large grouping of people who conceive themselves to have a communal past, including shared sufferings and shared achievements, from which past is derived a common culture which represents a form of cultural continuity uniting past and present and capable of being projected into the future. This continuity is not a static one, but is in a sense 'organic'. The common culture, the common way of doing and living, the common language (though nations need not be identified with a single language, e.g., Switzerland), have changed over time, but the changes occur within and make sense within an uninterrupted tradition, and stem from each generation's own choices, as distinct from having been imposed *ab extra*.

Crucially and centrally this involves having a common name: 'we in this nation call ourselves English, Scots, Swiss, or whatever'; and this in turn implies some notion of kinship, in the sense that members of the nation are all, however remotely, kin one with another, whether by birth or (as indeed in the parallel case of the family) by adoption. When, as is usual, the group is associated with, or lays claim to, some tract of territory, that, too, bears the common name, England, Scotland, Switzerland, or whatever.

As is indicated by my citation *in English* of the name of Switzerland, outsiders to a particular nation, in recognizing it for what it is, also have a name for it, not necessarily the same name as the members of the nation use. 'Germany' is a most obvious case of this phenomenon. Thus, although the essential feature of a nation is a common form of consciousness of members of a group, the existence of a nation is not a purely subjective fact. It is capable of objective—at least inter-subjective—recognition and thus subject to the use of common, publicly understood, names.

The point of all this was more elegantly put by Lord Simon of Glaisdale in his speech in the House of Lords case of *London Borough of Ealing* v. *Race Relations Board*[2] in 1972:

'Nation' and 'national' in their popular . . . sense are also vague terms. They do not necessarily imply statehood. For example, there were many submerged nations in the former Hapsburg empire. Scotland is not a nation in the eye of international law; but Scotsmen constitute a nation by reason of those most powerful elements in the creation of a national spirit—tradition, folk memory, a sentiment of community. The Scots are a nation because of Bannockburn and Flodden, Culloden and the pipes at Lucknow, because of Jenny Geddes and Flora Macdonald, because of frugal living and a respect for learning, because of Robert Burns and Walter Scott. So, too, the English are a nation—because Norman, Angevin and Tudor monarchs forged them together, because their land is mostly sea-girt, because of the common law and gifts for poetry and parliamentary government, because (despite the Wars of the Roses and Old Trafford and Headingley) Yorkshireman and Lancastrian feel more in common than in difference, and are even prepared at a pinch to extend their sense of community to southron folk. By the Act of Union English and Scots lost their separate nationalities, but they retained their separate nationhoods.

Tradition and folk memory, to which Lord Simon refers, are of course a matter as much of myth and heroic legend (Bannockburn, Flodden, Flora Macdonald) as of sober his-

[2] [1972] AC 342 at 364.

torical truth. As we see from such documents as the Declaration of Arbroath of 1320, the Scots of the time of Bannockburn had their own mythology going back further from their time than Bannockburn is from ours. And some of it belonged to the realms of pure fiction—perhaps even then it was not seriously believed that the highly Normanized if not in some cases purely Anglo-Norman signatories of the declaration were literally lineal descendants of a people who had made their way laboriously from Scythia to the Atlantic North-west of the British Isles.

But the fact that mythical history contains elements of pure fiction does not detract from the fact that it is held and asserted as a common myth or tradition. And the latter is the key fact for this discussion. For in such shared consciousness inheres the sense of a common identity which is what we signify by ideas like nationhood.

Why, then, should this be so? Why is it something about which people care? A part at least of the answer to that must, I suggest, lie in the way in which, for each of us, our sense of individual personality and identity is derivative from a social context. Even our personal names are conferred on us, not (in most cases) personally chosen. We 'place' ourselves through family, local community, nation, citizenship, religious affiliation, education, job, work community, and so forth. Of course, individuality goes beyond all that—but not in a way that renders all that superfluous or meaningless; human individuality presupposes social existence.

What is more, it is only through our membership of significant groupings that we can transcend the constraints of place and time. Each human being as an individual has no more than a short (no one knows how short) duration of life, and can never be in more than one place at a time. For each of us, then, a 'nation' (but not only a nation) can provide a conceptual framework which allows us to comprehend our own existence as belonging within a continuity in time and a community in space. Here it is vital to observe that the sense of a common past which Renan identified has as its corollary a hope or will for continuity into the future. In being conscious of, and perhaps even taking pride or pleasure in, the links of tradition and community which we have with the past, each of us has the

possibility of conceiving his actions and activities carrying that
continuity into the future, changed and improved perhaps, but
changed in a way which adds to rather than abolishes the
richness of tradition. In the same way, because one is a member
of a community, there is some common link between what one
does here and others do elsewhere. Consciousness of belonging
to a nation is one of the things which enables us as individuals in
some way in this earthly existence to transcend the limitations
of space, time, and mortality, and to participate in that which
had meaning before us and will continue to have meaning
beyond us.

Nations are not the only unities which can give this sense of
continuity beyond an individual's own life-span. Families and a
'sense of family' can have similar significance. Nor is this confined necessarily to aristocracies. My own father used to be set
on his grandmother's knee in a humble house in Mull and
asked, Co tha thu (Who are you)?'; 'Cha n-eil fhios agam (I
don't know)'; 'Is tu Iain mac Dhomhnuill 'ic Neill 'ic Iain 'ic
Dhughaill . . . (You are John, son of Donald, son of Neil, son of
John, son of Dugald . . .)'—and so on went the genealogy up to
thirty-three generations, no doubt some of them fictitious. I
have inherited a similar conception of having a familial past and
(as it were) a hope for a familial future. The huge success of Alex
Haley's *Roots* suggests that I am not alone in being glad to know
my roots (and not only in the patrilineal line), and thus of
having some small sense of contributing to a continuity, not
merely seeing out my three score years and ten, if I get that far,
for what it may serve me.

Churches, trade unions, political parties, schools, universities, firms, supranational groupings, empires, and all such
durable and significant human groupings (whether or not
inspired with intimations of divinity) can have a like significance to human beings in just the same way as can nations or
families. What is more, such collectives may matter at least as
much to their members as either nation or family. So all the
more can and should the concept of belonging to mankind, and
sharing a small planet with other animals and organisms.

'Patriotism is not enough', said Edith Cavell. And she was
right. A sense of inclusion in any unity entails a sense that others
are excluded. I am a MacCormick or a Scot in a way which

necessarily implies that others are not. For any such x those who are x are x to the exclusion of others who are not x. And this can itself be taken as a ground for unfavourable differential (or worse) treatment of the outsiders. Hence the need for deeper and wider moral loyalties than those of nation, family, church, or whatever.

It is not so much a paradox as a perennial moral problem that undue love of one's own can lead to hatred or contempt of others. Family pride can degenerate into snobbery, love of one's university into an élitist contempt for the unscholarly, honourable national sentiment into the unspeakable evil of Nazism, firm religious commitment into harsh sectarianism.

Hence it is said by some that all such exclusionary sentiments are necessarily evil. We must abandon any particularistic love and give ourselves over only to universal love. But that seems falsehood to me. It is, I suggest, those who have a decent and moderate love of their own family, country, colleagues, co-religionists or whatever who can alone recognize as equally legitimate (because the same in kind) the love others bear for their own. Could one learn to love mankind universally if one had not first learned to love people in the concrete in the narrower range? What is more, respecting other people entails respecting the things they value. If I have no sense of what is my own to which I have special regard, I can hardly respect your sense of special regard for what is your own. 'Patriotism is not enough . . . I must have no hatred in my heart.' But that does not imply that there is no place for patriotism and like sentiments.

Equally, because there is more than one form of grouping within which individuals may find a sense of identity and of community with others, it seems wrong to rank them in terms of more or less absolute claims of loyalty. Sometimes it has been held that a claim made by or on behalf of 'the nation' (such claims may be made by governments in nation states, for example) necessarily and absolutely overrides every other possible claim on an individual—whether of family, of religious commitment, of friendship, of political loyalty, of professional or scholarly ideals, of solidarity with workmates, of personal conscience. That is a morally intolerable claim. If nationalism implies ascribing that sort of absolutist, overrriding force to the claims of 'the nation', then it is indeed a morally intolerable philosophy. But what is morally intolerable is the assertion of the *overriding* force of the claim, not the suggestion that some such claims are morally valid and politically justifiable.

Sometimes 'nationalism' is taken to mean adherence to just that morally intolerable principle, that the claims of a nation on its members override any other claim. This principle is commonly in turn grounded (or alleged by its proponents to be grounded) on the thesis that the nation is the highest form of human association, through which and only through which human perfection can be achieved, each human being having moral significance only as part of greater units, themselves only part of this greatest unity, the nation. It is but a short step from this to the view that nations in turn may be ranked in hierarchical order, superior nations having rights of domination over inferior ones.

As is well known, doctrines of that very kind arose within political philosophy towards the end of the eighteenth and beginning of the nineteenth century. They emerge in various forms from the writings of thinkers such as Rousseau, Lessing, Hegel, Fichte, and von Savigny. Hence it has become in our own time something of a commonplace that, as Eugene Kamenka puts it, 'Nationalism . . . is a modern and intially a European phenomenon, best understood in relation to developments that produced, and were symbolized by, the French Revolution of 1789.'³ Kenneth R. Minogue argues the same thesis in his admirable *Nationalism*.⁴ And in the volume in which this essay first appeared A. J. P. Taylor propounded a similar case.⁵

There is, as Mr Taylor points out, an important connection between such doctrines and various forms of democratic theory. If 'the nation' has overriding claims on its members, and just claims as against other nations, whether equal or inferior, the issue poses itself how we can identify the claims of a nation. The

---

³ E. Kamenka (ed.), *Nationalism, the nature and evolution of an idea* (London, 1976), p. 4. See pp. 12–13 for discussion of Renan's 'Qu'est-ce qu'une nation?'.
⁴ K. R. Minogue, *Nationalism* (London, 1967)' and of R. L. McLaughlin, 'Aspects of Nationalism', in *The Scottish Debate*, ed. N. MacCormick (London, 1970).
⁵ See 'Nations in History', *The Crown and the Thistle*, ed. C. MacLean (Edinburgh, 1979), pp. 1–8.

answer, obviously, is that they must be expressed by the nation, the whole nation, the sovereign people. The claims of a nation are, to use Rousseau's term, expressed in deliverances of the 'general will' of the people. It is only a slight irony if we discover that this can in turn seem to justify the effective subjection of the entire people to a charismatic leader, Napoleon or Hitler, who is deemed to express and interpret the pure will of the people in a manner which transcends the mere squabbling of pseudo-democratic parties. But, be that as it may, the evident need that the nation be free to express its will leads logically to the view that there must be self-determination of nations and that, since the sovereign state is the supreme form of politico-legal order, each nation must be or become a sovereign state.

(Conversely, and not surprisingly, we find that wherever there are sovereign states, they (which is to say, their governing authorities) seek to legitimate themselves by adopting the rhetoric of nationhood and portraying the state as the institutional embodiment of a postulated nation. Since such rhetoric is powerful and since the citizens of a state do necessarily have at least legal institutions and defensive arrangements in common, and since nationhood postulates the existence in a group of people of a shared consciousness of historical and cultural continuity, it is not surprising that states do in fact succeed in generating nations. The combination of their very existence and their official rhetoric creates the conditions for emergence of the relevant forms of consciousness. That there has been a United Kingdom for 270 years makes it unsurprising, and a fact which in itself demands respect, that so many adhere to a belief in and declare their loyalty to the 'British nation'.)

It is certainly true that the term 'nationalism' first came into currency as a term of art in political discourse during that period in the early nineteenth century to which what I shall call the 'orthodox theory' ascribes the beginnings of nationalism; and some variant on the principles I outlined above and stigmatized as morally intolerable has been held by many who have called themselves nationalists.

But the orthodox theory seems to me misleading in restricting the meaning of the term nationalism—which is in common use in a far wider sense, even among scholars—to denoting only principles such as those propounded by the early nineteenth-century theorists of nationalism. The orthodox theory certainly admits of the existence, prior to 1789, of nations characterized by a sense of nationhood, coupled with ideas of patriotism, even chauvinism and xenophobia. These are recognized as primitive forerunners of nationalism proper, yet they did, it is suggested, undergo a revolutionary sea-change in or after 1789, when in France first of all subjects became citizens, the state became a nation, and the sovereign nation arose to fill the void left by the demise of the absolute monarch. 'France', as Mr Taylor puts it, 'became the title of a country not a king.'[6]

What all this seems to me to render wholly obscure is the fact that long before then, and in different political systems and traditions, the concept 'nation' figured significantly in political rhetoric and political argument. And it did so precisely by way of making the case that it was wrong to pursue political objectives aimed at absorbing one nation into another, or subordinating one to another. The distinctiveness of nations was, long before 1789, advanced as a reason why they ought to live under their own kings subject to their own laws; this was advanced as a matter of right, of the right of a people to live under their own laws and customs; and conversely it was represented as injustice if this were not allowed.

I can speak only of what I know, and I make no claim to expertise as a historian, but it seems to me that there is in the history of Scotland an abundance of evidence for the statements I have just made. And I see no reason at all to suppose that concepts and forms of argument which were evidently in common currency among the Scots were peculiar to them alone. I shall outline some of that evidence in a moment, but before doing so I shall explain why I think the point important.

No term seems as appropriate as 'nationalism' to describe political principles which justify forms of government on grounds of their appropriateness to the distinctiveness of nations, or on grounds of the rights of nations. All such principles have it in common with the more virulent (and morally intolerable) principles advanced in the nineteenth century in the name of 'nationalism', that they assume or assert

6 Ibid., p. 3.

the existence of nations as a politically significant fact, and as a ground both of collective and of individual rights. To apply a commonly accepted philosophical usage, we may say that within the concept of nationalism the nineteenth-century theories express but one conception of nationalism. There have been and are other conceptions of nationalism, and it remains an open question whether any of those others is morally acceptable. The orthodox theory errs in confusing the nineteenth-century Hegelian conceptions of nation and nationalism with the concept itself.

Now for the evidence of the pre-1789 sense of nationalism, which as I said I cull from my reading of Scottish history:

Let me commence by recalling the sixteenth-century attempts of Henry VIII to procure forcibly a union of England and Scotland through the 'rough wooing' of the infant Mary of Scots on behalf of Henry's young son Edward. The 'wooing' proceeded by way of devastation of southern Scotland, and it provoked from an anonymous writer a pamphlet entitled the *Complaynt of Scotland*, from which I quote:

There is nocht tua nations vndir the firmament that ar mair contrar and different fra vthirs nor is Inglismen and Scottismen, quhobeit that thai be within ane ile and nychtbours and of ane langage. For Inglismen ar subtil and Scottismen ar facile. Inglismen ar ambitius in prosperite and Scottismen ar humain in prosperite. Inglismen ar humil quhen thai ar subieckit be forse and violence, and Scottismen ar furius quhen thai ar violently subieckit. Inglismen ar cruel quhene thai get victorie, and Scottismen ar merciful quhen thai get victorie. And to conclude, it is onpossibil that Scottismen and Inglismen can remane in concorde vndir ane monarche or ane prince, because there naturis and conditions ar as indefferent as is the nature of scheip and woluis.[7]

A better authority than I (the late Professor G. S. Pryde) says that the above 'no doubt . . . accurately reflected at this time the sentiments of Scotsmen'.[8] But one does not even have to believe that, far less to believe in the truth of the statements in the *Complaynt*, in order to believe that the concepts used and the principles tacitly appealed to in the *Complaynt* were available to

[7] This extract is taken from G. S. Pryde, *The Treaty of Union of Scotland and England, 1707* (London and Edinburgh, 1950), p. 3.
[8] Ibid.

its writer. Plainly the writer thought such ideas sufficiently current in his own community to make them worth using in a political pamphlet. A little later in the same century we find the same ideas far more elegantly and just as explicitly employed in George Buchanan's *De Jure Regni apud Scotos.*[9]

Nor is this in the sixteenth century an exclusively Scottish thing. Read Spenser's *Faerie Queen*; read Shakespeare's histories. Are not these two greatest poets of the century profoundly moved by a sense of the English nation and of pride in its qualities and achievements? The elaborate allegory of Spenser perhaps brings this out most clearly, Gloriana serving at once to personify the true faith and the nation of England, and to justify the independence of both from the tentacles of Rome.

This is not a novelty in the sixteenth century either. Hector Boece's early sixteenth-century history of Scotland may be unreliable as history, but it is enormously revealing in the concepts of the antiquity and independence of the Scottish nation which it deploys.[10] Barbour's *Bruce*, the late fourteenth-century epic of the early fourteenth-century war of independence, though much concerned with knightly virtues and feudal conceptions of 'freedom', is by no means silent on the nationalist points, as these lines may show.

> To Scotland went he [King Edward I] in high
> And all the land gan occupy . . .
> And stuffyt all with English men.
> Sheriffs and baillies made he then
> And alkyn other officeris
> That for to govern land afferis
> He made of English nation;
> That worthyt then so ryth fellone . . .
> That Scottis men might go na thing
> That ever might please to their liking.[11]

[9] Discussed and cited in ch. 4 above.

[10] Rosalind Mitchison, writing of Scotland in the later fifteenth and early sixteenth centuries, says: 'Nationalism, as distinct from patriotism, was an emotion of the time and the Scots shared it . . . [A]t the end of the fifteenth century, under Hector Boece, an able Latinist and an unscrupulous historian, [they] started inventing their own history.' *A History of Scotland* (London, 1970), p. 80.

[11] *The Bruce* by Master John Barbour, ed. W. W. Skeat for the Scottish Text Society (Edinburgh, 1893–4) bk. I, lines 183–4, 189–94. I have slightly modernized the spelling.

Most resonant of all, needless to say, is the famous letter of 1320 composed by Bernard of Linton, Abbot of Arbroath, for signature by the Scottish lords and despatch to the Pope, making out the case for papal recognition of and support for Robert Bruce as King of Scots. The so-called Declaration of Arbroath—our declaration of independence—is a magnificent piece of rhetoric, as the following extract may show:

The divine providence, the right of succession by the laws and customs of the kingdom (which we will defend till death) and the due and lawful consent and assent of all the people, made him [Robert] our King and Prince. To him we are obliged and resolved to adhere in all things . . . as being the person who hath restored the people's safety in defence of their liberties., But, after all, if this prince shall leave these principles he has so nobly pursued, and consent that we or our kingdom shall be subjected to the king or people of England, we will immediately endeavour to expel him as our enemy, and as the subverter both of his own and of our rights, and will make another king who will defend our liberties. For so long as there shall but one hundred of us remain alive, we will never consent to subject ourselves to the dominion of the English.[12]

This ringing assertion follows upon a historical sketch tracing the antiquity of the Scottish nation and its uninterrupted independence under its own chosen rulers.

Nor is this out of touch with the spirit of the time. Professor G. W. S. Barrow's *Robert Bruce* [13] demonstrates elaborately and at length that although the Anglo-Scottish war of the late thirteenth and early fourteenth century, whose turning-point was at Bannockburn, arose from dynastic pretensions of Edward I to overlordship over Scotland, it was throughout seen from the Scottish side as primarily a national struggle. That the issue was focused upon the rights of the King of Scots as an independent sovereign tells us nothing more remarkable than that in contemporary political theory kingship was of the essence of the governance and constitution of an independent community. Nowhere is this more clear than in the period dominated by the military leadership of William Wallace, who

[12] Quoted from G. W. S. Barrow, *Robert Bruce* (2nd edn., Edinburgh, 1976), p. 428, the translation of the Latin text being that printed in *Miscellanea Scotica* (Glasgow, 1820), iii. 126 of the first print.

[13] Op. cit., see esp. chs. 1–6.

at no time purported to act as anything other than guardian of the kingdom on behalf of the king, lawfully appointed by 'the community of the realm of Scotland'.

That the Declaration of Arbroath was in the form of a letter to the Pope has significance, too. Since the plea for recognition of their king and for support against the English is explicitly founded on the national distinctiveness and immemorial laws and customs of the Scots, it appears that the composer of the letter supposed such to be a recognizable and adequate political justification for a political claim. He took it for granted that the principles at stake were ones which would commend themselves to any reasonable contemporary, and *a fortiori* to the Pope. Again, the Scottish context does not imply that the principles involved were the exclusive property of Scots at that time.

Faced with such evidence at this, I cannot believe it reasonable or appropriate that the present orthodoxy as to the meaning of 'nationalism' or its temporal location only in the period since 1789 be accepted. The principle that those who belong to distinct nations ought to have distinct governments based on their own distinctive laws and customs is far older than that. And there is no reasonable description to attach to such a principle other than to call it a 'nationalist' one. To that conclusion it is quite irrelevant that the term 'nationalism' as a term of art in political theory comes into general usage only in the nineteenth century; and it is equally irrelevant that in its usage then it was taken to denote only a particular and, as it happens, morally unacceptable conception of national rights and their political implications.

Nevertheless, in any context 'nation' is a term which has *some* political implications. This is a point which must be made in order to complete the analysis offered earlier, which while differentiating 'state' and 'nation', failed adequately to differentiate nations from other communities distinguished by a form of historical and cultural consciousness. Apart from possible linguistic and/or territorial connections, the idea of a nation is that of a grouping which has or aspires to or conceives itself entitled to some form of specifically appropriate governmental or institutional expression. (I do not exclude from such 'institutional expression' the possibility of a distinctive form of

church or of religious organization; the significance, historically, of the Jewish faith, of the Catholic Church in Ireland, or
in Poland, of the Church of Scotland, and (in a negative sense)
of the Welsh movement for disestablishment of the Church in
the nineteenth and early twentieth centuries, is very obvious in
this context.) The mode of consciousness which constitutes a
national identity includes a consciousness of the need for a form
of common governance which recognizes and allows for the
continued flourishing of the cultural and historical community
in question.

In this there lies the germ of a principle which, unlike the
absolutist conception of nationalism, is—far from being
morally intolerable—morally acceptable or even mandatory.

The Kantian ideal of respect for persons implies (as I
suggested earlier) an obligation in each of us to respect that
which in others constitutes any part of their sense of their own
identity. For many people, though quite probably not for all, a
sense of belonging to some nation is an element in this precious
fabric of identity. This comprises, as I suggested before, not
merely a consciousness of a continuity with the past, but also a
will or hope for continuity into the future; and also consciousness of a form of cultural community which requires protection
and expression in appropriate institutional forms.

The doctrine of state sovereignty and the world order of
mutually independent sovereign states—more commonly than
not, soi-disant 'nation states'—which have emerged in and
dominated the politics of the modern world, owe much to the
'nationalism' embraced by nineteenth-century theorists. In the
light of the past two centuries of history, neither can be said to
have made a decisive contribution to the peace and happiness of
mankind. For that reason one cannot but warmly welcome the
hesitant moves of the past two or three decades towards a new
form of world order, of which, in our corner of the world, an
example is provided in the supra-national confederation
towards which the European Community is groping. Lord
Soames, Lord Hailsham, and Sir Monty Finniston have all in
different ways alluded to this phenomenon and rightly
commended it.[14] A diffusion of governmental power among

---

[14] See *The Crown and the Thistle*, ed. C. MacLean, essays by authors named.

various levels of government, rather than a concentration of power in centres of local omnipotence, seems eminently desirable.

Yet if this newly emerging order is to be morally acceptable, to say nothing of its durability, it must fully allow for the rights of nationalities, and create the conditions of mutual respect and self-respect among the members of diverse nations, as the foregoing argument implies. I assert it as a principle that there ought to be respect for national differences, and that there ought to be an adoption of forms of government appropriate to such differences.

Arguing from these principles as a Scotsman of the late twentieth century, I contend that the constitution and government of the United Kingdom as they function at present do not adequately fulfil these requirements. Within the past hundred years, the languages of both my patrilineal and my matrilineal ancestors have been all but extinguished under the educational policy set by agencies of the state. The media of mass communication present a continuing rhetoric of 'national' (that is, UK-wide) versus 'regional' which consistently devalues the status of the 'community of the realm of Scotland' and implies that only what emanates from London is 'national'. The Scottish institutions which there are have had defined for them, and have to some extent co-operated in defining themselves as having, an essentially parochial and provincial function and status. There is little or no prevailing sense of metropolitanism or cosmopolitanism anywhere or in any walk of life or institutional establishment within Scotland. Out of the remarkably rich cultural heritage of the country, what is most commonly recalled or resorted to by way of celebration and entertainment is the most cheap and meretricious; this might be summed up as the 'Scotland the Brave' syndrome; 'here's tae us, wha's like us', being a question to which the true answer may be unpalatable.

The comparatively modern growth of state centralization—along with industrial and economic centralization—has contributed much to this. Equally significant has been the dominance, almost inevitable and certainly not founded in ill will, of a somewhat anglo-centric conception of Britain. Lord Hailsham hits the nail on the head when he refers to the way in which, out of deference to the sensibilities of Scots and Welsh, the English had changed the name of their country to 'Britain'.[15] That is just why the presently dominant spirit of British nationalism, expressed and embodied in the major institutions of the state, is profoundly inimical to the continuity into the future of 'Scotland' and 'Wales' as anything other than geographical expressions with historical connotations capable of being preserved or resurrected for the amusement of tourists.

This opinion is not without support from external and thus more objective observations. For example, in the work quoted above on *Nationalism*, Eugene Kamenka remarks that 'Political power, aided by geography, created the English nation out of Britons, Angles, Saxons, Jutes and Danes and succeeded in absorbing the Norman conquerors, as it is absorbing the Scottish and, with somewhat more trouble, the Welsh, today.'[16] To agree with that, one does not have to dislike or disrespect England, English people, the English way of life, or any such thing. One can, as I do, genuinely love and admire the richness of the English tradition, the splendid tolerance and peacefulness of the English way of life, the almost infinite (despite present 'racial' problems) ability of England to welcome and assimilate new elements from abroad into the nation, and a host of other excellences down to the English pub; one can love and admire all that, wish indeed to adopt and adapt to some of these English excellences; and yet wish to be, and go on being, something recognizably different.

It is also true that there is genuinely something in common among all parts of the United Kingdom, to which Lord Hailsham has alluded with appropriate indefinition as 'the British thing'.[17] One must recognize how much of this stems from a common loyalty to a common monarch and more generally to a more than admirably constitutional royal house.

But it remains the case that the present governmental system of the UK is profoundly inimical to the continuing existence of the nations of the Scots and the Welsh, or so it appears. One form of change which is, from this point of view, desirable is constitutional and governmental change.

[15] 'The Nation and the Constitution', in *The Crown and the Thistle*, pp. 71–80.
[16] Op. cit., p. 13.
[17] 'The Nation and the Constitution', p. 71.

The principles put forward here do not, however, establish *what* sort of change ought most to be favoured. They certainly do not support the facile assumption that sovereign statehood is the only acceptable status fitted to the essence of nationhood. The concept of a 'sovereign state' is of much more recent vintage than that of a nation, and developments such as that of the European Community suggest that it may have already had its day. It seems to me obvious that the nations of the United Kingdom have so many common interests as to require and justify some common political institutions, whether through common membership of the European Community or through specifically British institutions such as a common crown, or both. If those political parties which favour schemes of devolution, 'home rule all round', or some kind of internal federation within the UK do devise, and press forward with, some such scheme otherwise than as a mere tactic to dish the SNP electorally, I for one will be happy to see the new political order given a full and fair trial. But previous experience does not encourage optimism that the British Parliament will itself be eager to do much if anything on these lines without the strongest of political pressure from Scotland and Wales.

Be that as it may, I hope that the principles stated here can be accepted not only as compatible with but also an essential complement to those stated earlier in the book. If so, that very acceptance may in a small way help to foster a more genuine willingness to take seriously the rights of small nations as well of individual persons. Some may think this too weak a version of nationalism to merit the name, others that any version of nationalism is merely a stalking horse for chauvinism and xenophobia. To both I would say that in this and in other matters there is much to be said for a golden mean.

INDEX OF NAMES, CASES AND STATUTES

SUBJECT INDEX